# The Immigrant Other

*LIVED EXPERIENCES IN A*
*TRANSNATIONAL WORLD*

*Rich Furman, Greg Lamphear,*
*and Douglas Epps, editors*

 COLUMBIA UNIVERSITY PRESS   NEW YORK

COLUMBIA UNIVERSITY PRESS
*Publishers Since 1893*
New York   Chichester, West Sussex

Library of Congress Cataloging-in-Publication Data
The immigrant other : lived experiences in a transnational world /
   Rich Furman, Greg Lamphear, and Douglas Epps, eds.
      pages cm.
   Includes bibliographical references and index.
   ISBN 978-0-231-17180-9 (cloth : alk. paper) — ISBN 978-0-231-17181-6 (pbk. : alk. paper) —
   ISBN 978-0-231-54113-8 (ebook)
   1. Immigrants—Social conditions—Cross-cultural studies. 2. Immigrants—Cultural
assimilation—Cross-cultural studies. 3. Transnationalism—Cross-cultural studies.
I. Furman, Rich, editor. II. Lamphear, Greg, editor. III. Epps, Douglas,
   editor.

   JV6225 .I43 2016
   304.8—dc23

                                                                    2015024325

TO MY DAUGHTERS,
REBECCA AND MYAH—
I WILL ALWAYS BE YOUR *NEW DAD*.
TO BROWNIE,
THIS BOOK WAS CONCEIVED WITH YOU ON MY LAP,
AND FOR YOU, I WILL ALWAYS BE GRATEFUL.
YOU WERE A HECK OF A DOG.
—RF

TO MIGRANTS EVERYWHERE, BOUND FOR PARTS UNKNOWN.
—GL

TO MARIE AND LIAM,
FOR *ALWAYS* BELIEVING IN ME.
TO RICH,
FOR SHOWING ME WHAT'S POSSIBLE.
—DE

# CONTENTS

*THE IMMIGRANT OTHER*

# 1

# Introduction

*MULTIPLE TRUTHS AND PRIVILEGED COLLABORATIONS IN A TRANSNATIONAL WORLD*

▸ RICH FURMAN, GREG LAMPHEAR, DOUGLAS EPPS, AND IMAN UJAAMA

AN APTLY TITLED BOOK SHOULD hint at the intentions of the authors and editors. Perhaps more so than with many books, the title of our book, *The Immigrant Other: Lived Experiences in a Transnational World*, articulates our intentions for the overall nature of our volume and for each individual chapter. In this introduction we will explore some of the key themes this edited book addresses: the importance and centrality of the lived experiences of immigrants, the notion of immigrants being marginalized or "othered," how understanding these lived experiences is predicated on an appreciation of the transnational nature of this moment in history, and finally, how criminalization is not a binomial phenomenon but instead is relative and exists along a (nonlinear) continuum. Before addressing these three substantive areas, we would like to share with you how this book came about, as this history will help you understand the perspectives of the authors and why we chose our focus.

The idea for this book emerged during the production of another of the first editor's books, *The Criminalization of Immigration: Contexts and Consequences* (Ackerman & Furman, 2014). That volume's chapters explore the various policies and systemic and legal mechanisms by which immigration is criminalized. Chapters focus on various states in the United States, such as Arizona and Alabama, which have been systematically constructing barriers to vulnerable immigrants by hampering their ability not only to live with dignity and respect but to actually survive. The book also explores how policies and practices criminalize immigrants in various countries around the world. These policy- and practice-oriented chapters provide valuable insights into the problem of the criminalization of immigration.

Yet the chapters that were most compelling to Rich Furman, coeditor of that previous volume, were those that moved beyond legalistic and policy frameworks to describe the *lived experiences* of the impact of these laws, systems, and structures. For example, Douglas Epps, one of the editors of the book you have in your hands, wrote an autoethnography exploring his experiences as an immigration detention officer. Now a social worker, Douglas's powerful narrative provided us with a surprising view of the consequences of a dysfunctional, criminalizing system not only on immigrants but also on detention system workers themselves. His narrative provides an evocative and emotional lived and performed example of what David Gil (1992) refers to as "structural violence," a characterization of organizations and systems that thwart the humanity of all those involved. Structurally violent organizations and social structures systematically compel participants to enact various covert and overt forms of violence not only against others but also against themselves. This structural violence, as our chapters describe, is endemic within various systems that interact with immigrants.

Even more compelling were the stories and narratives the authors used to present the personal, day-to-day, lived consequences of state and national policies on immigrants who have been increasingly marginalized or "othered" over the last several decades. These became our favorite chapters, as we were moved by the evocative, emotional truths of people's lived experiences. We lamented that more of our chapters did not privilege the voices of immigrants. This lament sparked an idea. That idea became a proposal. The proposal led to a contract. A contract led to contacts. And now, after a great deal of hard work and long nights by our most talented, expert authors, we present to you this book.

One final note about the composition of the chapters. You will note that perhaps more than many edited books on immigration-related issues, there is a strong presence of scholars who are social workers and community activists, as well as chapters that reflect experiences that occur within community-based contexts. This is a natural consequence of our focus on the lived experiences of undocumented people in transnational spaces. Undocumented people express their resistance not in isolation but collectively, with and within the groups that seek to serve and empower them. This book's first editor is a social work scholar, and the volume is being published as part of Columbia University Press's social work list. While the audience will most certainly include students, practitioners, and scholars from many disciplines, it has been crafted with an eye to influencing those who work with those who provide services to undocumented people and also those who teach those who will engage in this work. All names of the research participants in this book have been changed to ensure confidentiality.

## "THE IMMIGRANT OTHER"?

When our book proposal originally went out for review, one of our reviewers bristled at the phrase "the immigrant other." He or she suggested that the phrase was largely pejorative, labeling immigrants in a way that marginalizes and positions them as existing outside society and community. We are in complete agreement with this assessment; the reviewer's reticence and moral discomfort reflects our experience of what happens to undocumented immigrants, and frequently, what happens even to those documented immigrants who come from diverse communities. Various laws, policies, and practices intentionally or unintentionally cast immigrants into a liminal state of marginalization and "otherness" (Sekhon, 2003). Consider the most common term for undocumented immigrants in the United States—"illegal alien." An alien is some "thing" (as opposed to someone) from another world (Mehan, 1997), separate, tragically different, from those who are included—the "us" or the "we." Not only are they separate and different, but they are also viewed as threats that place at risk the very survival of the "us" or the "we" (Furman, Ackerman, Loya, Jones, & Negi, 2012).

Marginalizing others, or "othering," occurs not only within the realm of immigration policy and practice. The othering of human beings has also been a powerful tool of overtly oppressive regimes and, sadly, of governments that are more, at least on face value, democratic. The linguistic and structural mechanisms for the othering of individuals were powerfully explored in Frantz Fanon's (2004) classic text on the mechanisms of colonialism, *The Wretched of the Earth*. Fanon highlighted the importance of language in the creation of group and individual identity and the mental health of both the "colonizer" and the "colonized," each internalizing the social constructions of each "role." Oppression, therefore, is not only facilitated by the laws and policies of a society but can also exist long after policy implementation as a sort of intrapsychic and social hangover performed by both oppressed and oppressor (Grygier, 1954).

As you will read in the following chapters, various policies and practices associated with the criminalization of immigration situate undocumented immigrants (and documented immigrants and even citizens) as threatening "others." This othering has powerful implications not only for immigrants and their families but also for all of our notions of justice, social change, and a just society. We adopt the nomenclature of the *immigrant other* as a means of highlighting the ways of framing the experience of courageous people who encounter nation-states and groups that seek their exclusion. These sometimes desperate, always courageous people fight for survival in an increasingly complex, transnational, and global world that is not constructed to contend with the problems of those who cross nation-state boundaries.

### THE TRANSNATIONAL/GLOBAL WORLD

The term "globalization" is frequently used so casually that it has become almost meaningless (Negi & Furman, 2010). It is so frequently and unabashedly thrown about as a glib explanation for a myriad of social forces, dynamics, or problems that it appears to be causal to nearly every human condition. Globalization—the increasingly interconnected nature of financial, social, political, business, and organizational life—has, however, transformed the very nature of our political and social worlds.

This transformation is particularly salient for immigration. Readers of this book will find that more traditional patterns of immigration have often shifted to a pattern of movement that has been referred to as *transmigration* (Portes, 1997). While traditional migrants move from one nation-state to another and largely sever (or reduce) connections to their country of origin, transmigrants continue to live, work, and/or maintain familial connections in both their sending and receiving countries. Their lives truly exist in and between two or more nation-states. Even though transmigration is often necessitated by economic realities, it is facilitated and encouraged by the free movement of capital and made increasingly easy through inexpensive communication technologies (i.e., Skype, Facebook, and Internet forums). Such technologies increase the capacity of transmigrants to maintain close family ties (Madianou & Miller, 2011), develop sophisticated cross-border social networks, and more easily discover time-sensitive information about border crossing and employment opportunities.

Sadly, their lives are frequently criminalized when these migrants cross borders from sending to receiving country and back again. Therefore, transnational spaces become contested spaces where the confluence of global factors renders transmigrants neither here nor there but existing within a complex synthesis of two or more nation-states (Simon, 1998). Transmigrants live not only lives of "here and there" but also "neither here nor there."

Globalization and transnationalism are intertwined and must be understood together. Opponents of globalization view it as little more than a form of neocolonialism or neoimperialism (Reitan, 2012). From this perspective, the function and aim of globalization is for corporate elites to access and exploit the cheapest labor possible, integrate the global poor into the world market, help them become more invested in lifestyles congruent with the marketplace, and sell products back to the masses at a high profit margin. Yet what is known about such policies is that even when they do work to raise the per capita income of a nation, they do not reduce poverty for all (Kaplinsky, 2005). In fact, the most vulnerable and marginalized populations in society are often deeply impacted by rapid changes in social spending and changes in the market. These changes, regardless of whether their long-term effects are positive or negative, lead to social dislocation. When such forces impact groups who perceive a better life in a nearby country, there exists a confluence of push/pull factors that markedly increase transmigration. Of course, this is not the only recipe for transmigration, yet it is a powerful one.

Given the choice, the vast majority of transmigrants would prefer to stay in their own countries and earn a *livable wage*; few wish to live in a transnational netherworld of frequent violence, poverty, and risk away from those they love. Globalization and transmigration go hand in hand. The dramatic shifts caused by globalization fuel undocumented immigration. Paradoxically, some proponents of globalization make classic neoliberal arguments about the importance of free markets, the need for free flow of capital for investment purposes, and the value of the integration of world economic structures to reduce poverty. Yet, even more paradoxically, few of these proponents seem to recognize a fundamental truth of economics: labor follows jobs regardless of laws and policies to the contrary (Pries, 2004). Those in need will seek to survive. Transmigrants exist with and between the politics, policies, and laws of two (or more) countries. This reality too frequently ignores a fundamental truth: transmigrants are usually poor people who are compelled to move across borders for their own survival.

Of course, the dynamics of globalization and transnational migration are far more complex than portrayed in this brief introduction. For example, historically disenfranchised groups and communities are now able to see their products in a global marketplace through the Fair Trade movement (Le Mare, 2012). Additionally, the globalization of communication and technology has provided the platform for the transnational indigenous rights movement, which seeks to shape the nature of our rapidly globalizing world (Bellier & Preaud, 2012).

Yet in spite of these potentially liberating movements, globalization has placed many of the poor in the global South at risk. The following brief exploration provides students and those new to the study of undocumented immigration a global, transnational framework to contextualize the rest of the chapters. Developing an understanding of the macro, global factors that influence undocumented immigration should encourage readers to begin to understand the lived experiences of transmigrating peoples in a context that helps view them as heroic and not as criminal.

## NARRATIVE, TRUTH, AND THE LIVED EXPERIENCE

In the social and behavioral sciences, the notion of truth has been greatly contested. In an age that fetishizes science and technology and reifies evidence-based practices, a hierarchy of knowledge has prevailed that privileges an empirically verified truth, a truth based on sample size, sufficiently powerful statistics, and other procedures of science that lead to universally generalized truths (Furman, 2009). Without question, the advancements derived from science have been profound. Biomedical science has done much for curing disease and relieving suffering. If this is so, why create a book that seeks to infuse narratives into its very fabric? How can we "trust" these highly individual, subjective stories? Should we not have edited a volume dedicated to survey research alone?

Narratives explore the complexity of life in ways that traditional data cannot. People's lived stories transcend the portrayal of facts or even qualitative categories that are empirically derived. Narratives present the complexity of people and their contexts and portray them in all their humanity. This is especially true for those who are different from us, the "other." Facts or discrete data points portray tendencies about groups of people, yet they can rarely help us understand the lived experiences of individuals. They also tend to "blame the victim" by divorcing motivations and behaviors from historical trends that influence the lives of individuals. Taken to its extreme, decontextualized data can lead to the type of generalizations that foster practices used to oppress whole groups, such as with racial profiling of Latinos at traffic stops (Nier, Gaertner, Nier, & Dovido, 2011). Supposed facts (frequently dubious to begin with), for example, about the negative economic impact of undocumented immigrants decontextualize the complex, transnationally situated reasons for immigration. These reasons and knowledge lie only within lived stories, stories performed each day on the global and transnational stage. Facts divorced of context, of story, often mean very little.

Those who work with and provide services to the people whose lives are presented in the following chapters will gain powerful insights through attending to the stories portrayed here with an open mind and a listening heart. We ask you to appreciate without analyzing, to attempt to see the full humanity of those whose lives are lived precariously across and between borders. By allowing their lived stories to be heard and felt, by exploring their full humanity, you will help eliminate the marginalization, the "otherness," portrayed in these stories.

### A CONTINUUM OF CRIMINALIZATION

One of the powerful lessons for us during the editing of this book was that the criminalization of immigration is not a binomial phenomenon. Social policies and practices do not either criminalize or not criminalize; their potential impacts are more varied and nuanced. Instead, various policies and practices range in the degree and vary in the manner in which they criminalize the lives of undocumented people, documented migrants, and those from various ethnic and diverse communities.

Overt criminalization is easy to identify. For instance, a law that states that undocumented immigrants are to be sent to immigration detention centers or automatically deported clearly positions undocumented immigration as a criminal act. Less direct examples of criminalization include practices that profile racial and ethnic groups who may be documented or undocumented immigrants, laws that create sanctions for service providers who work with those who may be undocumented (Furman, Langer, Sanchez & Negi, 2007), and policies that sanction the employment (read: financial survival) of undocumented people (Bloch, Kumarappan, & McKay, 2014), along with many other policies and practices.

As you will discover throughout this book, the ways in which people's lives are criminalized are often easy to miss and insidious, creating social contexts and relationships that not only harm undocumented people but also the very civility and "culture" of societies. To treat other human beings as criminal others merely due to their existence on a particular spot of real estate on our planet is to devalue and dehumanize all human life. Being born into poverty in a transnational world in which fast-moving and unstable markets may mean one's sole source of employment disappears overnight, therefore mandating one migrate to another country in order to help one's family survive, does not make one a criminal. When assessed from outside the rhetoric of a nation-state discourse or provincial party politics, such behavior can only be viewed as heroic. Fundamentally, this is a book of stories about heroes.

## CHAPTER OVERVIEWS

The chapters are organized into two sections: those exploring the lived experience of the criminalization of immigration within the United States and those focusing on other parts of the world. Given that some of the issues explored are truly transnational in nature, this distinction is at times arbitrary.

The authors of the chapters you are about to read have been privileged to witness, hear, and investigate the lives of some of the most vulnerable people on this planet, people who have been systematically criminalized, disenfranchised, and dehumanized simply by virtue of the randomness of their place of birth and moment in history. The authors of each chapter, as you will soon see, have a deep and profound respect for this privilege, for being entrusted with the stories told to them, in privileged collaborations. They are privileged in the sense of not only being honored but also in having status. And with privilege and collaboration comes responsibility. Our authors' responsibility, their task at the outset, was to make the stories of "immigrant others" central to their chapters. They were responsible for treating these stories with honor, with dignity, and with recognition that these stories were indeed as "true," if not more so, than results validated by statistical measure. They are true because those who lived them and performed them say they are so; they are true because they resonate—they resonate within our hearts. With that in mind we share with you the chapters of this book.

Tanya Golash-Boza's chapter, "National Insecurities: The Apprehension of Criminal and Fugitive Aliens," presents a rich and nuanced exploration of the consequences of federal laws in the United States. Through her evocative narratives and keen insights deconstructing U.S. laws that seek to identify and deport "criminal" and "fugitive" aliens, Golash-Boza deftly shows how policies that are intended to make "us" safer very often do not. Her chapter explores how these laws merely pay lip service to national security. However, research demonstrates that the majority of those deported are typically law-abiding people whose lives are devastated by their criminalization.

Throughout history psychiatric hospitals have often been used not only as places of treatment for those possessing mental health disorders but also as depositories for those society deems deviant (Jackson, 2001). This *criminalization without criminalization* has been applied too frequently not only to undocumented immigrants with mental health concerns, some of whom could benefit from gentle and therapeutic inpatient care, but also to those for whom inpatient hospitalization adds to their experience of crisis, trauma, and illness. Nora Kenworthy's heart-wrenching chapter explores how psychiatric hospitals have become a largely unknown and tragically hidden "space of abeyance" from which undocumented people with psychiatric illnesses have little hope of appropriate discharge due to their immigration status. Kenworthy presents narratives from 2 years of interviews with a group of individuals who were or had become undocumented and had histories of significant mental illness that led to extended hospitalizations in state facilities in Massachusetts.

Lesbian, gay, bisexual, and transgender (LGBT) people in many countries face a number of abuses, including sexual harassment, physical and sexual abuse, and even violent death. In response, many seek asylum in countries presumed to be more open to LGBT people. Sadly, while some receiving countries may be open to LGBT people, they may not treat LGBT immigrants without proper identification as we would hope all asylum seekers would be treated. Nadine Nakamura and Alejandro Morales present a tragic and evocative case example of a Central American LGBT activist and her journey toward asylum in the United States. Subjected to many of the

indignities and abuses that LGBT people are forced to endure in their sending countries, "Scarlett" tells of her journey, a journey that exemplifies the
revictimization many LGBT people experience in immigration detention.
Scarlett's story evocatively illustrates not only the transnational nature of the
criminalization of immigration but the transnational nature of violence.

"Terrorist, foreigner, anti-American, antidemocratic, and misogynist"
writes author Saher Selod about the prevailing perceptions of Muslim American men in the United States. Based upon qualitative interviews in two large
cities in the United States, the author explores the ways that the criminalization of immigration, or the "war on immigration" as it has been called
(Sinnar, 2003), intersects and collides with the post-9/11 War on Terror
(Tumlin, 2004). The author investigates the perceptions of Muslim American men as they struggle to live and find meaning within their communities. Selod explores their perceptions regarding how prevailing prejudices and
discourses impact their movement in global spaces (e.g., via air travel). Selod's
interviews and commentary provide insights on the complex confluence of
citizenship, religion, and notions of belonging. We are excited by this chapter, as it cogently investigates ways that immigrants and those perceived to be
"different" are "othered" and marginalized at this moment in history.

In explorations of the deleterious effect of social policies and oppressive
practices, immigrants are often presented as semi-passive victims. While
undocumented immigrants are most certainly victimized, as you will see
throughout this book, they frequently are anything but helpless or passive.
Undocumented immigrants have personal and collective agency, which
becomes evident as you read stories of positive adaptation and resistance.
The collective agency and capacity to organize for social change is palpable
in the chapter written by Kathleen Staudt and Josiah Heyman. Using participant observation to explore how community-based organizations resist
the criminalization of immigration at the U.S.–Mexico border, the authors
provide guidance and insight with powerful implications for advocates and
scholars alike.

> No, it's even. You're only safe in your own home. Well, who's safe? Because
> for one, we don't have papers, we're illegal. They could get us at any moment.
> If not immigration, the police, yeah, I don't feel so safe, yeah. No, we don't
> know what our fate will be here . . . they're never going to give us papers.
>
> (Undocumented immigrant)

This candid revelation was taken from a qualitative interview with a Nicaraguan Latino day laborer in San Francisco. Kurt Organista and coauthors present us with a chapter full of the multiple psychosocial effects of the criminalization of immigration on Latino day laborers. Latino day laborers have been an essential driver of the U.S. economy for more than a century. They largely form the backbone of the construction, agricultural, and other sectors of the economy that would potentially collapse without them. The reality of their contribution is contrasted with their treatment. Organista and colleagues, one of whom has been a Latino day laborer, present the lived consequences of this horrible paradox.

Connie Oxford's chapter, "'It's Like You Are a Criminal': Asylum Seekers and Immigration Detention," explores the narratives of three African woman as they navigate asylum in the United States. The chapter evocatively illustrates the lack of awareness that asylum seekers have about the often confounding nuances of U.S. immigration law. These revelations challenge notions regarding the intentionality of immigrants and their actions vis-à-vis U.S. law; that is, their actions are not based upon a rational assessment of the consequences of what could happen to them in the United States but instead on the deleterious consequences of what might happen to them if they stay in their sending countries. This dynamic challenges the notion that U.S. federal and local policy will serve as deterrents for the most vulnerable populations. Oxford's chapter also speaks to the problematic micro practices that further criminalize asylum seekers. Oxford profoundly observes:

> Perhaps what is most problematic is that the practice of detaining asylum seekers consequently equates them with criminal detainees. Immigrant detention in the United States is in dire need of reform so that an asylum seeker can seek freedom from persecution without feeling like a criminal.

Cynthia Howson and Ashley Damp present us another important work with clear practical implications in their chapter "Hybrid Governance and the Criminalization of Somali Refugees Seeking Social Services in a Midwestern Town." While the chapter explores the experiences of documented Somali refugees in the United States, it demonstrates the ways in which the criminalization of immigration impacts even those who have a legal right to residency. Many of those interviewed had family members still living as undocumented, highly criminalized people in refugee camps in Kenya and Ethiopia; the psychological (and at times financial) toll of having family members living within these transitional, unstable, and often dangerous places is profound. The transnational relationships these families maintain, existing within the larger framework of the criminalization of immigration, demonstrate the need for more transnationally oriented global policies that transcend often shortsighted national laws. The authors' interviews with refugees and social service providers also explore the confluence between poverty and the criminalization of immigration and how nontraditional receiving communities struggle with the social integration of new immigrants.

Perhaps more so than any other ethnic group, Filipinas live highly transnational lives. In the first author's recent research trip to the Philippines, nearly everyone he encountered had close family or friends living abroad, usually supporting or at least contributing to their families through transnational labor. Indeed, the Philippine government has a number of policies that encourage the transnational migration of Filipinas and encourage a conceptualization of the "great Filipina worker" as a national hero (Guevarra, 2010). Valerie Francisco and colleagues, in their chapter, "Filipina Lives: Transnationalism, Migrant Labor, and the Experiences of Criminalization in the United States," explore the paradoxical and complex values and personal struggles that lead to Filipina sacrifice through their entry into the transnational labor system. The interviews also elucidate the abuses many Filipinas must endure, as the project of the criminalization of immigration impacts them and their families back home. Another example of the subtle and incidental effects of the criminalization of immigration, this chapter's analysis is powerful, as are its personal stories.

"Who will take care of me if she doesn't come back? Will you take care of me?" These painful words were spoken by a 4-year-old Brazilian child to an attorney's assistant, who looked after the child as her mother faced immigration officials. Her father had already been taken into custody by immigration officials during an immigration hearing that he had excitedly prepared for, as he was assured by his attorney that he would be granted legal residency and would be granted an opportunity to work for citizenship. Kara Cebulko and Heloísa Maria Galvão's poignant chapter, "The Criminalization of Brazilian Immigrants," presents this evocative and heartbreaking narrative of the unintended consequences of the criminalization of immigration on Brazilian immigrants in Massachusetts. In their research, the authors focus on the deleterious effects of the threat of deportation. The threat itself serves as a powerful mechanism that controls, marginalizes, and pacifies undocumented immigrants (Ackerman, Sacks, & Furman, 2014). In spite of the powerful forces of criminalization, Cebulko and Galvão's respondents demonstrate a powerful capacity for resistance, resilience, and adaptation.

In the final chapter in this section, we present the lived experience of immigrants whose lives began to be criminalized by another "war on"—the "war on drugs." In "Living with Drug Lords and Mules in New York: Contrasting Colombian Criminality and Transnational Belonging," Ariana Ochoa Camacho explores how social conceptions of Colombians have led to their ongoing criminalization. She traces this criminalization's origin to the 1980s, when popular portrayals of the drug cartels in Colombia became ubiquitous on U.S. television. This equating Colombians with drugs and violence has had significant impact on the lives of Colombians today and their struggles to live constructive transnational lives. Her chapter demonstrates the powerful confluence between the "War on Drugs" and the "War on Terror." As the culminating chapter in this section, it helps us view the risks of stereotypes and generalizations and their relationship to social policy, and how their adverse social conceptions impact the lives of hardworking, honest people in transnational spaces. The structural violence of U.S. society against many immigrants may serve as a form of revictimization against those whose lives were profoundly affected by violence in their countries of origin.

Mexico is the sending country for one of the largest migrations in the world—Mexicans into the United States. For more than a decade, the migration discourse in the United States has been on the "problem" of undocumented Mexicans entering the country. Few in the general public, however, understand the complex dynamics of transnational migration from, and through, Mexico. Sonya Wolf's chapter, "Mexico's Transmigrants: Between Los Zetas and the Iron Fist of the State," helps elucidate some of these dynamics. Presenting the case example of two Honduran immigrants and their journey from their violence-torn country, through Mexico, toward the United States, the chapter adds a human layer to a "problem" that has largely been decontextualized and dehumanized. Transnational gangs, drugs, and undocumented immigration are not merely concerns that the United States innocently receives; U.S. law, policy, and social realities are largely implicated in their creation and maintenance.

Paolo Boccagni's chapter, "Stigmatized, Segregated, Essential: The Position of Immigrant Live-In Care Workers Vis-à-Vis Formal Social Work Provision in Italy," forces social workers and other helping professionals to assess their relationships with undocumented people. Boccagni insightfully contends that "as a result of their pervasive contribution to domiciliary care provision, immigrant women are simultaneously 'alien' and 'intimate' to the everyday social reproduction of a number of Italian households." This seemingly contradictory and paradoxical relationship exists in most Western and privileged countries; we are highly dependent on immigrants, documented or otherwise, for various types of care. Yet how is this care reciprocated? How do the helping professions conceptualize their ethical responsibilities in this context? This chapter explores the essence of these conundrums.

Spain is the country that currently has the largest influx of undocumented and documented immigrants in Europe. Situated along the Mediterranean Sea, just north of Africa, Spain has been a country profoundly affected by immigration for millennia. Maria Aysa-Lastra's chapter, "Immigrants' Experiences with Law Enforcement Authorities in Spain," intelligently investigates the historical and present dynamics of undocumented immigration in Spain as they are lived by immigrants and law enforcement officers. In-depth interviews were conducted not only in the community but within immigration detention centers as well. The author also examined court records to provide additional depth and texture to her interviews. The chapter examines the current changes in immigration law in Spain and presents us with important lessons that are generalizable to many nation-state and transnational contexts.

Australia, like the United States, is a nation founded by immigrants. As in the United States, Australia's treatment of its indigenous people has frequently been harsh at best and genocidal at worst. Currently, Australia's treatment of perceived others is under scrutiny. Linda Briskman and Lucy Fiske's chapter, "Creating Criminals: Australia's Response to Asylum Seekers and Refugees," not only gives a powerful assessment of national policy but demonstrates the transnational implications of domestic laws. Australia's immigration policy has profound implication for immigrants, refugees, and asylum seekers from many nations in South Asia. The authors cogently and lucidly explore the ways in which asylum seekers and refugees are criminalized in spite of their legal status. The authors observe:

> Although seeking asylum in Australia (including when arriving without documentation or prior authorization) does not break any law, the use of the language of "illegality" by politicians and the media creates perceptions of criminal activity.

Francesca Meloni's chapter, "Longing to Belong: Undocumented Youth, Institutional Invisibility, and Ambivalent Belonging in Canada," explores the plight of undocumented youth in Canada through what can best be described as an existential lens. She explores how the consequences of existing in an illegal state has powerful implications for one's sense of "being in the world." This illegal state and its inherent liminality has powerful implications for a young person's sense of being and belonging and his or her sense of identity and vision of the future. Meloni describes the powerful dialectic between hope and disconnection and between hope and despair, each caused by the liminal status of undocumented youth. It is impossible to read her chapter and not be inspired, touched, and angered by her respondents' sense of hope—touched by the powerful humanity of their stories; inspired by their powerful resilience; angered by the horrible existential consequences of shortsighted national policies that neglect to account for whole families as they navigate transnational spaces.

Andrew Gardner is one of the world's authorities on immigration into Qatar. His long history of ethnographic research has focused on labor migration into the Gulf States from the perspective of both the migrants themselves and Qatari citizens. Gardner and his colleagues bring this complexity and subtlety to their analytical gaze in the chapter "Migrants and Justice in Qatar: Time, Mobility, Language, and Ethnography." In the authors' words, the chapter addresses

> the challenging task of navigating the threshold between legality and illegality, and . . . doing so in a complicated foreign environment. More directly, the chapter explores the governance of foreign migrants and the criminalization of the portions of migrant agency that conflict with the interests of the state, with those of corporations and migrants' employers, and with some of the citizens and foreigners who profit from these migrants' labor.

Greece historically has not been viewed as a common destination for immigrants. This changed radically during the 1990s, as political turmoil in Albania led to a huge influx of undocumented immigrants. Greece's response was particularly severe, a response that Georgios Karyotis and Dimitris Skleparis analyze in an impeccably researched chapter, "Resistance to the Criminalization of Immigration: Migrant Protests in Greece." The authors deftly explore the political and cultural factors that undergird Greece's responses to the most recent wave of immigration. This context serves as a background for their presentation of qualitative interviews with immigrants engaged in a hunger strike in response to increasingly restrictive proposed legislation. Their content analysis provides valuable findings about the specific ways in which criminalizing laws impact the lives of undocumented immigrants. It also further serves as a reminder of the agency of oppressed people and the importance of partnering with them in working toward social and political change.

Finally, we believe you, dear reader, are also a privileged witness to and privileged collaborator with those you are reading about. Your response, dare we say your obligation, we hope, is that you choose to act. Your practice as social workers, advocates, community leaders, or as citizens affords you opportunities to challenge the powerful, complex forces that lead to the criminalization of and marginalization of other human beings.

**REFERENCES**

Ackerman, A., & Furman, R. (2014). *The criminalization of immigration: Contexts and consequences.* Durham, NC: Carolina Academic.

Ackerman, A. R., Sacks, M., & Furman, R. (2014). The new penology revisited: The criminalization of immigration as a pacification strategy. *Justice Policy Journal, 11*(1). Online before print. www.cjcj.org/uploads/cjcj/documents/ackerman_new_penology_final_formatted.pdf.

Bellier, I., & Preaud, M. (2012). Emerging issues in indigenous rights: Transformative effects of the recognition of indigenous peoples. *International Journal of Human Rights, 16*(3), 474–488.

Bloch, A., Kumarappan, L., & McKay, S. (2014). Employer sanctions: The impact of workplace raids and fines on undocumented migrants and ethnic enclave employers. *Critical Social Policy.* Online before print. http://csp.sagepub.com/content/early/2014/09/05/0261018314545600.abstract.

Fanon, F. (2004). *The wretched of the earth*. New York: Grove.

Furman, R. (2009). Ethical considerations of evidence-based practice. *Social Work, 54*(1), 82–84.

Furman, R., Ackerman, A., Loya, M., Jones, S., & Negi, N. (2012). The criminalization of immigration: Value conflicts for the social work profession. *Journal of Sociology & Social Welfare, 29*(1), 169–185.

Furman, R., Langer, C. L., Sanchez, T. W., & Negi, N. J. (2007). A qualitative study of immigration policy and practice dilemmas for social work students. *Journal of Social Work Education, 43*(1), 133–146.

Gil, D. (1992). *Unraveling social policy*. New York: Schenkman.

Grygier, T. (1954). *Oppression: A study in social and criminal psychology*. New York: Routledge.

Guevarra, A. (2010). *Marketing dreams, manufacturing heroes: The transnational labor brokering of Filipino workers*. New Brunswick, NJ: Rutgers University Press.

Jackson, R. L. (2001). *The clubhouse model: Empowering applications of theory to generalist practice*. Boston: Brooks/Cole.

Kaplinsky, R. (2005). *Globalization, poverty and inequality: Between a rock and a hard place*. Malden, MA: Polity.

Le Mare, A. (2012). Show the world to women and they can do it: Southern Fair Trade Enterprise as agents of empowerment. *Gender & Development, 20*(1), 95–109.

Madianou, M., & Miller, D. (2011). *Migration and new media: Transnational families and polymedia*. New York: Routledge.

Mehan, H. (1997). The discourse of illegal immigration debate: A case study in the politics of representation. *Discourse & Society, 8*(2), 249–270.

Negi, N. J., & Furman, R. (Eds.). (2010). *Transnational social work practice*. New York: Columbia University Press.

Nier, J. A., Gaertner, S. L., Nier, C. L., & Dovidio, J. F. (2011). Can racial profiling be avoided under Arizona immigration law? Lessons learned from subtle bias research and anti-discrimination law. *Analyses of Social Issues and Public Policy, 12*(1), 5–20.

Portes, A. (1997). Immigration theory for a new century: Some problems and opportunities. *International Migration Review, 31*(3), 799–825.

Pries, L. (2004). Determining the causes and durability of transnational labour migration between Mexico and the United States: Some empirical findings. *International Migration, 42*(2), 3–39.

Reitan, R. (2012). Theorizing and engaging the global movement: From anti-globalization to global democratization. *Globalizations, 9*(3), 323–325.

Sekhon, V. (2003). The civil rights of "others": Anti-terrorism, the Patriot Act, and Arab and South Asian American rights in post-9/11 American society. *Texas Journal on Civil Liberties & Civil Rights, 8*(1), 117–148.

Simon, J. (1998). Refugees in a carceral age: The rebirth of immigration prisons in the United States. *Public Culture, 10*(3), 577–607.

Sinnar, S. (2003). Patriot or unconstitutional: The mandatory detention of aliens under the US Patriot Act. *Stanford Law Review, 55*(4), 1419–1454.

Tumlin, K. C. (2004). Suspect first: How terrorism policy is reshaping immigration policy. *California Law Review, 19*(4), 1175–1240.

# National Insecurities

## THE APPREHENSION OF CRIMINAL AND FUGITIVE ALIENS

▸ *TANYA GOLASH-BOZA*

ICE [Immigration and Customs Enforcement] makes America safer by identifying, apprehending, and removing criminal and other illegal aliens from the United States.
(U.S. Department of Homeland Security FY 2011 budget request, p. 66)

A top priority for ICE has been to target the "worst of the worst" in the illegal population—criminal aliens incarcerated in U.S. prisons and jails; . . . and fugitive aliens who have been ordered removed from the United States but have failed to depart.
(ICE FY 2008 annual report, p. 13)

ONE SUNDAY MORNING IN 2009, immigration agents pounded on Vern's door. When he opened the door, they arrested him—in front of his wife and two children, ages 12 and 9. They took Vern to a detention center and deported him to Guatemala a few days later.

Vern had lived in the United States for nearly twenty years. When he first arrived, he applied for political asylum. The Immigration and Naturalization Service issued him a work permit while his case was being processed. Vern found a job in a frozen-food plant in Ohio, where he met a Honduran woman, Maria, also applying for political asylum, with whom he became romantically involved. Each year, Vern and Maria renewed the work permits that allowed them to continue working legally. Confident they would eventually achieve legal permanent residency, Vern and Maria married and had their first child in 1996.

In 1998, Vern received a notice that he should leave the United States—his asylum application had been denied. Vern was devastated; he had established a life in the United States and had few ties to Guatemala. He decided to stay, hoping his wife's application would be approved, and that she could apply for him to legalize his status. They had another child and continued to build their lives in Ohio. Vern and his family had a comfortable life, but Vern lived in fear that immigration agents would come for him. To avoid this, he stayed out of trouble. He did everything he could to avoid problems with the police—he never drank, avoided committing traffic violations, and abided by the laws at all times. He learned English, took his kids on outings every weekend, and tried to blend in as much as possible.

Vern's attempts to live under the radar and be a "model citizen" were not enough to prevent his deportation. Immigration agents targeted him because, by ignoring his deportation order, Vern became a "fugitive alien." Once he was arrested, there was nothing he could do to prevent his 1998 deportation order from being carried out.

The U.S. Department of Homeland Security (DHS) claims to be engaging in more effective immigration law enforcement by deporting the "worst of the worst." The "worst of the worst" includes any noncitizen convicted of a crime, people the administration calls "criminal aliens," and any person who has missed his or her immigration court date, people the administration refers to as "fugitive aliens." In many cases, criminal aliens' convictions are minor; moreover, they often are long-term legal permanent residents who have children and families in the United States and no ties abroad. As for "fugitive aliens," many of them spent years in the United States waiting for their court date, only to be denied legalization after establishing families in this country. Enforcement and Removal Operations (ERO) is the division of ICE that carries out arrests. On an average day, ERO officers arrest 471 immigrants with criminal convictions and deport 1,120 people (ICE, 2012).

To target criminal and fugitive aliens, ICE has implemented several programs, including the Criminal Alien Program (CAP), National Fugitive Operations Program (NFOP), Secure Communities, and the 287(g) Immigration Enforcement Authority. Through these programs, ICE has been able to increase the number of people deported from inside the United States. According to ICE, these tactics are making America safer.

These programs represent a merger between immigration law enforcement and criminal law enforcement. The CAP screens all inmates in federal, state, and local prisons, ensuring that noncitizens who pass through the criminal justice system are deported if they are eligible for deportation. The Secure Communities Program builds on CAP by targeting noncitizens in custody of local, state, and federal law enforcement authorities. The 287(g) program allows state and local law enforcement to cooperate with immigration authorities and check suspects' immigration status in any law enforcement encounter. The NFOP targets people like Vern who have been ordered deported but who have not left the country.

CAP, Secure Communities, and 287(g) work together to create a situation in which any noncitizen who comes into contact with law enforcement authorities can be checked to determine his or her eligibility to remain in the country. These programs ensure that convicted murderers and rapists are deported after serving their time in prison. However, they also ensure that when a police officer stops a Latino for an alleged traffic violation, the police officer can do a routine immigration check while writing a speeding ticket. If it turns out that the driver has a deportation order, then this routine traffic stop can turn into a "fugitive alien" being deported. If it turns out that the driver was convicted of possession of marijuana in 1986, then this stop can turn into a "criminal alien" being deported. And if the driver overstayed his tourist visa, then he or she also faces deportation as an "illegal alien."

In its reports and budgetary requests, ICE uses this dehumanizing language of criminal, fugitive, and illegal aliens and argues that it is making America safer by removing these noncitizens. There is little evidence, however, that these noncitizens are actually dangerous. In fact, only 12% of deportees in 2013 had been convicted of what ICE refers to as a "Level 1" offense (Transactional Records Access Clearing House, 2014). And although "fugitive aliens" sounds ominous, it refers to people like Vern who were released from ICE custody and did not report back for their immigration hearings.

Since taking office, President Barack Obama has argued that his immigration law enforcement has focused on dangerous criminals. In April 2012, Obama again defended his deportation policy, saying his tactic has been to target "criminals, gang bangers, people who are hurting the community" (Hing, 2012). In November 2014, Obama reiterated that immigration law enforcement focuses on "felons, not families" (Acosta and Collinson, 2014). The president alleged that catching criminals was the primary focus of deportation policy and promised it would remain that way.

The evidence that the DHS has been doing exactly the opposite is hard to ignore. Vern's story provides one example. Although Vern did not have so much as a traffic ticket, somehow his case made it to the top of the enforcement priority list, and he was deported to Guatemala.

On April 6, 2014, the *New York Times* reported that nearly two-thirds of the two million deportations since Obama took office have involved either people like Vern with no criminal records or those convicted of minor crimes (Thompson & Cohen, 2014). Just two days later, the Transactional Records Access Clearinghouse (TRAC), based at Syracuse University, issued an even more detailed, and more damning, report (TRAC, 2014). The report, which looks at deportations carried out by ICE, found that 57% of ICE deportations in 2013 were of people who had criminal convictions. However, this statistic hides the fact that most of these convictions are minor. The authors write:

> ICE currently uses an exceedingly broad definition of criminal behavior: even very minor infractions are included. For example, anyone with a traffic ticket for exceeding the speed limit on the Baltimore-Washington Parkway who sends in their check to pay their fine has just entered ICE's "convicted criminal" category. If the same definitions were applied to every citizen . . . evidence suggests that the majority of U.S. citizens would be considered convicted criminals. (TRAC, 2014)

In other words, not only have nearly half of all deportations involved people with no criminal record, large numbers of "criminal" deportations involve people with traffic offenses. The TRAC report is notable, because it provides a close look at the criminal convictions of deportees—data that has not previously been available.

The data reveal that about half of the two million people deported during the Obama administration, like Vern, had no criminal convictions. According to the TRAC report, each year of the Obama administration, the percentage of deportations that involve a criminal conviction has increased.

However, most of these convictions were minor. Some of these convictions would only be considered criminal in a very broad definition of the term. For example, about a quarter of the criminal convictions involved the immigration crime of "illegal entry." The difference between a person deported on noncriminal grounds for being undocumented and one deported on criminal grounds for "illegal entry" is almost entirely a question of prosecutorial decisions. In other words, these 47,000 people deported for illegal entry were converted into criminals for reporting purposes.

The next largest category is traffic offenses—the majority driving under the influence or speeding—which account for nearly another quarter of all criminal deportations. Although safe driving is valued in this country, in common parlance in the United States, we do not generally refer to people with traffic convictions as "criminals." The third largest category is drug offenses. Notably, the most common offense in this category was marijuana possession, which has been legalized in Washington, Colorado, and other locations.

The TRAC (2014) analysis renders it clear that the increase in the number of noncitizens who have been deported on criminal grounds under the Obama administration is mostly a consequence of an increase in the deportation of noncitizens with immigration and traffic violations—convictions that are only considered criminal in a very broad definition of the term. In fact, based on ICE's own definition of a serious or "Level 1" offense, only 12% of all deportations in 2013 were of people convicted of such offenses.

### IS MASS DEPORTATION MAKING US SAFER?

How does the United States get away with a policy of mass deportation that almost exclusively targets people from Latin America and the Caribbean, that tears apart families, and that occurs with almost no constitutional protections? The United States is able to do this by framing mass deportation in terms of national security. This raises the question: Does mass deportation make us safer? If the question is asked in terms of protecting the United States from terrorist attacks, the answer is clearly "no." Massive roundups of Latin American workers are unrelated to the prevention of terrorist attacks.

Under U.S. law, you do not have to have been convicted of a crime to be deported; you only have to be undocumented. However, with 10 million undocumented immigrants, the executive branch has to set priorities.

The goal of immigration law enforcement is not to deport all 10 million undocumented immigrants. Instead, the stated goals are twofold: (1) to deport 400,000 people a year and (2) to focus on noncitizens convicted of crimes. It appears that those two goals are at odds. In trying to reach 400,000 deportations a year, many immigrants without criminal convictions have been caught up in the deportation dragnet.

In an internal memo made public in March 2010, ICE director James M. Chaparro reminded ICE field office directors that they have goals they need to meet. The first goal for FY 2010 was to deport 150,000 criminal aliens. The second was an overall goal of deporting 400,000 people. As made evident in this memo and in ICE annual reports, ICE prioritizes the capture of criminal aliens. The focus on criminal aliens has allowed ICE to claim it is enhancing national security by removing record numbers of criminal aliens. The rate of removal of criminal aliens in FY 2010 was 60% higher than in the last year of the Bush administration (TRAC, 2010).

The quota of 400,000 deportees is an arbitrary number, based on estimates of ICE's capacity, not on actual numbers of immigration law violators. For this reason, the quota has not decreased, even though the U.S. Border Patrol apprehended one-third fewer people in 2010 than it did in 2008 (DHS, 2012, table 35). The failure to reduce the quota has meant that increasing numbers of deportees are people who have lived in the United States for decades and who have strong ties here.

Let's take a closer look at these programs so we can see how these programs operate and what happens when people are deported. These examples of deportations of criminal and fugitive aliens provide a human face to this issue. I gathered these narratives from deportees in Guatemala, the Dominican Republic, and Jamaica as part of a research project designed to understand what happens to people once they are deported.

### NATIONAL FUGITIVE OPERATIONS PROGRAM: DEPORTING FUGITIVES WITH FAMILIES

In 1986, Rafael witnessed an extrajudicial killing in his home country of Guatemala. Once the assassins learned who he was, he began to receive death threats. Rafael fled to the United States. His wife, Mariluna, and their two children, Katy and Alejandra, came soon afterward. They made a life for themselves in Louisiana, and Rafael set up a successful car-detailing business. All they had built crumbled, however, when immigration agents raided their home in 2000.

Mariluna told me: "They came in, as if we were criminals, as if we were murderers." When Mariluna recounted the story to me, her voice broke and tears streamed down her face. When their home was raided, the immigration agents told them two family members needed to be taken into custody to ensure the family would depart. Rafael surrendered, and they had to choose whether to send Mariluna or their daughter Alejandra to immigration detention, as Katy was still under the age of 18. Alejandra volunteered and was taken to a county jail.

The immigration agents took Rafael to an immigration detention center. However, there was not a center for women close by, and Alejandra had to spend 4 days in the county jail. She was 20 years old. She still has nightmares about the experience. Another inmate tried to rape her when she was inside, but she waited years before telling her parents about the incident, as she did not want them to feel guilty. When Mariluna recalled that her daughter had been taken to prison, tears streamed down her face.

With Alejandra and Rafael in custody, and her life in shambles, Mariluna was in shock. Her friends helped her pack her things, but she could barely think straight. With four days to do everything, Mariluna was not able to get all of their belongings shipped to Guatemala. She was able to get a few things into a container and to pack eight suitcases, only six of which she was able to take with her. They left their house and five cars in Louisiana.

When they were deported to Guatemala, Katy could not believe how drastically her life had changed. They were fortunate that they had a place to go—Katy's grandmother had left them a house. However, it was a simple dwelling, with adobe walls and a tin roof. Katy went from living in a spacious, luxurious home in Louisiana to a one-bedroom shack with an outdoor toilet in Guatemala City. It is already difficult to be an adolescent, and Katy did not deal well with this fall from riches to rags. She fell into a deep depression, and barely left the house for over a year. Unable to read or write Spanish, she never went back to school. In the United States, Katy had only finished the ninth grade.

In Louisiana, Katy excelled in school, was popular with her friends, and never got into trouble. She had dreams of becoming a veterinarian, and her sister was already studying to be a doctor. When they were deported to Guatemala, her dreams were shattered.

When we spoke, they had been back in Guatemala for nine years, but the wounds were deep, and Katy still hurt from what happened to her when she was 15. She shed tears for most of the interview. Just thinking about what happened to her and her family was too much to bear.

The deportation of this family happened through the predecessor to the NFOP—an abscondee removal team. Since its creation in 2003, NFOP has expanded this sort of arrest dramatically. A recent report by the Migration Policy Institute criticizes the program, primarily because of its failure to arrest dangerous fugitives—"NFOP has failed to focus its resources on the priorities Congress intended when it authorized the program. In effect, NFOP has succeeded in apprehending the easiest targets, not the most dangerous fugitives" (Mendelson, Strom, and Wishnie, 2009, p. 2). Although NFOP is designed to deport dangerous criminals, nearly three-quarters of the people they apprehended between 2003 and 2008, like Rafael, had no criminal records. In 2007, with a $183 million budget, NFOP arrested only 672 fugitive aliens that ICE considered to be dangerous. The other 30,000 arrested were people with deportation orders (15,646), undocumented migrants (12,084), or noncitizens who had been convicted of nonviolent crimes, such as shoplifting (2,005). Mendelson and colleagues of the Migration Policy Institute point out that "the number of fugitive aliens with criminal convictions arrested . . . remained relatively constant between FY 2004 and FY 2008. Congressional allocations to NFOP, by contrast, grew 17-fold over the same period" (2009, p. 15).

Rafael had requested asylum once he arrived in the United States. Nearly a decade after he applied for asylum, his application was denied. By that time, Rafael had already set up a successful business in Louisiana. He could not imagine uprooting his family yet again, and they decided to stay. With outstanding deportation orders, Rafael and his family were "fugitive aliens" and thus made it to the top of the priority list.

### 287(G): WALTER, A CRIMINAL ALIEN GUILTY OF IMMIGRATION FRAUD

Walter, a citizen of the Dominican Republic, took a boat to Puerto Rico when he was 15 years old and attempted to enter the United States illegally to join his brother who lived in New York. However, he was caught and deported. When he was 19, Walter decided to try to emigrate again and made it all the way to New York City. Two years later, Walter met and married a U.S. citizen and obtained legalization in 1998 through family reunification laws. He intended to make his life in the United States; he worked at JFK airport to support his wife and their two children. In 2004, Walter was stopped by police officers for a traffic violation. When they checked his immigration status, the officer discovered he had an immigration hold. It turns out that Walter had an order to appear at immigration court because immigration investigators discovered that Walter had failed to mention on his application for legalization that he had been deported from Puerto Rico when he was 15. This accusation of immigration fraud resulted in Walter's residency being rescinded. Walter spent four years fighting his case, but in 2008 he lost and was deported to the Dominican Republic—as a "criminal alien." His crime: immigration fraud. One out of six people deported on criminal grounds are deported for immigration crimes such as these.

Walter was deported after being pulled over by a local police officer. When local police officers collaborate with immigration law enforcement, tensions between police officers and community members increase, as does the distrust people feel toward law enforcement. ICE officials argue that collaboration between local and immigration law enforcement is important, because it gives police officers the resources they need to fight human trafficking and organized crime. In theory, interagency collaboration could enhance national security. In practice, the adoption of 287(g) decreases local-level security.

Under 287(g), police officers have the authority to call immigration agents to find out whether any person they encounter is undocumented. This means that people who are undocumented or whose loved ones are undocumented will be less likely to call the police to report crimes, even when they are the victims. Because of the heavy policing of Latino neighborhoods, 287(g) could even lead to people being scared to take their children to the hospital.

When I lived in Little Village, a primarily Latino community in Chicago, one of my neighbors recounted to me what happened when her daughter fell off of a piece of playground equipment. The girl came home crying that she was hurt, and my neighbor rushed her 9-year-old daughter to the hospital. Doctors put a cast on the girl's arm, and eventually she healed. Because of this incident, a police officer came to question the mother to find out whether there was a case of child abuse in the home. The officer determined there was not, and that was the end of the investigation.

My neighbor remembered this vividly, and it was well known in this neighborhood that when any accident happens, police can get involved. In another case, my other neighbor came home from drinking with friends and injured his arm when he fell on a wire gate. Police officers subsequently interviewed his wife to find out whether there had been any domestic violence. Both my neighbor who took her daughter to the hospital and my neighbor whose husband injured his arm are undocumented. If Chicago police were to cooperate with immigration law enforcement agents, people in immigrant communities might think twice about calling an ambulance or taking their loved ones to the hospital after experiencing an injury.

### CRIMINAL ALIEN PROGRAM—THE WORST OF THE WORST?

CAP is designed to apprehend convicted criminals serving time in federal and state prisons. ICE touts this program as identifying the "worst of the worst" in the noncitizen population. However, many of the people identified in this program are in fact long-term legal permanent residents of the United States who are deported for relatively minor crimes. Whereas undocumented people can be deported regardless of whether they have criminal convictions, legal permanent residents only face deportation if they have been convicted of a crime. In these cases, they are deported after serving time for their criminal convictions.

O'Ryan, for example, moved to the United States from Jamaica when he was 6 years old. When he was in his early twenties, O'Ryan was a passenger in a car where drugs were found. He was sentenced to 3 to 9 years for drug trafficking. He chose to do boot camp, so he only spent 18 months in jail. After serving his time, he was deported to Jamaica. All of O'Ryan's family members are U.S. citizens—his mother, his sister, his fiancé, and his daughter. He also had applied for citizenship, but the application was still pending when he was arrested. O'Ryan has only distant relatives in Jamaica. When I met him, he had been in Jamaica for 7 years and saw his deportation as a cruel punishment for a mistake for which he had already paid.

Human Rights Watch (2009) reports that 897,099 people were deported on criminal grounds between April 1, 1997, and August 1, 2007, and that 94% of these people were from just 10 countries—Mexico, Honduras,

El Salvador, Dominican Republic, Guatemala, Colombia, Jamaica, Canada, Brazil, and Haiti. Just under 10% of those people—87,844—were legal permanent residents of the United States, and about 20%—179,038—were legally present in the United States as either legal permanent residents, asylees, or parolees, or on a temporary visa. Very few of the "criminal aliens" who are deported are people who present any real danger to society. In fact, their deportations often have negative consequences for the family members they leave behind. O'Ryan, for example, left behind his newborn daughter—who will now be raised by a single mother.

The majority of criminal deportees were long-term residents of the United States—half of the people deported between 1997 and 2006 for aggravated felonies had spent more than 14 years in the United States (TRAC, 2006). The fact that increasing numbers of deportees are people who have been in the United States for extended periods of time means that deportations affect more people in the United States and that the effects are more widespread. For example, if a migrant farmworker comes to the United States to work for 6 months and is deported after 3 months, he and his family in Mexico feel the most immediate harm. The principal effect of this deportation is the loss of the wages for the farmworker and the loss of labor to the farm owner. This is quite distinct from the deportation of a person who has been in the United States for two decades, has children in the United States, and has strong community ties. His deportation entails much more than the loss of wages. His children lose a father, his wife a husband, and his community members a valuable and productive member.

## SECURE COMMUNITIES—SUSPECTED, ARRESTED, DEPORTED

When I was in Guatemala in 2009, I witnessed thousands of deportees returning to their country of birth. Four to six planeloads of deportees arrive at the Guatemalan air force base each week—a total of more than 44,000 people displaced in 2013 ("Más de 44 mil deportados," 2013). Eric is one of the deportees I met at the Guatemalan air force base. When we met, I asked if I could contact him after he had a chance to get settled in. He agreed.

Just over a month after Eric arrived, we met up in Metro Norte, a modern shopping center in one of the rougher neighborhoods of Guatemala City—Zona 18—close to where Eric was staying. Eric told me he had traveled to the United States when he was 11 years old, to join his mother, who had left three years before. He went on an airplane alone, with a tourist visa, as his undocumented mother could not come for her son or apply for an immigrant visa for him. Eric enrolled in middle school in Inglewood, Los Angeles, where his mother worked at a garment factory. In his last year of high school, Eric's mother injured her back and was unable to continue working. Eric had to drop out of school and get a job to keep the family afloat. He had no trouble finding low-wage work and worked two jobs. He met a Salvadoran woman who is a legal permanent resident of the United States, and they got married.

Once Eric had a job, he purchased a car to drive to work each morning. On weekends, Eric spent time with his wife and friends. One Saturday afternoon, Eric's friend asked him for a ride, and Eric took him to the other side of town. Shortly after he dropped his friend off, a police officer pulled Eric over and arrested him as an accomplice in the car theft his friend had allegedly committed. The police checked Eric's immigration status, as the police district participated in the Secure Communities Program. This program, designed to find and deport dangerous noncitizens, enables police officers to determine whether an arrestee is in the country legally. The police discovered he had overstayed his visa and held him until immigration agents came to take him into custody, even though the car theft charges had been dropped. Immigration agents took Eric to a Corrections Corporation of America detention center and held him until he was deported from the United States. Neither Eric's innocence of car theft nor his pending application for legalization on the basis of his marriage prevented his deportation, and he had to leave his mother and pregnant wife behind.

In Guatemala City, Eric moved into his aunt's house, where he had lived before leaving the country (when he was 11). Soon after arriving, Eric secured a job at a call center where he answers calls from customers in the United States. As a bilingual deportee familiar with the United States, he is an ideal worker for this transnational corporation. His labor is also significantly cheaper than it would be in the United States: his job pays just $400 a month.

Once Eric was arrested, deportation was practically inevitable. When he was taken into custody at Los Angeles County Jail, because of the Secure Communities Program, they ran his fingerprints through an immigration database, which revealed that Eric had overstayed his temporary visa and was eligible for deportation. The police officers thus held Eric—even though there were no criminal charges against him—until immigration agents arrived and took Eric to an immigration detention facility.

### CONCLUSION

Most criminal and fugitive aliens do not present a threat to society. The main reason that ICE targets criminal and fugitive aliens is that doing so allows them to claim they are making America safer through the use of dehumanizing rhetoric that conjures up images of malignant characters. The reality is that criminal and fugitive aliens are often people with families in the United States. Their deportation does not make the country any safer, yet often has pernicious effects on their families.

The cooperation between criminal and immigration law enforcement agents means that many of the problems we have with our criminal justice system are exacerbated. After riding in a car where drugs were found, O'Ryan not only spent over a year behind bars, he also was deported. Eric seems to have been a victim of racial profiling—police officers saw two young Latinos driving in Los Angeles and suspected they had been involved in a car theft. In addition to the hassle involved in being arrested and taken downtown, Eric was deported. Walter was pulled over for speeding. The propensity of police officers to pull over African Americans more often than whites is so prevalent that the moniker "driving while black" has emerged to explain this phenomenon. In the early 1990s, statistician John Lamberth conducted a detailed investigation of police stops on the New Jersey Turnpike. This study revealed that only 13% of all cars on the New Jersey Turnpike had a black driver or passenger, but 35% of those stopped on the turnpike were black, and 73.2% of those arrested were black. Blacks were much more likely than whites to be stopped, even though blacks and whites violated traffic laws at almost exactly the same rate (Lamberth, 1994). Racial profiling also extends to Hispanics. A study in Volusia County in Florida, for example, revealed that blacks and Hispanics were more likely to be pulled over and, once pulled over, were much more likely to be searched than whites (Mauer, 1999). When deportation is a collateral consequence of racial profiling, the consequences of this profiling are exacerbated.

The removal of these men from their communities will have reverberating effects. Vern may never see his children again. Walter's wife was obliged to turn to public aid after his deportation, as her minimum-wage job did not pay enough for her to support their children. O'Ryan's daughter has grown up only knowing her father as a voice on the other end of the telephone. Eric's wife was pregnant when he was deported, and he may never meet his child. In addition to the immediate effects felt by these families, the stories of their deportations circulate in communities, leading to fear and resentment—especially with regard to local law enforcement. Police cooperation with ICE thus leads to less—not more—secure communities.

In November 2014, Jeh Johnson, secretary of the DHS, issued a memo that announced that that the Secure Communities Program would be replaced with the Priority Enforcement Program (PEP). In this memo, Johnson indicated that ICE should only go to jails to detain people who have been convicted of an offense that is a high priority for ICE removal. Under this new program, people should only be placed in removal proceedings if they have been convicted of a felony or more than one misdemeanor. As of this writing in April 2015, PEP is still being implemented, and it is too early to tell whether this change in priorities will mean that people like Eric will not be deported.

The narratives and data presented in this chapter make it clear that immigration reform is necessary. However, insofar as immigrants continue to be conflated with criminals, fugitives, terrorists, and gang members, it will be difficult to get comprehensive immigration reform through Congress. There is a paradox wherein U.S. citizens who know immigrants often consider those immigrants to be upstanding members of the community. However, many U.S. citizens continue to imagine immigrants as "other," as unassimilable foreigners who come to this country to wreak havoc and take advantage of public aid. Shifting this discourse will be a hefty task. However, it is hard to imagine how we will be able to achieve immigration reform without changing how we talk about immigrants.

## REFERENCES

Acosta, J., & Collinson, S. (2014, December 20). Obama unveils new immigration plan. CNN. www.cnn.com/2014/11/20/politics/obama-immigration-speech.

Hing, J. (2012, October 17). Who are those "gangbangers" Obama's so proud of deporting? Colorlines. Retrieved on June 13, 2014, from http://colorlines.com/archives/2012/10/who_are_those_gangbangers_obamas_so_proud_of_deporting.html.

Human Rights Watch. (2009). Forced apart: By the numbers. *Human Rights Reports*. New York: Human Rights Watch. Retrieved on June 13, 2014, from www.hrw.org/sites/default/files/reports/us0409web.pdf.

Lamberth, J. (1994). *Revised statistical analysis of the incidence of police stops and arrests of black drivers: Travelers on the New Jersey Turnpike between exits or interchanges 1 and 3 from the years 1988 through 1991*. West Chester, PA: Lamberth Consulting. Retrieved on June 1, 2012, from www.lamberthconsulting.com/uploads/new_jersey_study_report.pdf.

Más de 44 mil deportados de Estados Unidos durante 2013. (2013, November 18). América Economia. Retrieved on June 13, 2014, http://americaeconomia.com/node/105264.

Mauer, M. (1999). The crisis of the young African American male and the criminal justice system. *Sentencing Project*. Retrieved on June 1, 2012, from www.sentencingproject.org/doc/publications/rd_crisisoftheyoung.pdf.

Mendelson, M., Strom S., and Wishnie, M. 2009. *Collateral damage: An examination of ICE's Fugitive Operations Program*. Washington, DC: Migration Policy Institute. www.migrationpolicy.org/pubs/NFOP_Feb09.pdf.

Thompson, G., & Cohen, S. (2014, April 6). More deportations follow minor crimes, records show. *New York Times*. Retrieved on June 13, 2014, from www.nytimes.com/2014/04/07/us/more-deportations-follow-minor-crimes-data-shows.html.

Transactional Records Access Clearinghouse. (2006). How often is the aggravated felony statute used? *TRAC Reports*. Retrieved on June 13, 2014, from http://trac.syr.edu/immigration/reports/158.

——. (2010). Current ICE removals of noncitizens exceed numbers under Bush administration. *TRAC Reports*. Retrieved on June 13, 2014, from http://trac.syr.edu/immigration/reports/234.

——. (2014). Secure communities and ICE deportation: A failed program? *TRAC Reports*. Retrieved on June 13, 2014, from http://trac.syr.edu/immigration/reports/349.

U.S. Department of Homeland Security. (2012). Yearbook of immigration statistics: 2012: Enforcement actions. Retrieved on June 1, 2012, from www.dhs.gov/yearbook-immigration-statistics-2012-enforcement-actions.

U.S. Immigration and Customs Enforcement. (2012). Fact sheet: A day in the life of ICE Enforcement and Removal Operations. Retrieved on June 11, 2014, from www.ice.gov/doclib/news/library/factsheets/pdf/day-in-life-ero.pdf.

# 3

# Unexpected Asylums, Tenuous Futures

## HELD IN ABEYANCE AT A STATE PSYCHIATRIC INSTITUTE

▸ NORA J. KENWORTHY

FOR MANY UNDOCUMENTED IMMIGRANTS, LIFE seems suspended, and the period before documentation, before official belonging, easily acquires permanence. Being "held in abeyance" (Hopper & Baumohl, 1994; Mizruchi & Schwartz, 1983) shapes the logic of everyday life: families wait decades to be reunited, bureaucratic processes drag on without resolution, and mass detention resembles incarceration. (Here, I am not referring to "abeyance" in the legal sense of awaiting ownership. Rather, I am interested in abeyance as a bureaucratic strategy of temporary removal or suspension that all too often becomes permanent.) Immigrants often find themselves existing in a state of in-betweenness—not yet exiled but not at all belonging—and it is this state of liminality and limbo that so heavily impacts the undocumented immigrant experience.

This chapter explores an unlikely space of abeyance: a northeastern state psychiatric facility where immigrants have little hope of discharge, because they are undocumented and thus unqualified for other forms of care. (The hospital's name, its location, and the names of key collaborators who work at the facility must remain anonymous to protect participants from deportation or other negative consequences.) This group of immigrants occupies an anomalous intersection of two institutional bureaucracies—the legal webs of the U.S. immigration system and the underfunded, overcrowded state mental health system. Though this situation is largely unknown to the broader U.S. public, it is shaped by two of the most prominent institutions of social management and control. While mental health officials are reluctant to discuss how undocumented immigrants receive care in other states, this situation is not unique to the hospital discussed here (Department of the Public Advocate, 2009).

## ASYLUM IN ASYLUMS

Immigrants show higher burdens of certain serious mental illnesses (Cantor-Graae & Selten, 2005; McKenzie, Fearon, & Hutchinson, 2008; Takeuchi, Alegria, Jackson, & Williams, 2007; Velig et al., 2008), face multiple barriers in accessing mental health services (Fortuna, Porche, & Alegria, 2008; Kim et al., 2011), and experience acute mental health challenges when held in detention facilities (Bridges, Andrews, & Deen, 2012; Coffey et al., 2010; McLoughlin & Warin, 2008). In addition, trauma (and evidence of trauma) in immigrants is deeply shaped by politics at home and abroad (Caple-James, 2010; Ticktin, 2006). But much less is known about the clinical trajectories of immigrants through psychiatric care: how they access care, what kinds of services they are offered, and how—and whether—they are able leave restrictive hospital settings. Between 2009 and 2011, research was conducted with a group of individuals who were or had become undocumented and had histories of significant mental illness that led to extended hospitalization in state facilities. Though the deinstitutionalization movement emptied out many state hospitals, replacing them with community-based services, state law precluded patients from being discharged without an appropriate outpatient treatment plan. State funds ensure undocumented patients are treated at psychiatric hospitals regardless of ability to pay, but community-based care is dependent on Medicaid and social security funds. Because undocumented patients rarely qualify for such social support, they end up stranded within the state hospital system. Hospital policies are more humane than measures taken at other medical facilities, from which undocumented patients have been deported (Mehta, 2010) or sent back to their countries of origin with the assistance of private "medical repatriation" firms (Sack, 2009; Silva, 2010; Vesga-Lopez et al., 2009).

Those interviewed for this study had primarily been "discharged" from the state inpatient hospital to a less restrictive facility on the hospital grounds. This residence facility did not provide the community integration or other opportunities that community-based facilities tend to offer: undocumented patients remained segregated in a full-time residence on hospital grounds and, perhaps most importantly, continued to *think of themselves* as hospitalized. As a result, undocumented patients became a disproportionately large group at the on-site residence, constituting about 20% of occupants. Though some participants in the study were also still residing within the inpatient hospital unit, most had been at the on-site residence for many years, and few foresaw any way to leave.

Though clinicians had been mostly compassionate toward these undocumented patients, discharge options were very limited. In rare cases in which a patient had family support nearby, the patient could be discharged to live with family, while the hospital continued to provide and pay for ongoing, backdoor medical care. Otherwise, staff could gently explore the option of "repatriation." This was a difficult subject to broach, as patients were frequently unwilling or unable to return to their countries of origin: in-country medical services were too limited, patients had lost contact with family, or else patients had been in the United States for so long that they hardly had a "home country" to which they could return.

Those who did not or could not explore these options remained marooned by default on hospital grounds. While the logistical and legal challenges of patients' situations are urgent (for more on this, see Kenworthy, 2012), their life stories offer an instructive look into immigrant vulnerabilities and the bureaucratic institutions that shape much of life's chances for people arriving, and surviving, in the United States. Some life trajectories were especially poignant: Jakov was an elderly Jewish man who had fled Hungary with his family in the 1950s; he was hospitalized at 18, shortly after he arrived in the United States. He spent the remainder of his life at the hospital and passed away as the study began. At the time of his death, most of his family members were naturalized citizens, and few had any contact with him. He was buried in the hospital graveyard.

Before turning to more in-depth life stories, a few methodological notes are important. As may already be clear, crucial details about individuals' lives and the institutions at which they resided have been withheld in an attempt to preserve confidentiality as much as is possible. Methods of data collection were multifaceted, including: culling and analyzing medical records for almost all undocumented patients throughout the hospital; conversations with staff and clinicians as well as key informants from other states and facilities; and in-depth life history interviews with 17 patients representing a range of backgrounds and characteristics.

It is all too common for immigrants and those diagnosed with mental illness to have narratives and accounts called into question, brought under a suspicious and authoritarian gaze. Though symptoms of illness shaded some narratives, and narrators sometimes struggled to recall details, I endeavored to embrace all accounts as valid and representative of life experiences and outlooks. While medical records helped to triangulate key dates and facts, they can have their own inaccuracies and serve purposes other than the accurate transcription of medical procedures (Garfinkel, 1967). Data from interviews were condensed and rewritten as personal life histories. Informants then collaborated in revising and elaborating the stories. The process proved especially helpful for those who struggled with oral communication because of illness or the long-term side effects of medication. The result was a set of narratives that interviewees thoroughly embraced as their own, even though they are more distilled than first-person quotations. The stories that follow are drawn directly from those cocreated narratives.

### Lisa

Lisa was born into a poor family in Seoul, South Korea, in the 1950s. Her parents had intermittent factory jobs, but she and her siblings often went hungry, and there was little money for education. Lisa did not finish high school, and when she left school, she found a job working in a food factory. When Lisa was 25 she met Paul, an American GI who was stationed in South Korea, and they quickly married. She joined him in the United States when she was 27.

After being stationed in Louisiana, Paul was discharged from the army, and he and Lisa found work in a meat-processing plant. It was grueling work, but after more than a decade in the factory, they were able to buy a house. About 15 years into their marriage, Paul unexpectedly had an affair and "got a girl pregnant." Lisa felt she had no choice but to "let him go."

After they divorced, Lisa moved to the city, hoping to find a job. She worked as a bartender, then in a massage parlor. Living alone with no family in the United States to fall back on, she knew she had to protect herself financially, and she carefully squirreled money away for retirement. After a while, however, she "got lost," and began using drugs—cocaine, then crack. Working in a massage parlor soon turned into sex work.

While working one night, Lisa was raped and badly beaten by three men. She became depressed and soon after started hearing voices. She attempted suicide, overdosing on drugs, and was hospitalized involuntarily for three agonizing months. By the time she was discharged, she had lost her home and all her belongings. For the next five years she was homeless—staying in cheap hotels when she could afford it, but mostly out on the streets. Throughout this period, Lisa continued to hear voices; it was hard to sleep or even sit still. She kept seeking care, from Korean doctors and during two additional hospital stays, but found little relief. It was, she says, "a very, very hard life."

Lisa struggled with mental illness and homelessness for more than two decades before she found any respite, and it took an event she described as "completely [losing] my mind" for her to find meaningful and effective treatment. She was finally booked into a large urban psychiatric hospital and transferred from there to the state hospital. She seemed to stabilize at the hospital, completing a drug treatment program and appreciating the care of her doctors. After nine months she was transferred to the on-site residence and has been there for the past 10 years.

At one point, of course, Lisa had U.S. citizenship. She remembers her naturalization ceremony with pride, and the feeling of having a social security number and driver's license. At some point, either during her lengthy homeless period or one of her transfers into or out of the hospital, Lisa lost all of her documents, the addresses of her family members, and her divorce papers. She says she was "so, so scared" when she lost touch with her family: now no one knew where, or who, she was.

It is especially difficult to reapply for immigration paperwork or reestablish an immigration claim from hospital grounds. Lisa first hired an immigration lawyer to find her paperwork, ultimately paying him $3,000. He told her he had found nothing, but she suspects he simply took advantage of her. Two years before our meeting, Lisa decided to try reapplying for her social security card. Since she lacked other documentation as well, Lisa tried going in person to Philadelphia, where she had originally received her card. Since none of the staff was willing to assist her with the trip, she simply called a cab and used all of her cash savings—$300—to pay the fare. When Lisa arrived at the Social Security Administration's regional offices to try reapplying for her card, she handed over the only

ID that remained in her possession: her hospital ID card. Her efforts were promptly rebuffed.

For Lisa, becoming redocumented is essential to her recovery process. Though she is deeply grateful for what the residence offers her—she reports she is "happy, thank God" to be there and refers to the staff as "beautiful people," she is bored, and wants to get a place of her own. But Lisa is trapped: having lived in the United States for so long and lost all contact with South Korea, she "can't go back, can't go back" without papers; she worries that discharge might force her back onto the streets. "I can't do that anymore," she says. Most of all, Lisa just wants to "keep on living," but without documents, "I can do nothing, you know?" Sadly, on another level, she wants her documents so that the residence staff "won't think I am sneaking into the U.S."

As Lisa's story demonstrates, one of the lamentable (and preventable) consequences of frequent hospitalization and homelessness is that crucial paperwork is often lost. A psychiatric break can ravage memory, and paranoia compounds suspicion that documents have been stolen or destroyed by family or care workers. For immigrants, illness can also imperil contact with far-flung family members.

Navigating government agencies to find lost documents or reinvigorate long-forgotten immigration claims is a necessary job skill for social workers at psychiatric facilities, though it competes with more pressing concerns in a perennially understaffed environment. By the time I met her, Lisa had more help than in the past but still felt overwhelmed by the process. Even basic application fees (which run $200 to $300) are exorbitant, and hospital funds for such expenses are scarce. Recovering lost documents is laden with difficulties, even for nonimmigrants (Wilson, 2009), requiring extensive capabilities, patience, and resources.

As long as Lisa is unsuccessful in reapplying for her papers, she will remain in the residence, regardless of her recovery. She may be off the streets, but living here is a suspension of life, an institutionalized existence that protects only "bare life" (Agamben, 1998). It is an acute, structural double bind: mental illness adds to the suspicion with which immigrant claims are regarded, but lack of documentation prevents discharge. Doubly unwanted and doubly held in abeyance: each status reinforces the other.

### Samad

Samad came to the United States as a refugee of the first Iraq War. Even more so than in Lisa's story, the damages of the American empire are writ large in Samad's life history. Samad suffers from acute memory loss—it is hard to say whether this is from medical issues, trauma, mental illness, or all three. While the details of his story are at times slim or incongruous, two themes remain constant: first, the power of bureaucratic institutions, which seem so irrational and unintelligible, in shaping Samad's life; and second, his deep fears about surviving in this country.

Samad grew up in a large Shiite family in southern Iraq, and his father served in the Iraqi army for more than 8 years, mostly fighting Iran. By the time Samad turned 17, he too had joined the army, and the Gulf War broke out shortly afterward. His memories of the war are fragmentary, full of gunfire, confusion, and prayer. He describes an "American army evil" that came and "put the bomb on Iraq." By the time he was 20, Samad was stationed in Kurdistan, fighting in the Iraqi–Kurdish civil war. Somewhere along the line, he was selected to join a large group of Iraqis who were offered asylum by the United States for their roles in assisting American military operations (U.S. Department of Defense, 1997). Since Samad's memories of his activities in the war are foggy, it is difficult to assess how he might have been selected for refugee status, or why.

While Samad had few qualms about leaving a war zone to come to America, the arduous journey and resettlement process soon raised doubts in his mind. Along with a large group of refugees, he was taken from Kurdistan and across the border to Turkey by bus, and then flown to Guam. The refugees were held in Guam for 3 to 4 months in what he describes as a highly militarized complex, where they were screened for asylum. Eventually, Samad was granted asylum and flown to the United States; given a green card, an ID, and a social security number; and settled with the help of a refugee services organization in the Southwest. His settlement process, as is true for many refugees, was difficult, and his transition was made all the more frightening by the voices he had begun hearing. "It was crazy," he remembers, "I walked around in the city, and I didn't even know who I was . . . I was so scared . . . I went to the hospital, and the hospital did nothing . . . [so I left the] hospital . . . [I was] crazy, crazy." At the time, he was living on a small stipend in an apartment he shared with five other people, and after a few conflicts with his room-mates, he left the apartment to seek out accommodations in the city's only homeless shelter.

Samad spent five months in the shelter, sometimes sleeping inside, some-times staying in the alley behind it. While he was sleeping outside one night, his wallet and all of his papers were stolen. "I thought to myself," he says about his stolen green card, "what to do . . . now? Where would I ask for it? When I asked for it, where would I put it [to keep it safe]?" He lost all touch with his family, because he had lost their contact information as well. His memory loss makes reapplying for documents especially difficult: "I don't know how long I've been in America, I don't know what date I came to America, I don't know what year it was . . . I don't know nothing," he insists morosely. During the same period, Samad was charged with crim-inal trespassing, charges that not only confused him but fed his paranoia and fear regarding the police. "I just don't know what the problem was with walking in the city." Later, he comments, "Maybe it [was] my fault. I just [didn't] know where I [could] go [to] eat."

Samad circulated between homeless shelters and the streets in cities throughout the southwestern United States for more than half a decade. Samad's stories from this time period are disjointed but consistently full of fear. The police hassled him relentlessly in encounters that he found threat-ening and overwhelming. He recalls that when he was in California he heard voices that told him to kill himself. The shelter he was staying in was particularly abysmal, and he felt perennially cold from sleeping outdoors. He walked into traffic and was hit by a car, which broke his leg. At another point, he ran into an Iraqi refugee he knew from his army service. The man was doing well, working for a bank, but he refused to speak to Samad, slam-ming the door in his face. It is these stories of assaults on his dignity that seem to stick most clearly in his mind.

Eventually, Samad made his way to the East Coast. Soon after, he was admitted involuntarily into an urban psychiatric hospital and from there was transferred to the state hospital for 8 months. Now in the residence, Samad enjoys a gentler life than the one he led on the streets. It is a good place to stay, and he has friends. But he misses his family, and his many letters home either go unanswered or (he suspects) are never sent. He can-not remember any addresses in Iraq. And though he misses his home coun-try, Samad is well aware of the conflicts that have raged through Iraq in his absence and is doubtful he could find a way to survive there, even if he did find his family.

### THIS IS MY GREEN CARD NOW

Like Lisa, Samad believes that his prospects of survival in the United States outside the facility are equally slim. When he speaks of life on the streets, he recalls seeing "people taking other people to work" and "people finding work," while "I didn't know where I could find work." Later, he asks, "Why would I see a lot of people in the city, doing good, [having] work, and they drink and eat. [But] I [would] see the police bothering me all day?" (Kenworthy, 2012, p. 127). In one telling conversation with Samad, he insists that he does not want a green card. It is difficult to assess whether he simply feels that there is no point to getting one or if he worries that getting one would mean he would have to leave the residence. "What to do with these papers," he asks me, especially when he is here? He tugs at the hospital ID on his chest: "This is my green card [now]." I tell him that other people do want to get their green cards, and he nods, "But I lost support when I came to America. All of it. I don't got a home, I don't got a work, I don't got—this is the [only] place [for me]" (Kenworthy, 2012, p. 127). Later, I explain that with a green card he could get social security. "Social security?" Samad asks, "Who would do that for me?" He believes he is undeserving of benefits, and given the institutional logistics he has encountered thus far, his skepticism is likely reasonable.

This is hardly the sort of "learned helplessness" that psychologists (Seligman, 1991; Wing & Brown, 1970) have long asserted keeps patients bound to institutions well after recovery or rehabilitation might have been expected. While immigrants come from countries with very different norms regarding the social contract, hospitalization, homelessness, and unbelonging teach a "learned unworthiness"—the sentiment that one does not deserve basic rights or entitlements. Nor is Samad's assessment of his chances of survival outside the hospital residence unreasonable. Rather, he seems to have carefully taken note of the lessons U.S. immigration and social service institutions have taught him by default: survival in the United States as an undocumented immigrant still struggling with mental illness is impossible but for the asylum provided by the hospital itself. Trajectories such as these repeatedly raised questions about whether patients' persistent challenges obtaining documentation also cut short trajectories of recovery from illness. Certainly, for patients like Samad, a reasonable hopelessness prevailed that extended beyond the usual illness symptomologies.

## SURVIVAL AND THE INSTITUTION

Despite the breadth of the stories collected in this project, nearly every single participant had experienced periods of homelessness and acute hardship, and many had been impacted by the wars or foreign policies of the United States. Homelessness sometimes preceded the first symptoms of acute mental illness and sometimes followed it; some lost documents during crisis, and some never had them to start with; some fled wars, and others fled economic crises spurred by neoliberal policies. So these individuals were not made vulnerable by a single social institution but by many. Most of all, they suffered from legal systems that penalize and criminalize immigration, poverty, and mental illness; their survival was imperiled by insufficient social services for immigrants, the unhoused, and those struggling with mental illness.

Yet even as institutions imperil survival, they preserve it, a situation that has become more and more common for populations of the vulnerable in the United States. In the hospital, undocumented patients find an unexpected safe harbor. And though many report that they are well cared for and appreciate the stability of this environment, such asylum comes at a steep cost to one's sense of self and one's hopes for the future. The "mortification rituals" Goffman (1961) so expertly described as part of one's entrance into hospitalization are here coupled with a tenure that lacks an endpoint—a landscape without a horizon. And while undocumented residents here are relatively insulated from deportation, their protection could at any moment vanish—if funding shrinks further, or public opinion turns against the use of state coffers for this purpose, or U.S. Immigration and Customs Enforcement begins taking note of this largely unrecognized population.

Such circumscribed, tenuous institutional survival is evident elsewhere: as Hopper (1990) notes, we serve most marginal populations in institutions ill-suited to their needs. These "hybrid institutions"—jails, emergency rooms, homeless shelters—act as overstretched safety nets for populations long since abandoned in the neoliberal turn away from more progressive options for the poor. The resulting circuits between street, jail, shelter, and hospital can deeply erode sense of self and contribute to loss of paperwork or status. At least one undocumented individual in the residence was a man who insisted he was, and appeared to be, a U.S.-born citizen. But a lifetime of mental illness and of strong antipsychotic medicines can ravage memory, and he had lost enough to make finding his records impossible. When convoluted institutional pathways are traced and retraced over the better part of a lifetime, past selves as well as paper trails can be lost. Thus, even as institutions provide a modicum of basic survival, they are corrosive to the self—the very self one must present as worthy, genuine, and legitimate in order to obtain (re)documentation.

Two distinctive poignancies intertwine here. The first is that undocumented residents may get better and more ample services here than they do elsewhere. In this sense the hospital ID does confer a circumscribed set of curious entitlements not always on offer to other immigrants (mental health care perhaps most important among them). But this is not care on one's own terms, and the second poignancy is that many patients are well enough to be discharged but are kept for lack of the documentation necessary to fund a pathway out of the hospital system and toward community-based recovery. And so at a facility where staff are keen to support recovery, and in a system in which community-based services are many times cheaper than hospitalization, patients are maintained at great cost to already dwindling state coffers, because those who are not "lawfully residing" cannot access adequate health coverage (Department of Health and Human Services, 2012).

As a result, residents enact the repetitive patterns of a moored, constrained life: killing time smoking outside under the silent watch of abandoned hospital buildings; squirreling away funds for a splurge on take-out Chinese or a weekly trip to the nearby pharmacy; gossiping, crafting, and pacing the hallways. Joseph, an immigrant from West Africa, surprises and delights us when he reveals that, unbeknownst to staff, he has been walking off hospital grounds each day to a nearby gas station, where he has a job pumping gas. He is paid in cash that he hides in his room and intermittently wires to extended family back home. But for those less enterprising, the task is simply to wait and to guard one's hopes.

To be documented, after all, is not simply to have a bureaucratic identity or a legal belonging. Rather, it is to be visible, to exist. Illegality and invisibility are not simply the result of lost documents or illness episodes but are produced by bureaucratic policies that are difficult to navigate and that link belonging to paperwork. As Darren, another resident, put it when discussing his missing birth certificate, "You see, it's as if I never existed. That's how it is . . . even in my own [home] country, it's as if I never existed. They don't have no documents on me." Such a situation invites the mental demons that make recovery all the more elusive. So residents spend their days doing battle with themselves, fighting despair, suspicion, and doubt. Darren, only in his early twenties, can hardly sort out anymore where he came from or where he really belongs. Without documents, "it's hard to know what to believe." As Darren reasons solemnly: "If you don't know your past, it's hard to figure out your future."

### REFERENCES

Agamben, G. (1998). *Homo sacer: Sovereign power and bare life.* Stanford, CA: Stanford University Press.

Bridges, A. J., Andrews, A. R., & Deen, T. L. (2012). Mental health needs and service utilization by Hispanic immigrants residing in mid-southern United States. *Journal of Transcultural Nursing, 23*(4), 359–368.

Cantor-Graae, E., & Selten, J. P. (2005). Schizophrenia and migration: A meta-analysis and review. *American Journal of Psychiatry, 162*(1), 12–24.

Caple-James, E. (2010). *Democratic insecurities: Violence, trauma and intervention in Haiti.* Berkeley: University of California Press.

Coffey, G. J., Kaplan, I., Sampson, R., & Tucci, M. M. (2010). The meaning and mental health consequences of long-term immigration detention for people seeking asylum. *Social Science and Medicine, 70*(12), 2070–2079.

Department of Health and Human Services. (2012, March). *Overview of immigrants' eligibility for SNAP, TANF, Medicaid, and CHIP* (ASPE Issue Brief). Washington, DC: Author. Retrieved on March 10, 2012, from http://aspe.hhs.gov/hsp/11/ImmigrantAccess/Eligibility/ib.shtml.

Department of the Public Advocate. (2009). *Undocumented immigrants in New Jersey's state and county psychiatric hospitals.* Trenton, NJ: Author.

Fortuna, L., Porche, M., & Alegria, M. (2008). Political violence, psychosocial trauma, and the context of mental health services use among immigrant Latinos in the United States. *Ethnicity and Health, 13*(5), 435–463.

Garfinkel, H. (1967). *Studies in ethnomethodology.* Englewood Cliffs, NJ: Prentice-Hall.

Goffman, E. (1961). *Asylums: Essays on the social situation of mental patients and other inmates.* Chicago: Aldine.

Hopper, K. (1990). Public shelter as a "hybrid institution": Homeless men in historical perspective. *Journal of Social Issues, 46*(4), 13–29.

Hopper, K., & Baumohl, J. (1994). Held in abeyance: Rethinking homelessness and advocacy. *American Behavioral Scientist, 37*(4), 522–552.

Kenworthy, N. (2012). Asylum's asylum. Undocumented immigrants, belonging, and the space of exception at a state psychiatric center. *Human Organization, 71*(2), 123–134.

Kim, G., Aguado Loi, C., Chiriboga, D., Jang, Y., Parmelee, P., & Allen, R. (2011). Limited English proficiency as a barrier to mental health service use: A study of Latino and Asian immigrants with psychiatric disorders. *Journal of Psychiatric Research, 45*(1), 104–110.

McKenzie, K., Fearon, P., & Hutchinson, G. (2008). Migration, ethnicity and psychosis. In C. Morgan, K. McKenzie, & P. Fearon (Eds.), *Society and psychosis* (pp. 210–234). Cambridge: Cambridge University Press.

McLoughlin, P., & Warin, M. (2008). Corrosive places, inhuman spaces: Mental health in Australian immigration detention. *Health and Place, 14*(2), 254–264.

Mehta, S. (2010). *Deportation by default: Mental disability, unfair hearings and indefinite detention in the United States immigration system.* New York: Human Rights Watch and American Civil Liberties Union.

Mizruchi, E. H., & Schwartz, M., eds. (1983). *Regulating society: Marginality and social control in historical perspective.* New York: Free Press.

Sack, K. (2009, November 20). The breaking point: Closing of dialysis unit hits illegal immigrants hard. *New York Times*, p. A1.

Seligman, M. E. P. (1991). *Helplessness: On depression, development, and death.* New York: Freeman.

Silva, C. (2010, March 7). Crackdown urged on undocumented migrants' medical healthcare. *Miami Herald*, p. A1.

Takeuchi, D., Alegria, M., Jackson, J. S., & Williams, D. R. (2007). Immigration and mental health: Diverse findings in Asian, black and Latino populations. *American Journal of Public Health, 97*(1), 11–12.

Ticktin, M. (2006). Where ethics and politics meet: The violence of humanitarianism in France. *American Ethnologist, 33*(1), 33–49.

U.S. Department of Defense (1997). Operation Pacific Haven wraps up humanitarian efforts (press release). Retrieved on April 5, 2014, from www.defense.gov/releases/release.aspx?releaseid=1218.

Velig, W., Susser, E., van Os, J., Mackenbach, J. P., Selten, J.-P., & Hoek, H. (2008). Ethnic density of neighborhoods and incidence of psychotic disorders among immigrants. *American Journal of Psychiatry, 165*(1), 66–73.

Vesga-Lopez, O., Weder, N., Jean-Baptiste, M., & Dominguez, L. (2009). Safe return to homeland of an illegal immigrant with psychosis. *Journal of Psychiatric Practice, 15*(1), 64–69.

Wilson, A. B. (2009). It takes ID to get ID: The new identity politics in services. *Social Service Review, 83*(1), 111–132.

Wing, J. K., & Brown, G. W. (1970). *Institutionalism and schizophrenia: A comparative study of three mental hospitals, 1960–1968.* Cambridge: Cambridge University Press.

# 4

# Criminalization of Transgender Immigrants

*THE CASE OF SCARLETT*

▸ *NADINE NAKAMURA AND ALEJANDRO MORALES*

IMMIGRATION IS A PHENOMENON IMPACTING the cultural climate of countries worldwide. Each year, immigrants from all over the world make a journey for a better future for themselves and their families. Some immigrants are motivated to leave their home countries in hope of economic opportunities, while others are forced to flee because of persecution and death threats (American Psychological Association, 2012). At the end of 2012, there were an estimated 928,000 asylum seekers worldwide (United Nations High Commissioner for Refugees, 2013).

In many countries, including Jamaica, Iran, and Sudan, lesbian, gay, bisexual, and transgender (LGBT) individuals are persecuted, imprisoned, and sometimes sentenced to death because of publicly expressing their sexual orientation or gender identity (Itaborahy & Zhu, 2014). For example, transgender men and women often flee their countries because of violation of their human rights by organized crime and police (Morales, Corbin-Gutierrez, & Wang, 2013; Reading & Rubin, 2011). Fearing for their lives, transgender individuals spend thousands of dollars to immigrate to the United States and face great risks en route to the United States, including being abandoned, raped, and murdered (Cantú, 2009; Heller, 2009; Toro-Alfonso, López Ortiz, & Nieves Lugo, 2012). Many of them, because of the political situations in their home countries, seek asylum.

Asylum seekers must demonstrate that they risk persecution in their home country if they want to be granted asylum. In many countries, transgender individuals may be victims of forced sterilization or castration, so-called "corrective rape," domestic violence, forced sex work, institutionalized violence, and death (Bach, 2013). Once they arrive in the country where they are seeking asylum, they still face additional gender identity–based violence, such as being abused in detention centers (Bach, 2013; Gruberg, 2013). According to Tabak and Levitan (2013), transgender women are 13 times more likely to be sexually assaulted compared with other detainees. In an effort to address or prevent this form of violence, many transgender detainees are placed into "administrative segregation," which is essentially solitary confinement and can exacerbate any preexisting psychological problems (Tabak & Levitan, 2013). As a result of the trauma faced in their home countries and in detention centers, many transgender immigrants suffer from psychological problems, including depression, anxiety, and posttraumatic stress disorder (Chavez, 2011; Robjant, Hassan, & Katona, 2009; Shildo & Ahola, 2013).

In addition to the problems that immigrant trans women often face in detention, many also struggle to find housing, employment, and sources of support (Chavez, 2011; Choudhury et al., 2009; Gehi, 2008). Due to xenophobia and trans phobia, immigrant trans women are discriminated against and often cannot find jobs. Among immigrant transgender women, it is common knowledge that once they have good places of employment, they do everything they can to keep their jobs (Cerezo, Morales, Quintero, & Rothman, 2014). Also, because of job discrimination, documentation status, language barriers, and limited social support, many transgender immigrant women are pushed to sex work as a means of survival (Gehi, 2012; Sausa, Keatley, & Operario, 2007). This exemplifies how trans immigrant women continue to be pushed toward criminalization due to lack of other options. Waiting for their asylum cases to be resolved is a long process, and some are unaware of the protections that exist while they are awaiting decisions on their cases. Thus, they would rather find ways to survive than rely on the government. However, sex work puts immigrant trans women at risk for arrest, sexual violence, sexually transmitted infections, kidnapping, and in some cases murder.

While the literature of immigrant transgender women is growing, little is known about the criminalization of immigrant transgender individuals. The purpose of this chapter is to bring to light and discuss how transgender individuals are criminalized and the impact this has on their lives. We present a case study of trans Latina immigrant that is part of a larger research study about the asylum-seeking process of LGBT immigrants.

The case study was selected because of its complexities as well the resilience that reflects what is often observed in immigrants and LGBT individuals. The chapter is divided into three major sections: (1) we provide a description of our case study of Scarlett; (2) we present themes from the interview, which include criminalization and resiliency, as well as subthemes; and (3) we discuss the implications of our findings on the criminalization of LGBT immigrants.

## SCARLETT: A HUMAN RIGHTS ACTIVIST

Scarlett (pseudonym) is a 35-year-old human rights activist from Central America who had been in the United States for less than a year at the time of the interview. Early on she focused her life on working with groups that advocated for the rights of transgender women in her home country. A transgender woman herself, she joined an organization that provided AIDS/HIV prevention and health education to trans women. Through her work Scarlett helped educate trans women on how to prevent HIV infection, how to avoid issues with the police, and how to keep clear of the violence directed at trans persons that can result, in some cases, in death. Many trans women are thrown out of their homes once they start their transition. Trans youth in particular are forced to live on the streets and engage in unsafe sex with random men. Every day trans women are brutally murdered in Scarlett's home country, and their murderers go unpunished. Despite these challenges, Scarlett stayed in her home country and advocated for the rights of transgender women.

Back in her home country, Scarlett had a job she loved and a supportive group of friends and family and was raising four children. These children were technically her nieces and nephews, but she raised them as her own when her sisters left for the United States. Her life changed completely the day she was approached by an organized gang wanting her to sell drugs to transgender sex workers. Scarlett refused any association with them. The gang retaliated by making death threats over the phone, promising to kill Scarlett and members of her family if she continued to refuse to cooperate with them. The gang also vandalized the organization that employed Scarlett. They destroyed the facility and stole computers, monitors, and other valuable equipment. Due to the nature of these events, Scarlett was forced to make a decision. Upon consulting with her coworkers, she filed charges against the individuals who harassed her and destroyed her place of work. Soon after, she fled her country.

Like many other undocumented Central Americans, Scarlett crossed two borders. With the assistance of a *pollero* (a smuggler), she crossed the border into Mexico and then the border into the United States. Crossing to Mexico was not as hard as entering the United States. When she was crossing the border between Mexico and the United States, she had to pass a river and then walk through the mountains. During this time Scarlett injured her leg. She mentioned that because of her injury and the machismo and trans phobia she encountered from the *pollero*, she was left behind. Not knowing what to do, she walked for three nights with no water or food until she found a road where she hoped that the U.S. Immigration and Customs Enforcement (ICE) would pick her up. The officers who found her took her to a detention center, where she was processed. Scarlett was placed in the section with the mentally ill. A man who appeared to be having a psychotic breakdown harassed her and grabbed her breasts aggressively on various occasions. She called an officer and reported the incident. The officer then removed the man. Because of her documentation status, Scarlett had to appear before an immigration judge, at which time she filed for asylum. She remembered filling out papers and speaking with a lawyer about her asylum case, but there was never a follow-up.

Scarlett was transferred to a prison in the southwestern area of the United States, where she was left in solitary confinement. She remembered feeling as if she was being punished for being transgender and undocumented. Scarlett felt she was losing her mind. She mentioned how horrific it was to have no human contact. With the assistance of a guard, she was able to make a phone call to her mother, who lives in the United States. Within days, her mother paid the bond for her release. Scarlett moved in with her mother and siblings. She felt that she was traumatized due to the treatment she received in prison and from the smugglers and the gang members in her home country who caused her to flee in the first place. These adversities did not stop her; rather, she continues to advocate for the rights of her fellow immigrant transgender sisters in the United States. It was her activism that allowed her to connect with an organization in the United States that helped her apply for asylum. At the time of this interview, Scarlett was waiting to hear about her case. She was hopeful and wanted to get asylum so she could work and start providing for her family in the United States and back in her home country.

In the following two sections, we present themes that emerged from Scarlett's interview. The themes and subthemes voice the traumatic experiences Scarlett had to endure and also highlight the strengths and resiliency of a transgender Latina immigrant. We present quotes to demonstrate each theme and subtheme and to let Scarlett's voice be heard as an example of the criminalization of LGBT immigrants.

### Criminalization

The theme of criminalization is apparent throughout Scarlett's story. It began in her home country, where gangs and police corruption caused her to flee to save her life, and continued as she paid smugglers to help her enter the United States. Those smugglers abandoned her before she reached the United States, and she purposefully sought out immigration officers to arrest her. This brought her into the criminal justice system within the United States, where she was housed apart from the general prison population. She was instead housed with mentally ill inmates and was physically attacked by a cellmate and later put into solitary confinement. She is currently seeking asylum and is awaiting a ruling by an immigration judge.

#### BEING TRANSGENDER IN CENTRAL AMERICA

While Scarlett lived in her home country she worked as a health educator for trans women and girls. She described the limited options available to trans women in her home country.

> Being transgender, no one gets jobs . . . They just look at their chest, and they look at their hair, and they make a face . . . They can't even go to school there—a transgender person can't go to school or work . . . That's why they opt for looking for sex work . . . Look, when the girls are rejected by their families and sometimes their own families even kick them out of their homes . . . So there are 14, 15-year-old girls and they are out on the streets prostituting themselves.

Discrimination against trans women limits their options for employment and means that many end up engaging in sex work. Thus, discrimination leads to the criminalization of trans women who lack "legitimate" employment options that would allow them to be law-abiding citizens.

### POLICE AND GANGS IN CENTRAL AMERICA

Scarlett's reason for leaving her home country was a direct result of the violence and victimization experienced by trans women there. She described how the police cannot be counted on for protection and that they are often the ones who commit violent acts against trans women. She stated,

> Life for us, transgender women, is very sad because of the police. The police violate our rights, they beat us, they rape us . . . We have a government where the police officers themselves are the delinquents. They are the ones that pursue us, they beat us, they force us to do immoral acts. They—they force us to do, what's it called? Sex at gunpoint.

Scarlett described how gangs run the streets in her home country and how they tried to recruit her to work for them:

> And they gave me a beating and then they told me that if I didn't do what they said, they were going to kill me . . . So then what happened is that I made—I tried to file a report and I went to the human rights commission, because that is the only place that helps us out a little bit. But when I told them that I had made—that I would complain to the police on the street and that what the police on the street would do is laugh at us and beat us instead of help us. So they told me at the commission that if I dared to file a report with the public prosecutor of the city, that I had to leave the country immediately, because it was a sure thing that the gang members and the police would find out and that I—I would be dead.

She went on to explain that the police are bribed by criminals to help them find their victims.

> In [my home country], someone can give a police officer 100 [pesos], and they've already bribed them and he'll do whatever the delinquent wants. So the police is [*sic*] actually pursuing us. They don't leave us alone over there.

### LEAVING CENT RAL AMERICA

This incident prompted Scarlett to leave for the United States. She described why she decided to come to the United States. She explained why immigrating to a neighboring Central American country is not an option for her:

> But all of Central America is the same. The discrimination against the trans. The gangs, the police they do nothing. I go . . . to those countries that are close to my country, and to be suffering the same crisis—they are suffering the same crisis that my country is suffering. No, the government doesn't help. There is no help at all. A lot of girls, from our friends, from [my home country] left because of the lack of resources—from not having anyone help them come to this country, they went to [a neighboring country]. A lot of them are now dead. Why? Because the—in [the neighboring country] it's the same or worse.

Scarlett paid smugglers to help her cross into Texas and noted "that because of the same machismo—the same machismo and the same discrimination that people have—towards us, all of the trans, the people who were bringing me were treating me very badly." Scarlett was again in a vulnerable position as a trans woman, as she had to rely on individuals who discriminated against her for help.

> With them, I was injured on my leg, I injured my leg . . . And I couldn't walk, so they abandoned me—they abandoned me in the mountain, in the—they left me in that scrubland. I walked for three days and three nights in that place and it was very sad for me. I thought I would never get out of there, because it was a place that I was unfamiliar with. And I would walk and walk and I didn't know where I was going.

About deciding to turn herself over to immigration, Scarlett said:

> So, I found the way to turn myself into immigration when I arrived to the street and I walked down the street, looking to see if I could find a patrol car. So then I waited until morning and I fell asleep on the street and in the morning when I woke up on the street, well, they—they were able to—the ones from immigration saw me—saw me and that's how I was detained by immigration . . . I looked for the way to find—well since immigration passes through that street looking for undocumented people, so I stayed—I stayed on the—perhaps putting myself at risk, because trailers would pass by, I mean large buses, and due to exhaustion, I fell asleep on the—what's it called—on

the pavement. So, I fell asleep unintentionally, I fell asleep. So in the morning when I woke up, the ones from immigration were asking me how I was feeling.

### DETENTION

Scarlett was taken to prison, where she was isolated from the general population and instead housed with mentally ill prisoners.

I asked them why they put me in that cell and they told me that I could not be—I could not be where the men were because they might harm me. But I told them, "But there are mentally ill people in this cell and they are also men." Because there were two men—and in fact I was assaulted by one of the men. Because the man pretended—he would sexually harass me. I was assaulted—I was—because he would beat—he would grab my breasts and he would grab them hard. And I told him to please stop bothering me, not to touch me, so he—that man beat me in front of the security there at the prison. They all saw when the man hit me and that he assaulted me really hard.

Once ICE deemed her case credible, Scarlett was moved to another facility, where she was kept in solitary confinement for a month.

That's where my nightmare began, where I was going crazy. Because they isolated me in a cell with mentally ill people where I was in a small cell, with four walls, all alone, with nobody, locked up with only a small bed and through a hole, they would pass me—through a small window, they would pass me my food. I would not see the light of day.

### SEEKING ASYLUM

Scarlett's mother paid $4,000 in bail to get her released from prison and hired a lawyer to represent her asylum case, which cost almost $4,000 more. Fortunately, Scarlett was able to connect with an LGBT immigration organization that provided her with pro bono legal representation during her asylum-seeking process.

Scarlett shared the difficulty she felt leaving her country, saying, "Of course nobody wants to leave their country, because my country is what I've loved the most, but now I am afraid to go back to my country."

If Scarlett is not granted asylum, she is in fear for her life, which she related by saying:

> Transgender people, who live in [my home country] are people who come in fear, with the horror of having to go back there, because if we go back, we are going back to hell. I was beaten, raped, I suffered all the worst mistreatments; psychological and physical and it was horrible. I believe that if I went back to my country, I would go back to death and I believe that it's something very unfortunate and I only hope to God that they can help us get our asylum.

### Resiliency

Despite the trauma that Scarlett faced both in her home country and in the United States, she still remains positive and hopeful about the future. Her resiliency seems to be fueled by her desire to help other people, as well as a strong connection with her religious beliefs. Despite the criminalization that she has experienced in the United States, she expresses trust in the U.S. government and criminal justice system.

#### DRIVE TO HELP OTHERS

Scarlett was previously a health worker in her home country, working with transgender sex workers to educate them about HIV prevention and health issues. Given her current immigration status, she is unable to work but says she desires to do so:

> Yes, I don't care if I have to wash floors, to clean, whatever. The important thing is to make some money to be able to help my mom and to help myself out with expenses and everything. Because my mother is a grown woman and she works too much. She works very hard at her job and that makes me very sad.

Scarlett also discussed her children, who remain in her home country, and said that she gains strength from fighting for them:

> And what is giving me strength is that I have to fight for the three kids that I left in [my home country]. Because to me, they are my kids and I have to fight for my life. Because if I go back to my country, I am going to die. And

that's what gives me strength, to fight here in this country to achieve something good for me. Because never—us trans have never had anything good in life. So we wait for hope.

### RELIGIOUS COPING

Another way that Scarlett exhibits resiliency is through her belief in God. She identifies as an Evangelical Christian, which is a conservative form of Christianity that is not traditionally supportive of LGBT individuals. Her ability to find a message of love and support from this religious tradition also speaks to her resiliency. She says:

> I was raised with Evangelical Christians and I believe that being what I am, I can also be a believer in God. Because God does not care about our diversity. What matters, what God cares about, is our hearts, our souls. I am a strong believer and that's what I think. I don't like, I don't know, I don't like bad things. I like to do everything right because I know that if I do everything right, at least no—God does not like what we do sometimes because of our sexual inclinations, but I think that God loves us. He does not love the sin, but he loves us. I am a strong believer and I hope that—I always have faith in God and thanks to God, he has always helped me. He took me out of that hell where the degenerates left me—those smugglers as they're called, they abandoned me in the scrubland—in some dirt. I walked for three days and three nights without eating. And so if God got me out of there, I think God will give me something good. Because if God didn't have something for me, I would have stayed there—I would have died in that place.

### TRUST IN THE U.S. GOVERNMENT

Despite the way that Scarlett was criminalized in the United States, she says she still trusts the U.S. government to not be corrupt like the government in her home country:

> That regardless, this country also has delinquency, but there's a government here—there is help for people here. If I call the police, I know that the police can't be bought. I know that the police in the United States is [*sic*] not going to be bought by a few bucks and do what the delinquent says.

## DISCUSSION

The theme of criminalization is salient throughout Scarlett's story. Crime in her home country caused Scarlett to flee to the United States. She was forced to leave when she refused to participate in criminal activities but did not have a safe, legal way to protect herself. Instead, she had to employ smugglers who mistreated her and ultimately left her to die. In order to save her life, Scarlett had to put herself in the path of ICE officers, and she was subsequently placed in detention. While in detention she was assaulted by another prisoner and was later placed into solitary confinement, treated as a criminal although her only crime was trying to escape being forced into criminal activity in her home country. Individuals like Scarlett are therefore in a no-win situation—they are damned if they do and damned if they don't. Scarlett awaits the judge's asylum ruling that will either allow her to legitimately stay in the United States or force her to return to her home country, where her life will once again be in jeopardy.

Some of the experiences that Scarlett endured are common among undocumented immigrants or asylum seekers who are fleeing from crime in Central America. Many Central Americans, including record numbers of unaccompanied minors, are leaving their countries of origin and heading north to the United States to escape gang violence, and many of these individuals end up in detention (Preston, 2014). However, Scarlett has faced additional challenges as a trans woman, including mistreatment by law enforcement, assault related to her gender identity, and solitary confinement in detention. Transgender asylum seekers also face unique difficulties in that other asylum seekers and immigrants often turn to their ethnic communities for support when they settle in a host country, but these communities are typically not accepting of transgender immigrant individuals (Shildo & Ahola, 2013). Lack of acceptance of their gender presentation and identity can create a barrier for transgender individuals, and rejection from one's ethnic community can be especially painful (Cerezo et al., 2014). While previous research has pointed to transgender immigrants finding strength through community (Cerezo et al., 2014), for transgender asylum seekers like Scarlett, language may be one of many barriers that makes the greater transgender community inaccessible.

The research evidence suggests that asylum seekers are at an increased risk for psychological problems (Robjant et al., 2009; Shildo & Ahola, 2013), but despite the multiple traumas Scarlett has experienced, she has not sought mental health treatment. Instead, she relies on her family for support. At the time of her interview, Scarlett had been in the United States for less than a year. If she is granted asylum, she will be in the position to build upon her social support system and hopefully receive the psychological support to address her past traumas and ongoing stressors. It is important for mental health service providers who work with immigrant communities and/or LGBT communities to consider the specific barriers that may exist for transgender immigrants and asylum seekers that may prevent them from accessing treatment. Some of these include language and physical access, as well as lack of cultural competence on the part of service providers. Therefore, as suggested by Cerezo and colleagues (2014), it is important that mental health service providers address their own biases toward both immigrants and transgender individuals. In addition, it is important for mental health service providers to be aware of the realities that transgender immigrants and asylum seekers face in order to be able to provide them with appropriate treatment and support.

Even though Scarlett has not received mental health treatment and does not have a community to support her, she still possesses a great deal of resiliency. This is evident from her desire to help others and her religious faith, as well as her belief that she will be treated better in the United States than she was in her home country. Previous research on transgender Latina immigrants has uncovered themes of resiliency related to the drive to help others (Cerezo et al., 2014). Perhaps, if Scarlett is granted asylum, she will be able to pick up where she left off in helping her community and her family through her work. This may give her a sense of purpose that will be helpful in her healing.

### REFERENCES

American Psychological Association. (2012). Crossroads: The psychology of immigration in the new century. Retrieved from www.apa.org/topics/immigration/report.aspx.

Bach, J. (2013). Assessing transgender asylum claims. *Forced Migration Review, 42,* 34–36.

Cantú, L. (2009). *The sexuality of migration: Border crossings and Mexican immigrant men.* New York: New York University Press.

Cerezo, A., Morales, A., Quintero, D., & Rothman, S. (2014). Trans migrations: Exploring life at the intersection of transgender identity and immigration. *Psychology of Sexual Orientation and Gender Diversity, 1*(2), 170–180.

Chavez, K. R. (2011). Identifying the needs of LGBTQ immigrants and refugees in Southern Arizona. *Journal of Homosexuality, 58*(2), 189–218.

Choudhury, P. P., Badhan, N. S., Chand, J., Chhugani, S., Choksey, R., Husainy, S., & Wat, E. C. (2009). Community alienation and its impact on help-seeking behaviour among LGBTIQ South Asians in Southern California. *Journal of Gay & Lesbian Social Services, 21,* 247–266. doi:10.1080/10538720902772196

Gehi, P. (2008). Struggles from the margins: Anti-immigrant legislation and the impact on low-income transgender people of color. *Women's Rights Law Reporter, 30,* 315–346.

——. (2012). Gendered (in) security: Migration and criminalization in the security state. *Harvard Journal of Law & Gender, 35,* 357–401.

Gruberg, S. (2013). *Dignity denied: LGBT immigrants in U.S. immigration detention.* Washington, DC: Center for American Progress. Retrieved on June 21, 2014, from http://cdn.americanprogress.org/wp-content/uploads/2013/11/ImmigrationEnforcement-1.pdf.

Heller, P. (2009). Challenges facing LGBT asylum-seekers: The role of social work in correcting oppressive immigration processes. *Journal of Gay & Lesbian Social Services, 21,* 294–308. doi:10.1080/10538720902772246

Itaborahy, L. P., & Zhu, J. (2014). *State-sponsored homophobia: A world survey of laws: Criminalization.* Geneva: International Lesbian, Gay, Bisexual, Trans and Intersex Association. Retrieved on June 22, 2014, from http://old.ilga.org/Statehomophobia/ILGA_SSHR_2014_Eng.pdf.

Morales, A., Corbin-Gutierrez, E. E., & Wang, S. C. (2013). Latino, immigrant, and gay: A qualitative study about their adaptation and transitions. *Journal of LGBT Issues in Counseling, 7,* 125–142.

Preston, J. (2014, April 10). Hoping for asylum, migrants strain U.S. border. *New York Times.* Retrieved on April 10, 2014, from www.nytimes.com.

Reading, R., & Rubin, L. R. (2011). Advocacy and empowerment: Group therapy for LGBT asylum seekers. *Traumatology, 17*(2), 86–98.

Robjant, K., Hassan, R., & Katona, C. (2009). Mental health implications of detaining asylum seekers: Systematic review. *British Journal of Psychiatry, 194,* 306–312. doi:10.1192/bjp.bp.108.053223

Sausa, L. A., Keatley, J., & Operario, D. (2007). Perceived risks and benefits of sex work among transgender women of color in San Francisco. *Archives of Sexual Behavior, 36*(6), 768–777.

Shildo, A., & Ahola, J. (2013). Mental health challenges of LGBT forced migrants. *Forced Migration Review, 42,* 9–11.

Tabak, S., & Levitan, R. (2013). LGBTI migrants in immigration detention. *Forced Migration Review, 42,* 47–49.

Toro-Alfonso, J., López Ortiz, M., & Nieves Lugo, K. (2012). Sexualidades migrantes: La emigración de hombres dominicanos gay. *Caribbean Studies, 40*(1), 59–80.

United Nations High Commissioner for Refugees. (2013). UNHCR statistical yearbook. Retrieved on June 22, 2014, from www.unhcr.org/52a7213b9.html.

# 5

# Criminalization of Muslim American Men in the United States

▸ SAHER SELOD

TERRORIST, FOREIGNER, ANTI-AMERICAN, ANTIDEMOCRATIC, and misogynist are just a few words that have become common characteristics associated with Muslims. In a post-9/11 society, Muslims have been confirmed as a threat to national security and Western values. Although these stereotypes did not magically appear on 9/11, myth became a reality, and the widely accepted belief that Muslims are a problem in society changed the everyday experiences of Muslims living in America. The creation of the U.S. Department of Homeland Security (DHS) and the federalization of security in airports via the formation of the Transportation Security Administration (TSA) reflect just a few of the changes in the American political sphere. This new political and cultural reality relies on a rhetoric of criminalizing Muslims to gain public support for intensified security policies and to justify the growth of these institutions. For example, in 2014 the TSA operated under a budget of $7.4 billion and employed 55,600 full-time employees (DHS, 2014). Additionally, corporations benefit financially from a culture of fear, because they create the tools and technologies (body scanners, surveillance tools) used for surveillance and security. Since 9/11, more than 2,000 private companies ventured into intelligence gathering for the state by securing government contracts and funding (Boghosian, 2013). Private citizens waver in their concern when it comes to surveillance. The data mining that occurs through social media sites for the purposes of marketing rarely creates a stir in the general public, but the idea that the government is collecting data on all citizens has led to some distress about privacy. When Edward

Snowden, a former systems administrator for the National Security Agency (NSA), leaked government documents to the media about the state spying on its citizens, concerns were raised about expansive government surveillance programs. While this was seen as an abuse of the power by the state, surveillance of people of color has historically gone on without much protest from communities not impacted by it. In a post-9/11 society, a Gallup poll in 2010 revealed that 71% of Americans support intensive security checks of passengers who fit the profile of a terrorist based on age, gender, and ethnicity (Jones, 2010). In this chapter, I demonstrate how Muslim American men are criminalized as potential terrorists and are not afforded the protections of citizenship because of the racialization of their religious identity. The criminalization of Muslims results in the treatment of Muslim Americans as potential terrorists.

### CRIMINALIZING MUSLIMS

Negative associations with Muslims did not magically appear on September 11, 2001. The social construction of a Muslim as violent and a threat to Western society has a long history that dates back to the middle of the ninth century in Europe. Although Muslims and Christians had a history of coexisting peacefully without major religious tensions prior to that time, the construction of Muslims as an enemy served several purposes in Europe. The promotion of anti-Muslim sentiments in Europe aided in unifying a divided Christian society that was undergoing internal conflict and strife. Focusing on a common enemy, Muslims, provided a shared ideology. After the ninth century, tensions between Muslims and Christians died down, but anti-Muslim sentiments were reignited around the fifteenth century. The First Crusade was launched against Muslims with the intent of minimizing Turkish military expansion in Europe and to again unify a divided Europe. Muslims were viewed as a barbaric, evil, violent, and godless people (Grosfoguel & Mielants, 2006; Mastnak, 2010; Rana, 2011). Thus, the social construction of Muslims as violent and barbaric has been around for centuries. In more recent years academics have played a role in perpetuating the construction of Muslims and Islam as a threat. Bernard Lewis's (1990) "The Roots of Muslim Rage" and Samuel Huntington's (1993) "The Clash of the Civilizations?" both characterize Muslims and Islam as antimodern, anti-Western, and a potential threat. Huntington (1993) predicted there would be conflict between the West and Islam. These arguments maintain the idea that Muslims are culturally backward and opposed to modernity. The government's response to 9/11 was congruent with Huntington's and Lewis's theses. Phrases such as "axis of evil" or "us and them" justified the military invasions of Afghanistan and Iraq. Support for these invasions was initially easy to gain because of the prevalent perceptions of Muslims. Since the early twentieth century, Arabs and Muslims have been portrayed as barbaric and as terrorists in films, television, and the news (Byng, 2008; Shaheen, 2008). Television shows such as *Sleeper Cell* and *24* are just a few examples of how the construction of the Muslim terrorist has become the norm in American culture. The perpetuation of this stereotype confirms for the American public that Muslims are a real threat and thus support for policies targeting a Muslim population ensues. For example, the establishment in 2002 of the Guantanamo Bay detention camp, where prisoners in the War on Terror have been detained, exemplifies the criminalization of Muslim men. The majority of these prisoners were Muslim men from several Muslim countries, including but not limited to Afghanistan, Iraq, Yemen, and Pakistan. Another policy that targeted Muslim men was the National Security Entry and Exit Registration System (NSEERS). NSEERS required immigrant men over the age of 16 from 25 countries to register with the government when entering or exiting the United States. Registering included being fingerprinted, photographed, and interrogated. Twenty-four out of the 25 countries on the list were Muslim-majority countries, revealing how this policy vilified Muslim men as a potential threat to national security. The cultural shift that occurred after 9/11 resulted in political initiatives that implicitly confirmed the association of Muslim men with terrorism.

In this chapter I will show how Muslim American men are criminalized and the impact it has had on their daily lives. Although this is a population that has been protected from some of the policies aimed at Muslim immigrants after 9/11 because of their status as citizens, they are still subjected to differential treatment by the state and their fellow private citizens because of their religious identity. The testimonies related here reveal that ordinary law-abiding Muslim men are routinely treated with suspicion and distrust. This has had a detrimental impact on Muslim men. It has left them feeling silenced, disempowered, and disconnected from their national identity.

## METHODS

The findings in this chapter are based on the lived experiences of 48 Muslim American men and women living in the Chicago and Dallas/Fort Worth area. I spoke with participants between 2009 and 2012 about their everyday experiences. The majority of the men and women I talked with identified as either South Asian or Arab American Muslims. Conversations lasted anywhere from 45 minutes to 3 hours. The majority of the participants were South Asian women born in the United States; however, for the purposes of this chapter, I am limiting the analysis to the experiences of Muslim American men who were among those interviewed. I conversed with these men and women in their homes, in coffee shops, over meals at restaurants, and at a community center in a suburb of Chicago that serves an Arab population.

After assuring the individuals I met and spoke with that I would use pseudonyms to protect their anonymity in the study, I told them I was going to ask them a series of questions about their experiences before and after 9/11. In addition to basic demographic questions, we talked at length about what their personal or professional relationships were like before and after 9/11. For example, they were asked whether they were friendly with their neighbors before 9/11 and whether this relationship changed after 9/11. They were also asked whether they had been questioned about their status as citizens or their patriotism.

## THE LIVED EXPERIENCES OF MUSLIM MEN: ASSOCIATION WITH TERRORISM

Since 9/11 the association of Muslims with terrorism has had detrimental consequences. Through interactions with their colleagues, friends, and government officials, Muslim men have become hyperaware of the repercussions. Several of the participants in the study stated they were targets of jokes that accused them of being terrorists. Although jokes may seem innocuous to some, the participants felt uneasy with these associations. Aman was a junior in college when I interviewed him. At the time, he was a pre-med major and revealed how he had become used to jokes made about him being a terrorist. He claimed the majority of these happened in high school, but some occurred in college as well.

AMAN: But the main difference was—it became mainly a joke, where people would joke to me, call me a terrorist, just like "Aman is with the Taliban," and stuff like that.

INTERVIEWER: Your friends? Or these are acquaintances?

AMAN: Like friends, mainly. Mainly [with] my friends. But yeah, that was pretty much it. I mean, I never really took offense to it. I just kind of laughed it off and stuff like that. And in some cases I guess I just laughed with them as well.

INTERVIEWER: So it didn't bother you?

AMAN: It wasn't necessarily something that bothered me at that time. Looking back on it, though, I think I should've stood up a little bit more.

While Aman stated this teasing was not a big deal, he also admitted he wished he had stood up for himself back in high school, indicating that these incidents did bother him. In a climate in which an association with terror has real judicial consequences, it was hard for the majority of the participants to view these jokes as completely harmless. Aman was not alone in being called a terrorist in a joking manner. Another participant admitted a partner at the consulting firm he worked at jokingly asked him where he was over the weekend after a bombing occurred in India. This incident made the respondent feel uncomfortable, and later in the interview he admitted he avoids talking about his religion or political views at work out of fear he will be seen as someone who sympathizes with terrorism. Because the War on Terror led the United States to invade Afghanistan and Iraq, participants were aware that disagreeing with the state's foreign policy could make them appear to sympathize with terrorism. After 9/11, America became a nation hyperconcerned with security. American citizens have been encouraged to report suspicious behaviors and activities. Because Islam is now viewed with suspicion, Muslim men are aware that being Muslim brings them under scrutiny. Thus, there is an underlying fear that these jokes could turn into something more serious, like being reported to the authorities.

Muslim men felt a sense of helplessness in their criminalization. Saleem, a young Lebanese American doctor, recalled an incident he had while traveling from Romania to Bulgaria by train when he was 18 years old. A Bulgarian officer came into the train at one of the stops and saw Saleem sitting in the train car. When the officer saw Saleem's passport, he began to interrogate the young doctor.

Kind of the first question he asked was "Where are the guns?," "Where's the coke?" They asked me whether I had cocaine on me, things of this sort. [It] was very horrible, because they tried to destroy my passport, my American passport. I was so naive—I actually went to the American embassy in Sofia to protest what had happened to me. I was literally told—and some people don't believe that I was told—"But you live in Lebanon," and I said, "Well, yes, because I'm in college, I'm studying at the American university. I'm pre-med there, and my family lives there." And he said, "Well, then, you don't live in America, and you live in an area of terrorism, and so you should expect to be treated like a terrorist."

(Saleem)

This statement was made to him prior to 9/11, revealing that Americans already had preconceived ideas of who fits the stereotype of a terrorist. Saleem's status as an American citizen did not protect him from being treated like a potential criminal. This interaction highlights how Muslim Americans are often denied the privileges associated with citizenship, such as the right to be seen as a law-abiding citizen. The official at the American embassy denied Saleem his status as an American citizen by telling him he should expect to be treated as a terrorist, because he lives in a country associated with terrorism. If Saleem were not a Muslim but a white American, he might have had his concerns acknowledged and addressed. This testimony showcases how Muslim men are not able to rely on the state for protection, because the state is often the perpetrator of their abuse.

Throughout the interviews I found that the majority of the Muslim men I talked with either had personally experienced or knew someone who had experienced profiling by the state. One participant revealed that he knew someone who had his bank account closed for no reason. Another participant shared the story of how the FBI came to her house because her 8-year-old son's name was on a terrorist watch list. Thus, the fear of the state is not irrational but a very real one for the Muslim community living in America. The most common experiences Muslims in this study had with the state occurred in U.S. airports.

### FLYING WHILE MUSLIM

Airports have become a site where the criminalization of Muslims is most visible. The policies and practices of the TSA forever changed flying for

Muslims after 9/11. The phrase "flying while Muslim" connotes the experiences Muslims have had with profiling in airports in a similar fashion to how "driving while black" reflects the experiences of black men with racial profiling by the police. TSA implemented several programs that target Muslim men. One program is Screening of Passengers by Observation Techniques (SPOT), in which TSA agents are supposed to watch out for suspicious behaviors in order to prevent another terrorist attack. SPOT has been criticized for allowing TSA agents to profile certain groups at airports, including Muslims. Another way TSA has attempted to curb terrorist activities is through the utilization of the No-Fly List, which is a document containing the names of individuals viewed as a potential threat to national security. The testimonies by Muslim men reveal these policies and programs implemented by the TSA are biased against Muslims.

I met Farooq, a 39-year-old computer programmer, at an Arab cultural center in a suburb of Chicago. The center serves an Arab American and immigrant population, and their services range from assisting victims of domestic abuse to helping the senior immigration population with their needs. I interviewed Farooq at this center the day he was volunteering there. We sat in the conference room and he told me about his experiences with air travel. He told me how, at his previous job, he had to travel to Dubai every two weeks for a few months. He told me his airline ticket had been marked with the letter $S$ on four occasions. These markings signal to TSA agents that a passenger should go through additional security, such as being pulled out of the security line and having one's luggage and body searched. Farooq is used to being stopped and searched at airports. He stated he endures this 70% of the time he flies. I found that almost all of the men who flew after 9/11 were told their names was similar to a name on the No-Fly List, resulting in them having to go through additional security. Most of the men were not able to use the self-service check-in kiosks for some time and were stopped, searched, and interrogated several times at airports.

Ahmed and I met at a coffee shop in Chicago one afternoon on a weekend in December. Ahmed is a Palestinian American doctor who moved to Chicago a few years before the interview took place. He and I talked extensively about his experiences after 9/11. He was one of the few male participants who spoke freely and openly about the discrimination he and his family faced after the terrorist attacks. Most of the men I interviewed were initially reluctant to talk about these experiences. He was in medical school when the attacks happened and remembered how tense it was immediately after the attacks. His experiences mirrored the majority of the Muslim men participants.

> Well, I was actually on a "No Fly List." So, actually, this was while I was interviewing for residency positions. What I found was that every time I'd get on a flight, I'd get searched on the way there, on the way back.

Ahmed also noticed an *S* on his ticket several times. He said his father's experiences were worse than his, because he would miss flights due to delays caused by profiling treatment. After several complaints to the airlines he found out his name was on a list provided to the TSA by the DHS. Ahmed is a law-abiding American citizen who is being treated with suspicion simply because he is a Muslim. His religious identity ignited suspicion of him by the state. Ahmed was one of the few respondents who was vocal about this treatment. He told me in response to this profiling he would ask to see the airline supervisor in order to demonstrate some agency.

> I always ask now. I even tried to look at the screen. I mean, I do everything I can. I used to make them bring the head of the, like, airline security of the airport. I used to make them bring him to the desk and explain to me face-to-face what they were doing. You know, because I wanted them to know— I wanted them to confront the people that they were affecting.

Ahmed felt compelled to confront the injustices he experienced. Although he was not shocked by this treatment, it did anger him. The majority of the Muslim men I interviewed did not share Ahmed's ability to demand an explanation for their treatment. A few of the participants admitted they expected this treatment, and even though it humiliated and angered them, they did not feel they were able to contest this profiling.

Naveed and I met for an interview at Chipotle one Sunday afternoon. I was given his e-mail through another participant. Naveed, who was in his early thirties at the time of the interview, is a Palestinian American. He described a time shortly after 9/11 when he and his sisters flew from Chicago to attend a protest in Washington, DC. They were all profiled at the airport. Naveed felt this profiling was justified, because their behaviors could be viewed as suspicious:

> [We] were going to purchase our tickets the morning of. We had no luggage. I had a backpack . . . my sisters probably had, like, a handbag or something. And we literally showed up at O'Hare. We purchased the tickets there at the airport for a flight leaving in a couple of hours, coming home the same day. Like, our flight was leaving at 6:00 a.m. coming home at, like, 6:00 p.m., you know, same day. I mean the only thing more suspicious would have been if it was a one-way ticket, you know. And our tickets actually had these huge stripes, these huge bars and boxes, for security. And we were all pulled aside, and we were frisked, and everything that we had was combed through. And my sisters were like this is because we're Muslim, and [I said] "No. It's because, we did exactly what the bombers did on 9/11." I mean the only thing different was they probably bought a one-way ticket.

Naveed understands and even accepts why he would be profiled at the airport. Although he has nothing in common with the 9/11 terrorists, it is curious he saw a justification for his profiling. Several of the terrorists checked in bags, and they all bought their round-trip tickets in advance, and not one shared Naveed's ethnic identity. What they did share was his religious identity, which was enough to make him and his sisters suspicious in U.S. airports. Yet this encounter did not fuel any ire or humiliation on Naveed's part, as it did for his sisters. In some ways he internalized his criminalization by viewing this profiling as justifiable in certain circumstances, such as buying a ticket for a flight the day of and flying without luggage, even though his flight had him returning the same day, making it perfectly understandable why he would not need a suitcase. And while Naveed felt this instance of profiling was defensible, he did not respond this way to all of the experiences he has had with profiling. A year prior to the interview he was profiled by American Airline agents in an airport in Panama.

NAVEED: Like, actually, I'd already gone through security, so this is where I got annoyed. I had already gone through security. I had a first-class ticket, so, like, I was sort of standing there ready to board, because they were about to announce boarding. And the lady just pointed at me, and she's, like, come here. And I actually thought that they were letting me board. And so I walked up to

her, and she started speaking, but I didn't really understand what she was saying. And then, the lady who checked me in at the front gate approached me.
And she took my ticket, and I was, like, okay, cool. And then I started walking
in and they all started screaming—not screaming, but, like, stop, stop, stop.

INTERVIEWER:  Was this in front of, like, other passengers?

NAVEED:  In front of everyone, yeah. The whole gate was watching . . . And I'm
just, like, I'm, like, wait, I'm not boarding. I'm, like, your best customer. I only
fly American Airlines. You are my only carrier. All my money goes to you.
So, I was, like, "Wait, so I'm not boarding?" "No, you have to go through extra
screening." And I'm, like, "Why? Why?" [And] then I was just, like, shut up.
Just go through the screening, you know . . . And they went through my bag,
and they frisked me again, and then I was just, like, what, is this really random?
Because it doesn't feel random to me.

Naveed reveals how frustrating and humiliating this process was for
him. He told me in the interview that he was a platinum member of
American Airlines and felt this would mitigate these experiences with
profiling, but it did not. Instead of receiving preferential treatment, he
was treated like a potential criminal. Even more telling is the recognition
that he was powerless in this situation. Most of the Muslim men in the
sample echoed this feeling of helplessness in the face of their criminalization. This sense of disempowerment is one of the major impacts of the
criminalization of Muslims.

### DISEMPOWERMENT, DISTRUST, AND ABUSES IN CITIZENSHIP

The impact of security has taken a toll on Muslims in the United States. In
an effort to make America safer and prevent another terrorist attack, practices and policies have been employed that unfairly target Muslims. Most
of the Muslim men I interviewed admitted they felt silenced for some time
after 9/11 out of fear of being associated with terrorism. They avoided talking about religion or politics, because they feared their religious association
along with their views on foreign policy, such as the invasion of Iraq or
Afghanistan and the Palestinian/Israeli conflict, could result in them being
seen as supporting terrorism. Hamza, a corporate attorney, told me he felt
"muzzled" for a while after 9/11. Aziz, a Pakistani American in his early
thirties, also felt the impact of the association with Islam in the workplace.

Although he is proud of his religious identity and is involved in religious organizations in his spare time, he admitted at work he avoids talking about religion and politics, a sentiment shared by the majority of the men interviewed.

> I definitely try to avoid the topic at work of me being Muslim. I do try and not talk about political things because I just feel like I'm just gonna get bucketed anyways as "Oh, he's a Muslim, so he's just taking that point of view." It's not gonna be that fruitful or productive, you know? That's just the feeling that I get that it's just gonna be my whatever views [that] would be dismissed or [viewed as] not in the best interests of America.
>
> (Aziz)

Aziz also admitted that before 9/11 he would not think twice about associating himself with another Muslim man who had a long beard, but since 9/11 he is aware that these associations can have deleterious consequences, such as being reported to the Federal Bureau of Investigation.

In a society in which prejudice and racism against Muslims is viewed as a necessity in the name of national security, Muslims have few avenues to pursue to protect themselves from this treatment. When Saleem went to the U.S. embassy to report the harassment he received from the Bulgarian police, he was told he should expect this treatment. While this happened prior to 9/11, the escalation of the criminalization of Muslims since the attacks has resulted in these incidents becoming more common. Although there are places to report discrimination, such as the American Civil Liberties Union and the Council on American Islamic Relations (CAIR), Muslims may not feel comfortable doing so. Saleem relayed an experience that happened 4 years after 9/11. He told me that a TSA agent in Houston marked through the expiration date and his birth date on his passport, making his passport invalid. As a result he was not able to board his flight in Houston, because the airline attendant could not read his birth date. When he went to make a complaint, no one would assist him; he was told it was an isolated incident and they refused to take a complaint from him. Saleem's experiences highlight how socially and politically acceptable it is to view and treat Muslims as suspects in the name of national security. Many of these abuses occurred at the hands of the state, through TSA policies and actions in airports. Muslim men do not feel protected from the state but rather feel a sense of persecution. It was recently reported that the NSA has been monitoring the e-mails of Muslim Americans, including those of the executive director of CAIR (Davidson, 2014). When the government spies on law-abiding Muslim American citizens, it validates the message that Muslims are to be distrusted. Furthermore, this revelation may prevent Muslims from turning to CAIR for protection when they experience civil rights abuses.

Treating Muslims as potential criminals violates their rights as American citizens. One of the privileges associated with citizenship is the right to protection by the state. Instead of being protected Muslims are being treated as though they are the enemy within. They are viewed with suspicion and are subjected to stops and searches at U.S. airports. Profiling not only strips them of their civil rights, it also reflects a prevalent perception of Muslims, that they are incapable of being loyal to the United States. This strips them of their national identity as Americans and makes them feel they are not valued members of society, something that citizenship should afford.

In a radicalized society, racism shifts and mutates. Although Jim Crow has been legally dismantled, segregation in education and housing is maintained in other ways, such as via mass incarceration (Alexander, 2010). September 11 forever changed the American political, economic, and social landscape. National security has become a billion-dollar industry that can only be sustained with the ongoing threat and fear of terrorism. The criminalization of Muslims has an economic and political motive. It justifies federal dollars spent on the defense industry. It enables the government to spend and expand the DHS, and it has been used by the United States to defend military intervention in places like Iraq and Afghanistan. Because Muslim Americans are not differentiated from Muslims living abroad, they are viewed as incapable of being loyal to the United States. The War on Terror implicates them as the enemy living within. What is often overlooked and understudied is the impact this has at the individual level. Hopefully this chapter aids readers in understanding the challenges facing a Muslim population in a post-9/11 society.

### REFERENCES

Alexander, M. (2010). *The new Jim Crow: Mass incarceration in the age of color-blindness*. New York: New Press.

Boghosian, H. (2013). *Spying on democracy: Government surveillance, corporate power and public resistance*. San Francisco: City Lights.

Byng, M. D. (2008). Complex inequalities: The case of Muslim Americans after 9/11. *American Behavioral Scientist, 51*, 659–674.

Davidson, A. (2014, July 10). The N.S.A.'s spying on Muslim-Americans. *New Yorker*. Retrieved on July 10, 2014, from www.newyorker.com/online/blogs /closeread/2014/07/the-nsas-spying-on muslimamericans.html.

Grosfoguel, R., & Mielants, E. (2006). The long-duree entanglement between Islamophobia and racism in the modern/colonial capitalist/patriarchal world-system: An introduction. *Human Architecture: Journal of the Sociology of Self-Knowledge, 5*, 1–12.

Huntington, S. (1993). The clash of the civilizations? *Foreign Affairs, 72*(3), 22–49.

Jones, J. (2010). Americans back profiling air travelers to combat terrorism. *Gallup Politics*. Retrieved on March 10, 2014, from www.gallup.com/poll/125078 /americans-back-profiling-air-travelers-combat-terrorism.aspx.

Lewis, B. (1990, September). The roots of Muslim rage: Why so many Muslims deeply resent the West, and why their bitterness will not easily be mollified. *Atlantic*. Retrieved on March 12, 2014, from www.theatlantic.com/magazine /archive/1990/09/the-roots-of-muslim-rage/304643.

Mastnak, T. (2010). Western hostility toward Muslims: A history of the present. In A. Shryock (Ed.), *Islamophobia/Islamophilia: Beyond the politics of enemy or friend* (pp. 29–52). Bloomington: Indiana University Press.

Rana, J. (2011). *Terrifying Muslims: Race and labor in the South Asian diaspora*. Durham, NC: Duke University Press.

Shaheen, J. G. (2008). *Guilty: Hollywood's verdict on Arabs after 9/11*. New York: Olive Branch.

U.S. Department of Homeland Security. (2014, May 10). *Budget in brief: Fiscal year 2014* (DHS Publications). Retrieved on May 10, 2014, from www.dhs.gov /sites/default/files/publications/MGMT/FY%202014%20BIB%20 -%20FINAL%20-508%20Formatted%20(4).pdf.

# Immigrants Organize Against Everyday Life Victimization

▶ KATHLEEN STAUDT AND JOSIAH HEYMAN

THE CRIMINALIZATION OF IMMIGRATION HAS reached unprecedented levels in the twenty-first-century United States, a phenomenon that Juliet Stumpf (2006) calls "crimmigration." We focus here on the everyday violence immigrants experience and on immigrants' organized agency to resist crimmigration in the central borderlands, particularly the Paso del Norte region of El Paso, Texas, and southern New Mexico. People exercise agency and leadership by using human rights and social justice agendas to mitigate some of the worst aspects of brutal enforcement processes.

This chapter is organized into three sections. First, we review the literature on the merger of local criminal law enforcement with federal immigration enforcement and, relatedly, the relocation of immigration enforcement into the sites of everyday life in the U.S. interior. Second, we provide a brief regional context. Third, we offer thick analytic descriptions of victimization as experienced in the Paso del Norte metropolitan region and the ways that two community-based organizations resisted local crimmigration: the Border Network for Human Rights (BNHR) in Chaparral, New Mexico, and two El Paso affiliates of the Industrial Areas Foundation (IAF) in El Paso, Texas. Also involved in Chaparral was a nonprofit legal agency, the Paso del Norte Civil Rights Project (PdN CRP).

Our methodology draws on participant observation and document analysis. Heyman works with the BNHR and chairs its board of directors. The BNHR is a large community member–based organization advocating for human rights, especially in immigration and border enforcement (Heyman, 2014). Staudt works with two affiliates of the Texas IAF network:

El Paso Interreligious Sponsoring Organization (EPISO) and Border Inter-faith (BI); in the latter she served as founding cochair. Heyman focuses on sheriff's raids in schools and homes in Chaparral, New Mexico, a *colonia* (unplanned settlement) located in Otero County, New Mexico, just north of the city of El Paso, using the documentary record created in a lawsuit. Staudt analyzes IAF's challenges to El Paso County sheriff checkpoints, resulting in deportation, through public accountability sessions during electoral campaigns. (BNHR was also involved in the response to the El Paso County sheriff's checkpoints, but for the sake of clarity and length, we set aside that part of the history.) Both organizations used access and leverage in the political context. We both live in the borderlands and teach courses on immigration and border politics; we have been immersed in the region for approximately 70 collective years.

### CRIMMIGRATION, FEDERAL–LOCAL LAW ENFORCEMENT LINKAGE, AND THE TURN TOWARD INTERIOR ENFORCEMENT

From the late nineteenth century on, U.S. federal immigration law enforce-ment, mostly administrative, was largely separate from state and local law enforcement. This changed with the 1996 Illegal Immigration Reform and Immigrant Responsibility Act and especially after 9/11 (Varsanyi, 2010). Developments included the Criminal Alien Program, which deports con-victed people after they have served their sentences; Secure Communities, which identifies, holds, and deports people before conviction, often for as little as a traffic violation; formal authorization of state and local police to enforce federal immigration laws (so-called 287(g) authority); state legisla-tion (e.g., S.B. 1070 in Arizona) mandating police detain supposed unauthor-ized immigrants for federal pickup and removal; and comparable informal state and local police practices (in some cases funded by federal or state law enforcement grants for other purposes, as in the cases we discuss here). Stumpf coined the term "crimmigration" for these developments (2006).

The spread of immigration enforcement across the U.S. interior has been intermixed. In the twentieth century, immigration enforcement focused on the dangerous but episodic border or near-border areas of unauthorized entry and only sporadically targeted interior community or workplace sites. Since 1996 and especially after 2005, however, interior immigration enforcement increased greatly (Coleman, 2012). This is significant, as interior enforcement impacts people in their everyday lives—in their houses and communities, while they are driving, working, shopping, attending school, worshipping, visiting family, and so forth (Coleman, 2012, p. 430).

Communities and families are typically composed of people of varying citizenship and immigration status, so the targeting of some individuals creates an atmosphere of insecurity for many people, though it also encourages mutual help and solidarity (Talavera, Núñez, & Heyman, 2010). Indeed, over 40% of ostensibly unauthorized immigrants turned over by local law enforcement to federal authorities turn out to be U.S. citizens or legal residents, mostly Latina/o, reinforcing this pattern of arbitrariness (Kretsedemas, 2008, p. 349).

The cases we deal with are a bit peculiar in this wider trend, insofar as they are close to an international border. While our cases are from the U.S. border with Mexico, they resemble events occurring at the northern border in states such as Washington and New York. Overall, our cases are broadly representative of how crimmigration, local police involvement, and immigration enforcement impact everyday settled life. Like Stuesse (2010), we examine the role of community organization in reversing the dynamic of fear created by arbitrary enforcement into everyday life.

## THE HISTORICAL CONTEXT OF THE INCREASINGLY SECURITIZED PASO DEL NORTE REGION

The central Paso del Norte region and its more than two million people consist of three parts: Ciudad Juárez, low-wage maquiladora capital of the Americas, where assembly-line workers earn US$40–50 per week; El Paso County, with 800,000 people, the vast majority Spanish speaking, more than 80% of whom are what the U.S. Census calls Hispanic; and southern New Mexico, which resembles El Paso.

Most of what is now known as the U.S. Southwest was once part of northern Mexico. With the Treaty of Guadalupe Hidalgo in 1848 and the Gadsden Purchase of 1853, Mexico lost nearly half of its territory to the United States (Martínez, 2006). At the border, which stretches approximately 2,000 miles from the Pacific Coast to the Gulf of Mexico, people moved back and forth partly in response to labor supply and demand. Only in 1924 was a Border Patrol established, initially under the direction of the U.S. Department of Labor, then the Department of Justice, and finally in 2003, in the mega-agency, the U.S. Department of Homeland Security (DHS). The Bracero Program (legal temporary labor) recruited workers from Mexico from 1942–1965, with Socorro as a major staging area in El Paso County.

U.S. immigration laws change periodically, but from the mid-1990s to the mid-2000s, the Pew Hispanic Institute estimated a rapid increase from 6 to 11 million undocumented people living in the United States, giving rise to mainstream political backlash and criticism about an inability to "control" the border in an increasingly polarized partisan political setting at the national level. A massive buildup of border enforcement directly on the boundary with Mexico began in late 1993, more precisely in El Paso, and then spread along the length of the border.

El Paso has been called the "Ellis Island of the Southwest" for its immigration gateway location, which continues into the twenty-first century, driven by low wages and everyday insecurity in Mexico and Central America. The official ports of entry in the El Paso sector have always been busy with people crossing in both directions to shop, work, and visit friends and relatives. These ports have been particularly congested since September 11, 2001, when U.S. policies began to conflate wars against terror with wars against drugs and against immigrants (Payan, 2006), destroying the beginnings of a binational approach to addressing immigration.

We now turn to cases that demonstrate people's agency to challenge injustice. The first is a lawsuit against the Otero County sheriff for harassment. The second case concerns accountability sessions with elected officials and relational power in El Paso County. Both cases had wide ramifications for reducing local law enforcement's involvement in crimmigration.

### Chaparral Case: The Border Network for Human Rights and the Paso del Norte Civil Rights Project

Our first case concerns Chaparral, New Mexico, an unincorporated settlement of 14,631 people split between two counties, Doña Ana and Otero. It is 84.1% "Hispanic," and the median household income is $26,441, quite low by U.S. standards (U.S. Census Bureau, 2014). Chaparral, located immediately north of El Paso, across the New Mexico–Texas state line, is far from the county seats of both counties. It is marginal in geographic, social, and power terms. The case concerns the Otero County portion of Chaparral. If not otherwise noted, all information comes from the documentary record of a settled lawsuit, not sealed and in the public domain, provided by one of the litigants (PdN CRP), and held in the files of Heyman (names are changed to preserve anonymity).

From May to November 2007, the Otero County sheriff's department conducted 27 de facto immigration raids that resulted in the turnover of at least 75 persons, including at least 28 children and two people older than 60, to the Border Patrol for removal from the United States. Law enforcement goals were minimal; there were seven arrests, mostly for warrants (Gilot, 2007b). One community-wide sweep, on September 10, 2007, resulted in 28 people being turned over to the Border Patrol, and 11 children being removed from Chaparral schools by sheriff's deputies and Border Patrol agents with parents or legal guardians present (Gilot, 2007a). Sporadic raids continued until 2008. Raids were halted by April 2008 through organized community resistance channeled into lawsuits (accompanied by street protests), and a settlement and formal consent order was accepted in March 2009 and has held to the present. The raids were conducted under the auspices of Operation Stonegarden, a federal grant program that pays state and local police officers overtime for general security operations in border counties. In 2007, Otero County was allocated $150,000 for overtime pay with the ostensible target being large-scale drug and human trafficking: "Combined efforts [Otero County Sheriff and DHS] will concentrate on known travel routes of smuggling activities . . . Staging of marked law enforcement units to observe, identify, and then intercept mobile loads of suspected illegal aliens, illicit drugs, and other criminal activity will be used for maximum effectiveness" (quote from Otero grant proposal, court record, file of Heyman). In fact, this is nothing like the low-level house and street searches carried out in Chaparral. Whether this was a deviation by the Otero County sheriff or an arrangement with DHS (or Border Patrol within it) is unclear. Certainly, once raids began, the Border Patrol assisted with them; an Otero County sheriff's lieutenant wrote that the Border Patrol "is aware of this operation and said they would have persons in the area in case of undocumented alien apprehensions" (Gilot, 2007b).

The Otero raids against settled immigrant families with virtually no linked criminal arrests scandalously ignored major drug organizations ("cartels") that conducted business regularly at illegal weekend cockfights in Chaparral, according to testimony at subsequent federal criminal trials (McKenney, 2013). This indicates the targeting (we might even say bullying) of the weak and avoidance of confrontation with the powerful and dangerous. Clearly, it deviated completely from the ostensible intent of the Stonegarden grants.

The sheriff's department used informants (in exchange, e.g., for waiving tickets) to identify specific people and households who were thought to be undocumented immigrants, without consideration of whether they were violating laws normally the concern of local law enforcement. They also stumbled on people in their ordinary lives, such as a family stopped with car trouble. They entered property and homes without warrants, in pushy ways, on flimsy pretexts, and demanded personal identification (a normal police request) but then ignored kinds of identification that would not reveal social security numbers, a clue to immigration status (in New Mexico, unauthorized immigrants can get driver's licenses, so the sheriff's department refused to accept licenses for identification purposes). They detained people for sustained periods of time with no reasonable suspicion of a crime until the Border Patrol arrived to conduct the actual task of immigration identification and removal. These abuses come out in several case studies selected from the lawsuit.

CASE 1: Domitilia was at home in her trailer talking to her sister Verónica and her mother María. When Domitilia left the trailer she noticed two Otero County sheriff's deputies approaching the home. One of the deputies asked Domitilia if she had "papers." Domitilia responded that she had "papers" but she did not have them with her. Hearing voices in their yard, Verónica and María went outside to investigate. One of the deputies told Verónica and María that they had a report that "illegals" were "hiding in trailers." When the deputies arrived, Felipe, Verónica's son, was talking to his neighbor in the adjacent yard. When Felipe saw the deputies approach his aunt, mother, and grandmother, he returned to his own yard to see what was going on.

When Felipe joined his family one of the deputies asked for his name. Felipe told the deputy his name, but refused the deputy's command to produce his ID. The deputy asked Felipe, "Are you American?" Felipe replied that he was. Then one of the deputies asked Verónica and María for their IDs. Verónica produced a New Mexico ID and María produced a Texas ID. After the women presented their IDs, the deputies moved on to a neighboring trailer where another Latino family resided. They saw the deputies take a man and his two children away. Meanwhile, Verónica, María, and Felipe went inside.

Several minutes later the deputies returned to the home and entered without knocking. Felipe said, "No. You cannot come in my house. You have to show me a report [warrant]." The deputies refused to show Felipe a warrant or evidence that they had received a report

about their home. Having barged into the home without warning, consent, or legal authority, and despite the residents' ability to produce valid identification, the deputies yelled
at Verónica and María, "Show me your papers! Are you Americans? What are your social
security numbers?" Verónica and María admitted they did not have "papers." Along with
their neighbor and his children, Verónica and María (who had been in the U.S. for 27 years)
were taken away by three U.S. Border Patrol agents waiting nearby.

**CASE 2:** José was enjoying a normal morning at home with his children when Otero County sheriff's deputies came to his door. The deputies asked him if he knew to whom the
stray dogs running around the neighborhood belonged. José and one of his children said
they were not their dogs and they did not know whose they were. The deputies left. The
dogs were taken away in what appeared to be an animal control truck. Several hours later
the deputies returned.

José's children were playing on the porch when the deputies asked one of them to go
get José. When José came to the door the deputies asked him about the stray dogs again.
José responded that he had already told them they were not his dogs and that the dogs were
already gone. Without warning, the deputies asked for José's ID. José produced his driver's
license. Not satisfied, the deputies demanded to see his social security card as well. Hearing strange voices, José's wife, Claudia, came to the door. The deputies asked her for her ID
as well. José could not produce a social security card and Claudia did not have an ID. When
they could not produce the requested documents, one of the deputies muttered, "Go back
to your country."

The deputies summoned U.S. Border Patrol agents, who again were apparently waiting
nearby. When José's sister-in-law arrived to take the plaintiffs' three children, who were
U.S. citizens, the deputies assaulted her with questions. "Where are you from? What is
your name?" The sister-in-law replied that she was an American citizen and she had come
to take the children. Instead, the deputies insisted that the children accompany Claudia to
detention and eventually to Juárez, despite the fact that their aunt, who was also a U.S.
citizen, was there to care for them (this is also a constitutional violation).

In these two cases, we notice that the sheriff's deputies indiscriminately
went after everyone around who was Latina/o; made prejudiced comments
centered on nationality/citizenship; created pretext rationales to initiate police contact; performed warrantless house intrusion; and refused to
accept legal identification. The real goal was to determine immigration status. On the part of the victims, we see evidence of vulnerability and naiveté
(with terrible consequences), but also we notice that individuals, families,

and neighbors made tentative if unavailing efforts at resistance, such as refusing a warrantless house entry. More organized and effective resistance, however, came from coalitions of community organizations.

Two lawsuits on behalf of sets of plaintiffs were filed in October 2007. One was filed by the PdN CRP and the BNHR; the other was filed by New Mexico American Civil Liberties Union (ACLU) and the Mexican American Legal Defense Fund (MALDEF). We concentrate on the first lawsuit, not only because we have the documentation created for the lawsuit, but also because BNHR's community-organizing method was important in creating an effective resistance movement and because the BNHR/PdN CRP lawsuit resulted in a strong and lasting final settlement.

BNHR uses a base community–organizing method (Heyman, 2014). Human rights promoters, who come from working-class immigrant backgrounds themselves, gradually assemble local committees that meet on a regular basis to discuss real-world applications of international human and U.S. constitutional rights. New promoters emerge from these committees. Committees are assembled into subregions and regions, ultimately feeding into the BNHR central office. In Chaparral this method meant, as in many other places, that committee members and human rights promoters, the grassroots level of the hierarchy, were already on the ground in marginal communities, ready to detect and spring into action when the Otero County sheriff launched his raids. BNHR in turn was able to connect organized community voices to a public interest law organization, PdN CRP, which had technical expertise (taking depositions, filing the lawsuit, doing discovery, crafting settlements and consent orders). In this way, disorganized vulnerability and improvised resistance was transformed into organized action. BNHR also carried out nonlegal responses, which may have assisted the lawsuit: an organizer was dispatched to Chaparral early on; an organized media campaign was launched within 5 days of the large raid of September 10, 2007, resulting in a wave of revealing media coverage; there were large public marches and meetings in September and October 2007; and Catholic church peace and justice networks were mobilized as support.

The New Mexico ACLU/MALDEF lawsuit was settled first with monetary damages to individual plaintiffs but a weak consent order. BNHR and PdN CRP held out for a stronger settlement, which was achieved in March 2009. While there is not room to review all 13 mandates to the

Otero County sheriff's department in the consent order, the key provisions address precisely the blurring of local law enforcement with federal immigration enforcement, the racial and other profiling involved, and the violations of constitutional and other legal rights and processes that occurred in this process. Though only applicable to one county, which of course is the limitation of this kind of struggle, the settlement has worked effectively to the present day on behalf of the people of Chaparral and all of Otero County, as have the policy changes introduced in El Paso County by Sheriff Wiles.

The lessons of the Chaparral case are that (1) unauthorized immigrants and their relatives and neighborhoods are vulnerable to unexpected and aggressive acts of victimization concerning immigration status by local law enforcement, although they also have a basic sense of rights and justice, combined with limited and fragmented capacity to resist; and (2) organized communities have much greater capacity to resist because (a) on-the-ground community organizations have the ability to detect rights violations and other issues, even in geographically and socially marginal communities (specialized advocacy groups with limited community presence may be less capable of this); (b) the organized community is more able to overcome fear, caution, and fragmentation in order to carry out effective acts of resistance, from marches to obtaining legal testimony; and (c) a community organization can bring in extra-community specialists, such as litigators, who have specific capacities not found in working-class communities. The trend toward crimmigration and the closely related trend toward interior immigration law enforcement can be blunted in specific sites via organized community resistance.

### El Paso Case: Industrial Areas Foundation Affiliates, El Paso Interreligious Sponsoring Organization, and Border Interfaith

The IAF, founded on principles that Saul Alinsky honed as far back as the 1930s, has spawned affiliates all over the United States, including Texas and the Southwest. Its base consists of member institutions such as faith-based organizations and teachers' associations. IAF organizers work with core leaders in these member institutions to identify and groom leaders who acquire voices and organizing skills through experience. Together they aim to change power relations in communities and in states through relationships with officials; public displays of power through numbers; and the expression of short, pointed stories and testimonials at these public accountability sessions. IAF agendas emerge from "house meetings" or small-group sessions in member institutions, wherein priority issues emerge in policy areas such as health, workforce, housing, and education. In Texas, and particularly in border IAF organizations, immigrant checkpoints emerged during house meetings.

In many faith-based institutions of multiple denominations, from synagogues to churches and Catholic parishes, congregants share core values around social justice concerns, including human rights abuses, low wages, and insecurities in everyday life. Congregants often come from multiple class/income, linguistic, and ethnic backgrounds within and across the coalition of member institutions, thus offering the potential to build social capital across class and ethnic lines. Congregations also offer safe places in which to articulate concerns, including those relating to ethics, morality, and justice.

In member institutions outside the city limits in the El Paso County, EPISO and BI leaders heard about harassment at checkpoints that the sheriff's deputies set up near and in *colonias*, outside the city limits (where the appointed police chief prevails) and inside the county (where the elected sheriff prevails). For example, when stopped at checkpoints outside the city in the county, drivers would be asked for not only their driver's license and proof of insurance but also for their social security card and documentation of citizenship. When the latter two documents could not be produced immediately, the sheriff's deputies would call the Border Patrol. In a 3-month period early in 2006, a total of 860 deportations occurred due to this strategy; many of those deported were breadwinners for their households and parents of U.S.-born children (drawn and updated from Staudt, 2008). As for the sheriff in Otero County, federal incentives for local law enforcement also proved enticing as a means to expand the El Paso County sheriff's department budget. But unlike the sheriff, city Police Chief Richard Wiles (with whom EPISO and BI had a relationship) adopted the "community-based policing" strategy instituted by many urban police departments in the 1990s. He directed his officers to create a victim- and witness-friendly community so that residents could report crimes and/or testify as witnesses without fear of deportation. In contrast, former El Paso County sheriff Leo Samaniego, a conservative elected as a Democrat, was proud to create so-called "secure communities" through deportation, though his checkpoints resulted in only four drug arrests and 0.6 pounds of drugs. During U.S. Representative James Sensenbrenner's swing through the United States to build support for his HR4437 in 2006, Samaniego testified at public hearings to an unfriendly audience of 400 El Pasoans at the Chamizal National Memorial; he used the words "terror" and "terrorism" no less than 17 times, while Police Chief Wiles testified that his community-based policing strategy resulted in El Paso's designation as the second-safest big city in the United States. El Paso has enjoyed first and second place status for nearly a decade (City Crime Rankings by CQ Press, 2013).

BI and EPISO leaders and member institutions spanned the city and county jurisdictional lines, so personal experiences of harassment by sheriff's deputies did not prevail for all. However, strong commitments to social justice and human rights exist; in one member institution, keen memories exist of the Nazis' incessant demands for "documents" during the Holocaust. Both institutions began their initial work in what IAF terms "relational" meetings. Leaders, including clergy such as priests, pastors, and rabbis, met with Samaniego to forge a policy with a written agreement to end checkpoints and initiate systems to report (i.e., to discourage or prohibit) the following (their language in bold).

1. Sheriff checkpoints **near schools**
2. Sheriff checkpoints **during** morning or evening **rush hours**
3. Sheriff's deputies **ONLY targeting older make cars** (all cars must be stopped at checkpoints)
4. Sheriff's deputies asking people who have NOT broken a law for their **social security cards** or proof of citizenship
5. Sheriff's deputies using **abusive language** or tactics

This document of March 8, 2007 (in Staudt's files) was circulated widely.

Despite the formal agreement, checkpoints continued. Thus, EPISO and BI leaders decided to include pointed questions and stories at public accountability sessions for candidates running in local and state electoral races. Public accountability sessions represent a hallmark strategy for the IAF: candidates are briefed about the organizations' agendas and the session format ahead of time; the events are carefully planned, timed, and scripted; and candidates (who receive the precise questions 24 hours before the events) get asked "yes/no" or "how" questions by clergy and other high-profile community leaders, with 1–2 minutes to explain their responses to a roused audience that averages more than 400 people who promise, in revival-like unison, to encourage 10 others to vote. IAF affiliates do not endorse candidates or parties.

Staudt vividly remembers observing and participating in several sessions at which Marcelino shared his story. A citizen, he drove his grandchildren to elementary school daily in an older car. In a 3-month period, he was stopped seven times. He was frightened, as were his grandchildren. His challenges were featured in stories in the media. Staudt also participated in the accountability session for candidates for sheriff in 2008, which included 11 candidates running as Democrats, including former police chief Wiles. (Samaniego had served six terms and was stepping down.) The candidates answered pointed questions about not only the agreement but its enforcement and the planned penalties for deputies who failed to comply with the policy. Not surprisingly, all candidates publicly stated their commitment to the policy and to penalizing deputies who failed to comply. Wiles, the front-runner and eventual victor in that election (and reelected in 2012), enforced the policy against checkpoints, and social security numbers (or citizenship documents) are no longer requested in routine traffic stops in the county.

The El Paso case offers several lessons. Like the BNHR, the power of collective organization has proven effective for challenging and changing enforcement policies. While sharing goals of changing local enforcement, IAF purses different but complementary strategies for change. First, large coalitions across ethnic and class lines provide a solid and political secure base from which to challenge injustices in local enforcement. Second, progressive clergy leaders offer a neutral, moral force and language that strengthen relational and public work. Third, electoral campaigns create regular, routine opportunities to make injustices public and to obtain public promises on which IAF leaders follow up, once winning candidates take office. Finally, relational work with public officials strengthens power in between elections.

### CONCLUSION

The Paso del Norte region is a place of unspeakable violence. Everyday security of people has have been challenged not only by poverty and flights from violence across borders but also by local county law enforcement, which in these cases violated constitutional, human rights and moral codes of social justice to harass and profile people in their homes and in the streets of their neighborhoods. Local officers did this with incentivized enthusiasm from federal resources in the stepped-up "wars" against drugs, immigrants, and terrorism.

Our analysis shows how local community organizations resisted and challenged unjust local law enforcement practices through documentation, lawsuits, public protests, electoral forums, and relational work. People of multiple backgrounds effectively halted unjust practices, helped inform voters about candidates' positions on the issue, and offered continuing oversight through grassroots expertise, activism, and relational work. Research ought to address and highlight not only victimization but also agency in resisting and challenging unjust laws. Paseños demonstrated some success in mitigating the worst of border enforcement abuses. Richard Wiles achieved national stature speaking against mixing local law enforcement and federal immigration enforcement, working closely with BNHR.

However, immigration policy and enforcement continue to threaten people and their everyday security in other border locations and in the U.S. mainstream. We operate under no illusions about the continuing injustices of harsh immigration policy, massive deportations, and extensive surveillance of life in the borderlands and mainstream of the United States. Local resistance and challenges demonstrate the axiom that "all politics is local," even for federal law, but local work cannot substitute for a thorough immigration policy reform that puts people, their dignity, and human rights before a harsh, militarized, border security–industrial complex. As part of wider immigration reforms, it is important to strengthen the separation between federal immigration enforcement and local public safety, including regulations that restrict local police from holding persons for identification by DHS without arrest on criminal charges and that likewise restrict local and state police from calling on DHS officers as translators, "back-up," and so on. Immigration is not and should not be a crime.

### REFERENCES

City Crime Rankings by CQ Press. (2013). Retrieved on July 2, 2014 from http://os
.cqpress.com/citycrime/2012/CityCrime2013_CityCrimeRankingsFactSheet
.pdf.

Coleman, M. (2012). From border policing to internal immigration control in the United States. In T. M. Wilson & and H. Donnan (Eds.), *A companion to border studies* (pp. 452–487). Malden, MA: Wiley-Blackwell.

City Crime Rankings by CQ Press, (2013). Retrieved on July 2, 2014 from http://os .cqpress.com/citycrime/2012/CityCrime2013_CityCrimeRankingsFactSheet .pdf

Gilot, L. (2007a, September 15). 28 deported after raid on Chaparral schools. *El Paso Times.* Retrieved on June 16, 2014, from www.elpasotimes.com /ci_6897970.

———. (2007b, November 12). Lawsuits claim Otero's Stonegarden violated civil rights. *El Paso Times.* Retrieved on June 16, 2014, from www.elpasotimes.com /news/ci_7437322.

Heyman, J. (2014). The Border Network for Human Rights: From community organizing to public policy action. *City & Society, 26,* 73–95.

Kretsedemas, P. (2008). What does an undocumented immigrant look like?: Local enforcement and the new immigrant profiling. In D. C. Brotherton & P. Kretsedemas (Eds.), *Keeping out the other: A critical introduction to immigration enforcement today* (pp. 258–290). New York: Columbia University Press.

Martínez, O. (2006). *Troublesome border.* Tucson: University of Arizona Press.

McKenney, D. H. (2013). *"Operation Stone Garden": A case study of legitimation of violence and the consequences for Mexican immigrants in Chaparral, New Mexico* (Unpublished master's thesis). University of Texas, El Paso, TX.

Payan, T. (2006). *The three U.S.-Mexico border wars: Drugs, immigration, and homeland security.* New York: Praeger.

Staudt, K. (2008). Bordering the other in the U.S. Southwest: El Pasoans confront the local sheriff. In D. C. Brotherton & P. Kretsedemas (Eds.), *Keeping out the other: A critical introduction to immigration enforcement today* (pp. 291–315). New York: Columbia University Press.

Stuesse, A. C. (2010). Challenging the border patrol, human rights and persistent inequalities: An ethnography of struggle in South Texas. *Latino Studies, 8,* 23–47.

Stumpf, J. (2006). The crimmigration crisis: Immigrants, crime, and sovereign power. *American University Law Review, 56,* 367–419.

Talavera, V., Núñez, G. G., & Heyman J. C. (2010). Deportation in the U.S.-Mexico borderlands: Anticipation, experience, and memory. In N. D. Genova & N. Peutz (Eds.), *The deportation regime: Sovereignty, space, and the freedom of movement* (pp. 166–195), Durham, NC: Duke University Press.

U.S. Census Bureau. (2014). American FactFinder. Retrieved on June 12, 2014, from http://factfinder2.census.gov/faces/nav/jsf/pages/index.xhtml.

Varsanyi, M. W. (2010). Immigration Policy Activism in U.S. States and Cities: Interdisciplinary Perspectives. In M. W. Varsanyi (Ed.), *Taking local control: Immigration policy activism in U.S. cities and states* (pp. 1–30). Stanford, CA: Stanford University Press.

# 7

# Undocumented Latino Migrant Day Laborers in the San Francisco Bay Area

## PSYCHOSOCIAL, ECONOMIC, AND POLITICAL CONSEQUENCES

▸ KURT C. ORGANISTA, LOBSANG MARCIA,
CARLOS MARTINEZ, MIGUEL ACALÁ,
AND JOSE RAMIREZ

THE PURPOSE OF THIS CHAPTER is to share the lived experience of undocumented Latino migrant day laborers (LMDLs) in the San Francisco Bay Area who left their homes in Mexico and Central America to pursue work in the United States in order to compensate for the lack of employment back home needed to support their families and livelihoods. More specifically, the consequences of being undocumented, as expressed and described by 51 LMDLs or *jornaleros* who participated in semistructured in-depth qualitative interviews, are shared and inductively discussed and analyzed in this chapter. These participants are part of a larger federally funded mixed-methods study designed to develop and test a structural-environmental model of alcohol-related sexual HIV risk (principal investigator: Organista; 1R01AA017592-01A2). This larger study has generated publications on LMDL sexual health (Organista et al., 2013) and alcohol use (Worby et al., 2014) and ways in which LMDLs negotiate discrimination (Quesada et al., 2014) under conditions of what we call *structural vulnerability* (Organista et al., 2012).

While the larger study from which the voices in this chapter come is *deductive* in nature (i.e., designed to develop and test a conceptual model), this book chapter was written *inductively*, as instructed by the book editors.

Hence, our qualitative database manager was tasked with generating any output pertinent to the consequences of being undocumented as discussed and expressed by our 51 LMDLs.

## APPROACH TO STUDY

A dozen pages of single-spaced output were generated from our qualitative database in an effort to capture the **Consequences of being undocumented**, as described and expressed by the 51 LMDLs in our sample. This new code was generated by searching the following existing codes that seemed most relevant: **Law enforcement**, which captures beliefs, attitudes, and behaviors pertaining to police; **Mobility** or movement within and between U.S. cities and states; **Stigma** related to being undocumented LMDLs, as described and experienced by participants; **Public**, which refers to dealings with the general public here in the United States; and **Housing** and **Work**, two codes that respectively refer to living and working conditions experienced by participants as well as related attitudes and beliefs. An additional four pages of a previously generated code, **Resilience**, was also reviewed for its relevance to coping with being undocumented.

Output for **Consequences of being undocumented** and **Resilience** was reviewed by five members of our research team: The principal investigator (PI), two interviewers trained in ethnography, who helped to collect the $N = 51$ of in-depth interviews; one interviewer trained in quantitative survey administration, currently interviewing day laborers; and one monolingual Spanish-speaking Mexican day laborer, living and working in San Francisco, recruited onto the research team 2 years ago to witness the research process, participate in the ethnographic phase or survey, and administer the quantitative survey instrument currently in progress. Most importantly, this *jornalero* provides his insider's knowledge of the local day laborer experience at critical junctures of the study (e.g., during the ethnographic phase, to provide input into quantitative survey development in subsequent years, etc.). All remaining authors are bilingual, bicultural Latino men.

The PI and each team member separately reviewed the **Consequences** data output and drafted preliminary thoughts and ideas about themes and quotes they believed supported the candidate themes. Next, the team met to share their notes and thoughts about possible themes and quotes in order to achieve consensus regarding those that best capture consequences of being undocumented in the sample of LMDLs. Three core themes were identified in this manner, and the first author assigned each to three team members with instructions to draft up results sections on these themes complete with supporting quotes. These drafted sections, one per theme, were reviewed by the first author, who provided feedback intended to: clarify wording of themes, question how well selected quotes support corresponding themes, and minimize overlap between themes. PI edits and feedback were next discussed in a face-to-face team meeting during which consensus was reached regarding directions for final drafting of the three sections. Also, each of the three team members discussed each of his or her sections with our day laborer team member to solicit any of his thoughts and observations on each of the themes, including any personal experiences he wished to share. The **Resilience** output was reviewed and presented to the team by one team member, especially interested in this topic, and discussed by the entire team until consensus was reached regarding how to define and illustrate this theme.

### FINDINGS

Our team achieved consensus on three central overarching themes within the **Consequences of being undocumented** output: (1) perceptions of San Francisco (and related areas) as a sanctuary city; (2) policing and hypervigilant self-policing to try and avoid deportation; and (3) emotional and psychological distress resulting from being undocumented. Additionally, **Resiliency** referred to coping with these three circumstances. Each of these four themes are defined and illustrated in the following sections.

### Perceptions of San Francisco (and Other Areas) as a Sanctuary City

This theme refers to day laborers' knowledge and awareness of San Francisco as a sanctuary city. Related perceptions and mixed feelings captured in the quotes below refer to both San Francisco and areas outside the Bay Area. In the two quotes that follow, similar positive beliefs are expressed about San Francisco by two Mexican day laborers with more 20 years and less than 5 years in the United States, respectively.

INTERVIEWER: What do you think about the police in San Francisco?

JORGE (MEXICO, 48 YEARS OLD, 22 YEARS IN THE UNITED STATES): I think that they are more tolerant. I also think that it is a sanctuary city for homosexuals and immigrants, perhaps gay immigrants.

INTERVIEWER: Have you had experience with police or immigration?

LUIS (MEXICO, 33 YEARS OLD, 4 YEARS IN THE UNITED STATES): No. That's one thing I like about San Francisco. Because as long as you're not getting in trouble, looking for it, they won't bother you. It's as if the cops didn't exist. Maybe immigration would like to but this is a sanctuary city. That helps a lot.

However, some LMDLs have become critical or even cynical about San Francisco, as suggested by the following:

INTERVIEWER: Have you seen the police get tougher with immigrants?

GILBERTO (EL SALVADOR, 56 YEARS OLD, 11 YEARS IN THE UNITED STATES): With the police here it is like they say, a sanctuary city, but now it is only the name. It is not a reality.

INTERVIEWER: Have you seen changes?

GILBERTO: Yes, the police do not tolerate anymore. I understand them because sometimes we do not behave, like we disrespect and sometimes they abuse us. Sometimes we are cool, just walking, and they stop us, and now they are deporting people. They are cleaning, to put it that way, just because they don't have documents. They are being deported, but the mass media does not communicate this.

INTERVIEWER: Do you feel safe in San Francisco, safer, compared to other places?

OSCAR (NICARAGUA, 55 YEARS OLD, 21 YEARS IN THE UNITED STATES): No, it's even. You're only safe in your own home. Well, who's safe, because for one, we don't have papers, we're illegal. They could get us at any moment. If not immigration, the police, yeah, I don't feel so safe, yeah. No, we don't know what our fate will be here . . . they're never going to give us papers.

While some undocumented LMDLs believe that San Francisco is no longer the sanctuary city it once was, it is perceived as far better than other U.S. cities and states, as expressed by the following:

LUIS (MEXICO, 33 YEARS OLD, 4 YEARS IN THE UNITED STATES): I've had to go out to San Jose, or whatever and a friend had a car, I was driving it, and he said, "No, be careful, immigration isn't like in San Francisco [no respeta como en

San Francisco]." So when you leave San Francisco you feel you're risking it . . . here you feel more protected.

Interestingly, San Jose is also a sanctuary city but is not perceived by Luis to be as tolerant as San Francisco. Whether this is true or not, remaining in San Francisco seems to make some day laborers feel safer. Staying out of Arizona is another way of avoiding police and deportation:

INTERVIEWER: In what part of Arizona did you work? What did Arizona seem like to you?

TORO (MEXICO, 29 YEARS OLD, 7 YEARS IN THE UNITED STATES): Um, to tell you the truth, there's lots of work in Arizona, yes, yes. So if they weren't having all those legal problems, you know, I would be working there and all . . . and I would live there but, yes, like you said just now just reminded me, right? So, it's fine, just that the only thing is . . . there is a lot of immigration and all that, how can I explain it? So, there's a danger that you'll be deported, just that, right? You know and . . .

INTERVIEWER: Do you know any of your friends who have been deported?

TORO: Yes, I mean, over there are lots of people. Lots of people are deported each day. For example, there are people who, let's say, are living with us, in a house. So, then one person says, "I'm going to the store, I'll be right back. I'm going to get a soda or something" and then after 2, 3, 4 hours, you don't come back because immigration has already . . . like, like, you know what I mean? That's difficult . . . I know lots of people like that, um, that's why, that's the same reason why I moved from there too.

### Threat of Deportation: Policing and Hypervigilant Self-Policing

Reflected in Toro's statements is a chronic anxiety experienced by LMDLs and precautions taken in the effort to avoid police and deportation. Such hypervigilant self-policing seems to influence everyday behavior, including socializing and drinking, as exemplified by a 30-year-old Guatemalan man, here since 2005:

INTERVIEWER: Do you drink when you go out dancing?

P: Yes, but not too much, maybe three or four beers. Yes, that's how I control myself. Well, it's hard because if I get too drunk the cops are waiting for you outside. If you're really drunk they'll put you in the patrol car and they won't put you in jail. Instead they'll turn you in to immigration. And once you're with immigration, there's no solution. You're headed back to your country. So that's why you only go out, relax, have fun, and have a few beers.

A 48-year-old Mexican day laborer who has resided in the United States since 2002 provides another example of self-policing:

I try to live a correct life, for me at least. I know that I am undocumented here so I know if the police catches you and you are drunk, you go to jail and ruin your record. I have tried to live a calm life. If you want to have a beer, I do it at home. If you want to have beer when I go out to dance, I do it but inside. I don't have car because of the same thing, I don't want to have problems with the police. And I don't like those kind problems. Another thing is that when I go out to dance and I drink 2 or 3 beers, I get a cab and then I go home. I don't go to Latino parties, because in the Latino parties there are drugs, beers, and fights and then the police show up.

The looming threat of deportation limits engaging in everyday activities, such as spending time in public spaces, which possibly leads to social isolation. One example is provided by this 56-year-old Salvadoran day laborer who has been in the United States for just over a decade:

Once in a while, it depends on the situation, because before I used to go to the park on 21st, but the police would go there often, so I don't go anymore there to avoid problems.

Fear of being outside the home is expressed by Pepe, a 55-year-old Nicaraguan day laborer residing in the United States since 1993:

PEPE:  You're only safe in your own home. Well, who's safe, because for one, we don't have papers, we're illegal. They could get us at any moment. If not immigration, the police, yeah, I don't feel so safe, yeah. No, we don't know what our fate will be here.

The simple act of being out in public can make an undocumented day laborer feel like a criminal. Interestingly, a 53-year-old Mexican man, living here since 2000, blames racial profiling on Guatemalans, by projecting his own discrimination toward this other Latino population, who he claims all have drugs.

Because where I live, if you're outside, cops [*chota*, slang for cops] think that you're using drugs, even more so if you are Latino, because within a couple of blocks there are almost only *Chapines* [slang term for Guatemalans] and they all have drugs. When I have my money, I buy my *caguama* [colloquial Mexican term for large bottled beer] and other necessities and I shut myself in my room, and that's it.

Implied above is the belief that, while he and other Mexicans are perhaps undeserving of racial profiling, Guatemalans are reasonable targets for police suspicion. Similarly, the statement below, by a 31-year-old Mexican man in the United States since 2010, implies that those who have been harassed by police and/or deported may have deserved it:

Up until now no police officer has bothered me, maybe because I haven't been doing anything bad. Maybe if I did something bad they would bother me . . . Ah ha. And what I've heard, the ones who drive and don't have a license are the ones who are afraid of the police. They're afraid of making a mistake and losing their car. That's it. If you don't get into fights, then you won't have problems with the police here.

Like the quote above, the following day laborer statement also seems to elevate the speaker above subjugated peers in an effort to differentiate him as undeserving of deportation.

LALO (MEXICO, 58 YEARS OLD, 22 YEARS IN THE UNITED STATES): I think that the law needs to be stricter, because there are bad people among the people. Among the immigrants, there are bad people. There are fucked up [*cabrona*] people and they need to obligate them to be straight, to respect the laws, because sometimes we think that we are still in our country, and we are in a country where there are laws, and it is a democracy, and there is more freedom.

### Emotional and Psychological Distress

Overlapping with the above is the emotional and psychological impact of the undocumented day laborer experience, including injury to self-worth, as articulated by Lazaro, a 57-year-old Salvadoran with 10 years in the

United States. In the following exchange the interviewer queries the participant's assertion that he is "no one."

INTERVIEWER: What makes you feel like you're no one?

LAZARO: When I feel like I'm no one [is] when I don't have the most important. . . . a job, am not in good health, you don't know the language, English, you don't have a place to spend the night. That you feel . . . like today I worked 4 hours . . . all week you worked 4 hours! When you have a job, yeah you feel tired but I feel better when I have a job. My mind feels clearer [*despejado*]. When I don't have anything, I think, your mind thinks a lot.

INTERVIEWER: What do you do when you feel these things?

LAZARO: Ah, there . . . there are times when you . . . when I feel like this . . . what I do, sometimes, I can go to the park and walk. But the economic problems make you think a lot in this country. Life for me gets complicated because I think lot. For example, my mom is older [*muy señora*] she needs for me to send her money, I need to pay for this, I need a place to live, and you don't have money. You don't have money, a job . . . you don't lead a calm life. You lead life thinking, that I can drive myself crazy. This country is very beautiful and gives you lots of opportunities. But those of us who don't have documents, it can be very difficult . . . because we're just surviving through God's mercy, what God wants [a la voluntad de Dios].

Lazaro's statement also captures a gnawing level of worry, usually about lack of work and money. Lack of access to a driver's license is also related to limited work opportunities with resulting anxiety sometimes related to drug and alcohol use.

INTERVIEWER: Where has most of your income come from then?

JUAN (MEXICAN, 37 YEARS OLD, 8 YEARS IN THE UNITED STATES): The last time was from the flea market [*la pulga*]. From sales, no, if I just relied on that I would starve . . . now the business is only on weekends . . . there are other flea markets that are all week in Oakland and elsewhere and it would get me out of here. But I don't have a car or a license, so I don't want to have anything to do with the police. You know, I mean even if you're here you're afraid. So you're not mentally free, we're not. We feel that way. . . . I think that the day we go back to our countries, it's going to be, like wow, like that burden is going to be lifted. We're carrying it, subconsciously we're carrying it and that also in the end leads us to drugs and all if someone isn't strong.

The following quote is from a man also making the connection between stress and drinking:

RAUL (EL SALVADOR, 58 YEARS OLD, 20 YEARS IN THE UNITED STATES): Yes, well [*sirens in the background*] I always stress and it makes me desperate [*desesperado*] so I drink. I drink and I drink and I'm with the hand with a beer and of course it's a different system here. In my country when the police come by it's a joke. Of course you're in the middle of the capital [and] it looks bad because there's women walking with their kids, pregnant with kids and it looks bad. It's another system but over there I'm walking down the street with a beer in hand with no problem.

### Resiliency and Coping with Challenging Circumstances

Resiliency refers to the ability to bounce back from setbacks and adversity, to persist with one's central goals, and to grow in the process (Zautra & Reich, 2013). Our team wondered about coping and resiliency in LMDLs in view of their formidable challenges and circumstances stemming from being undocumented. As reflected in the quotes below, *jornaleros* relied on coping resources and strategies within their control such as maintaining a positive disposition, taking comfort in their belief in God, and engaging in several activities with little or no cost attached. For example, optimism is expressed by a pair of day laborers regarding the future:

JAVIER (MEXICAN, 26 YEARS OLD, 8 YEARS IN THE UNITED STATES): Even if I don't have a job or with a job, I'm happy. A lot of people when they don't have a job say "Oh I'm desperate." Not me. When I have a job, wow; when I don't have a job, wow. Happy. In life, you have to laugh [hay que reir en la vida]. Being [happy] like that, just like that, better times will come.

FRANCISCO (GUATEMALA, 45 YEARS OLD, 20 YEARS IN THE UNITED STATES): Well, I try to be a little more realistic and . . . and to see the positive. In that, well, today maybe we didn't have work but, uh, tomorrow is going to be better. Um, maybe we couldn't pay off a loan, but maybe tomorrow. Um, it is possible to cover . . . uh, if I try to detach my mind I don't, for example . . . not to ignore what it is I'm living in the moment, but yeah, not to stay focused on that, where I am in that moment.

Other forms of coping include relying on social support, free activities, and entertainment outlets as illustrated in the following quotes.

FRANCISCO (GUATEMALA, 45 YEARS OLD, 20 YEARS IN THE UNITED STATES):
I try to . . . to detach my mind. Like . . . like that . . . go to the park, go playing soccer refreshes my mind. It makes me change a little bit, what I'm living, or if not I exercise, to get some fresh air, to walk, run, uh . . . that helps me a lot also. Another thing that helps a lot is, uh, surround myself with people with a positive attitude [rodearme de personas, uhm, que su mentalidad son positivas]. That helps me greatly because uh . . . uh, that gives inspiration to me as well, to be more positive. Yeah, that helps me.

DANIEL (GUATEMALA, 31 YEARS OLD, 9 YEARS IN THE UNITED STATES): Because [in the] afternoon it's hard to get work . . . You stay just joking around [*payasando*] . . . but, well, so you don't get bored at home. Sharing . . . because at least you go play soccer here in the park that's here. We've grilled up there and you spend time there and like I tell you . . . to see the good side of life [la cara buena de la vida]. There's no other choice, to smile, because there's no alternative.

INTERVIEWER: And do you ever have times when you're depressed?

MARTÍN (MEXICO, 31 YEARS OLD, 4 YEARS IN THE UNITED STATES): Yes, yes. That's how it goes. That does happen. But since I also am always in touch with my family [in country of origin], I talk to them and tell them and they also cheer me up some [dan un poco de animo].

LMDLs frequently rely on their faith in God, their spirituality, to help them cope, as evident in the following quotes.

MARTÍN (MEXICO, 31 YEARS OLD, 4 YEARS IN THE UNITED STATES): I'm a bit of a believer in God. So then, because look, here, I've felt that we all need each other. If you have family, maybe you'll need their help or someone's [help]. But the one who has helped me most has been God. And maybe that, maybe that source comes through . . . that . . . I'm estranged from church, but I do know that God is always with me because I feel he helps and comforts me.

LUIS (MEXICO, 38 YEARS OLD, 12 YEARS IN THE UNITED STATES): For years this corner here has been the goal. To come here . . . and the opportunity you're given . . . you are here to find work. The goal is to ask God and to go with faith to find an honest job like . . . like you should and to earn money honorably.

ERIC (MEXICO, 48 YEARS OLD, 22 YEARS IN THE UNITED STATES): Well . . . eh, with the faith that one has, I believe that Jesus Christ and God take care of you when you have a good heart with other people, toward the community, that as long as you are not out doing bad things [que no andas haciendo cosas malas] God takes care of your life.

INTERVIEWER: And what is your remedy in this situation?

LAZARO (EL SALVADOR, 58 YEARS OLD, 11 YEARS IN THE UNITED STATES): Ah, in this situation, asking God to keep me going [*alentado*] and to . . . and to ask God to get me a job . . . and be able to help others. Right, with what little I can do.

### DISCUSSION

The purpose of this chapter was to capture consequences of being undocumented for LMDLs living and working in the San Francisco Bay Area. Data from 51 LMDLs or *jornaleros* who participated in in-depth qualitative interviews were systematically reviewed, discussed, and analyzed for this chapter. A trio of major overlapping themes emerged from the creation of the qualitative database code **Consequences of being undocumented** that provided insightful descriptions of beliefs, attitudes, and behaviors related to: (1) how undocumented LMDLs view San Francisco as a sanctuary city, including comparisons with other areas; (2) the experience of being policed and how LMDLs try to avoid deportation; and (3) the emotional distress and psychological impact of being undocumented, including injury to self-worth. Coping and resilience were also analyzed in the effort to explore how LMDLs deal with their formidable circumstances (Figure 7.1).

Sanctuary cities such as San Francisco are a refuge for undocumented immigrants, because such cities do not allow municipal funds or resources to be used to enforce federal immigration laws (i.e., they do not allow police or municipal employees to inquire about an individual's immigration status). While sanctuary is not what it used to be, as the men in this study clearly convey, the San Francisco Bay Area may be "as good as it gets" for undocumented immigrants in comparison with other places, such as Arizona with its controversial Senate Bill 1070 (Quesada et al., 2014, p. 29). S.B. 1070 is a statewide law requiring law enforcement officers to determine the legal status of persons with whom they interact and

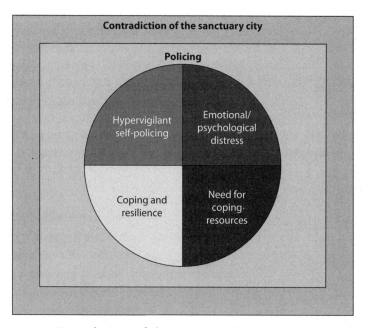

FIGURE 7.1. **Contradictions of the Sanctuary City.** The inductive model that emerged from an analysis of the overlapping themes regarding the consequences of being undocumented.

to arrest and detain the undocumented and turn them over to immigration control authorities (Legal Information Institute, 2010). Further, S.B. 1070 prohibits undocumented day laborers from seeking work in public and outlaws day labor centers that organize day labor work opportunities while providing other basic services (e.g., food, classes on health and occupational injury).

The mixed feelings expressed about San Francisco as a sanctuary city are understandable in light of recent changes in local and national laws and policies. For example, San Francisco's recent sit-lie ordinance is one that criminalizes people, such as the homeless, who sit or lie on public sidewalks for prolonged periods of time. San Francisco Board of Supervisors member David Campos asserted that LMDLs sometimes need to sit and rest while waiting for work for hours at a time, yet they are disparately affected by this ordinance (Quesada et al., 2014). Interestingly, San Jose, California, while also a sanctuary city, was described by one of the men as having harsher law enforcement. This may be attributed to personal experience, hearsay, or perhaps the illusion of safety that come from confining oneself to San Francisco.

At the national level, the Secure Communities (SC) program has contributed to San Francisco being among the top 13 counties in California deporting the highest percentage of noncriminal undocumented persons (Phelan, 2011). Implemented in 2008, SC requires local, state, and federal law enforcement to conduct Federal Bureau of Investigation background checks on individuals suspected of not being citizens, with reports automatically sent to Immigration and Customs Enforcement (Applied Research Center, 2011). SC operates in 44 states and since August 2011 has led to the deportation of 134,000 individuals. However, deportations have recently decreased in California due in part to the Trust Act, a new law limiting the state's cooperation with SC by limiting the detention of undocumented people in local jails for deportation purposes (California TRUST Act, 2014). Still, continued immigration control–related policing affects LMDLs in a variety of ways, as discussed later.

One response to the contradictory sanctuary city is hypervigilance on the part of LMDLs or the mix of anxiety, worry, and behavioral efforts employed to try and avoid deportation and interactions with law enforcement. Such worry and precautionary behavior pervade day laborers' mundane daily activities, such as the decision not to drive and to limit social activities to those less likely to garner police attention. Conscious efforts to avoid police include not drinking, drinking only at home, or drinking only with certain people in particular locations considered safer. While hypervigilance might limit deportation, it might also increase social isolation. As Quesada et al. (2014) explain, "In negotiating their position of vulnerability, day laborers simultaneously undertake a number of maneuvers such as managing their public image and conforming to social expectation through corporal management and self-discipline" (p. 42).

A subtheme of hypervigilant self-policing is the belief that those who have been deported or harassed by police probably brought it on themselves. Thus, the threat of deportation seems to inscribe strict guidelines into the dispositions and behaviors of day laborers such that it becomes commonly accepted that only by abiding by these guidelines can one hope to avoid deportation. Consequently, it becomes easier to accept that those who have been deported deserved it. Quesada et al. (2014) provide the following insight into self-policing on the part of LMDLs:

> One way discrimination is negotiated is to turn the critique of dominant society onto oneself; a sort of perverse internalized racism. Indeed, it is this form of symbolic violence when the critique is naturalized and accepted as fact that the negotiation is with oneself in the form of self-regulation. (p. 42)

Self-policing may also serve as a means for some day laborers to elevate their otherwise subjugated position above peers by differentiating themselves from others in their own segregated moral universe. The idea of what we have termed *deserved deportation* seems to serve as a reinforcing mechanism for day laborers to engage in self-policing. Ultimately, such symbolic violence serves to entrench and naturalize punitive neoliberal policies in the minds of day laborers. According to Bourgois (2001),

> The concept of symbolic violence was developed by Pierre Bourdieu to uncover how domination operates on an intimate level via the misrecognition of power structures on the part of the dominated who collude in their own oppression every time they perceive and judge the social order through categories that make it appear natural and self-evident. (p. 3)

Related to hypervigilance is emotional distress, including psychological injury to self-esteem resulting mainly from extremely limited access to work and to social services and resources (health and mental health services, etc.) to which citizens are entitled. The frustration of not being able to satisfy the most basic needs results in what the men describe as a "mental burden," which some cope with by drinking or using drugs. In the current study, injured self-esteem was reflected in statements such as feeling like "no one," rooted in the frequently thwarted goal of trying to support one's family and by making the sacrifice to leave home and seek work in the United States for months and years at a time.

In our efforts to capture how LMDLs cope with their challenging predicament, we conclude that their resiliency depends on the narrow set of coping resources within their control: trying to maintain a positive disposition, including optimism; focusing on the positive aspects of their limited lives; engaging in pleasant and distracting activities, including socializing with positive peers; and remaining in touch with family back home. Maintaining spiritual faith and taking comfort in a protective God was also commonly expressed. Such coping resources appear consistent with literature on core Latino values and cultural practices such as *familismo* or lifelong family interdependence as well as (predominately Catholic) religiosity that can enhance resiliency in the face of stress and adversity (Bermudez & Mancini, 2013).

While resorting to cultural resources is an adaptive response to harsh environmental conditions that include acculturative stress and discrimination (Padilla, 2002), we remain concerned about just how protective such coping resources can be considering the severe limitation of being undocumented. That is, because acculturative stress is exacerbated by the imbalance between high stressors and low resources (Miranda & Matheny, 2000), LMDLs remain at considerable risk given the broad array of coping resources for which they are ineligible. Thus, the few coping resources available to LMDLs are likely to have diminishing returns unless greater access to needed resources is secured.

The above findings are compatible with the structural vulnerability framework guiding the larger research project and from which the qualitative data come. That is, LMDLs are compelled to enter the United States without work authorization not simply because of the significant poverty in their countries of origin but by the poverty-exacerbating impact of NAFTA (North American Free Trade Agreement) on the Mexican economy, as well CAFTA (Central American Free Trade Agreement) on the economies of Central America (Bacon, 2009; Hing, 2010). That is, many industries and services in these countries have been devastated by free trade and the resulting widespread unemployment. Yet when migrants attempt to avail themselves of plentiful work opportunities in America, the cap on immigration visas is so severe that coming with documentation is virtually impossible—the result is living and working in the United States with all of the negative trappings of being undocumented (Organista et al., 2012).

## CONCLUSION

The single most powerful short-term intervention to alleviate poverty and distress in the lives of undocumented Latino migrant day laborers would be sufficient work authorization and visas, a structural intervention designed to regulate the flow of labor from Mexico and Central America in ways beneficial to both migrant workers and the U.S. economy. The single most powerful long-term intervention would be to amend free trade agreements in ways beneficial to the countries of Latin America as well as the United States. As such, *fair trade*, designed to improve work, credit, and the financial institutions of Mexico and Central America, would provide citizens with the desirable option of remaining in their countries of origin to support their families, pursue their livelihoods, and cultivate their own Latino dreams.

### REFERENCES

Applied Research Center. (2011). Shattered families: The perilous intersection of immigration enforcement and the child welfare system. *Research Reports.* Retrieved on May 11, 2014, from www.arc.org/shatteredfamilies.

Bacon, D. (2009). *Illegal people: How globalization creates migration and criminalizes immigrants.* Boston: Beacon.

Bermudez, M., & Mancini, J. (2013). Familias fuertes: Family resilience among Latinos. In D. S. Becvar (Ed.), *Handbook of Family Resilience* (pp. 215–227). New York: Springer Science+Business.

Bourgois, P. (2001). The power of violence in war and peace: Post-Cold War lessons from El Salvador. *Ethnography, 2*(1), 5–37.

California TRUST Act. (2014). California TRUST Act home page. Retrieved on June 4, 2014, from www.catrustact.org/about.html.

Hing, B. O. (2010). *Ethical borders: NAFTA, globalization, and Mexican migration.* Philadelphia: Temple University Press.

Legal Information Institute. (2010). Support Our Law Enforcement and Safe Neighborhoods Act of 2010. Retrieved on June 6, 2014, from www.law.cornell.edu/wex/support_our_law_enforcement_and_safe_neighborhoods_act_of_2010.

Miranda, A., & Matheny K. (2000). Socio-psychological predictors of acculturative stress among Latino adults. *Journal of Mental Health Counseling, 22*(4), 306–317.

Organista, K. C., Worby, P. A., Quesada, J., Arreola, S. G., Kral, A. H., & Khoury, S. (2013). Sexual health of Latino migrant day laborers under conditions of structural vulnerability. *Culture, Health & Sexuality, 15*(1), 58–72.

Organista, K. C., Worby, P.A., Quesada, J., Diaz, R., Neilands, T., & Arreola, S. (2012). The urgent need for structural-environmental models of HIV risk and prevention in US Latino populations: The case of migrant day laborers. In K. C. Organista (Ed.), *HIV prevention with Latinos: Theory, research, and practice* (pp. 1–39). New York: Oxford University Press.

Padilla, A. (2002). Hispanic psychology: A 25-year retrospective look. *Online Readings in Psychology and Culture, 3*(1). Retrieved on June 6, 2014, from http://dx.doi.org/10.9707/2307–0919.1025.

Phelan, S. (2011, March 31). SF in top 38 counties nationwide that deport "non-criminal aliens. *San Francisco Bay Guardian.* Retrieved on May 21, 2014, from www.sfbg.com/politics/2011/03/31/sf-top-38-counties-nationwide-deport-non-criminal-aliens.

Quesada, J., Arreola, S., Kral, A., Khoury, S., Organista, K., & Worby, P. (2014). As good as it gets: Undocumented Latino day laborers negotiating discrimination in San Francisco and Berkeley, California, USA. *City & Society, 26*(1), 29–50.

Worby, P. A., Organista, K. C., Kral, A. H., Quesada, J., Arreola, S. G., & Khoury, S. (2014). Structural vulnerability and problem drinking in Latino migrant day laborers in the San Francisco Bay Area. *Journal of Health Care for the Poor and Underserved, 25*(3), 1291–1307.

Zautra, A. J., & Reich, J. W. (2013). Resilience: The meanings, methods and measures of a fundamental characteristic of human adaptation. In S. Folkman (Ed.), *The Oxford handbook of stress, health and coping* (pp. 173–185). New York: Oxford University Press.

# 8

# "It's Like You Are a Criminal"

## ASYLUM SEEKERS AND IMMIGRANT DETENTION

▸ CONNIE OXFORD

### INTRODUCTION

IMMIGRANT DETENTION IS CURRENTLY THE fastest-growing form of incarceration in the United States (Dow, 2004; Epstein & Acer, 2011). Several watershed milestones have made immigrant detention part of the U.S. prison-industrial complex that exists today. In the 1980s, the Immigration and Naturalization Service (INS) joined the growing movement of prison privatization by outsourcing immigrants to facilities controlled by the Corrections Corporations of America (Welch, 2002). With the passage of the Anti-Drug Abuse Act of 1988, the policy of mandatory detention made certain migrants, those who were aggravated felons, ineligible for bond while they awaited their immigration court hearing (Mele & Miller, 2005). The Illegal Immigration Reform and Immigrant Responsibility Act (IIRIRA) of 1996 expanded the list of crimes that identifies an immigrant as ineligible for relief, making nearly all criminal aliens potentially subject to deportation. Those who commit any crimes listed in the statute are required to serve their sentences for their crimes and then are immediately transferred to detention and placed in removal proceedings (Dow, 2004). The terrorist attacks of September 11, 2001, ushered in further laws and practices that led to the detainment and deportation of immigrants (Golash-Boza, 2012a, 2012b).

While these laws and policies have contributed to the growing population of detained migrants, there are alternatives to detention, such as parole. Not all migrants entering the United States are detained. Moreover, of those who are detained, not all are subject to mandatory detention.

For example, on September 1, 2009, of the 31,075 migrants being housed across more than 300 detention facilities, 66% were subject to mandatory detention (Schriro, 2009). Although some migrants have legal options that either prevent them from being detained altogether or at least shorten their time in detention, restrictive immigration policies have led to the growing number of both detained migrants and the facilities that house them. In 1981, there were 18 immigrant detention facilities that housed a daily average population of 54 immigrants. These numbers increased dramatically to just over 200 facilities housing more than 32,000 immigrants daily in 2011 (PBS, 2011). The changes in policies and practices that led to the escalation of detaining immigrants in the United States have reverberated across the globe. According to the Global Detention Project, U.S. policies have shaped how other nation-states have responded to migration patterns, consequently giving rise to the current global immigrant detention phenomenon (Flynn, 2014).

Immigrant detention is particularly problematic for asylum seekers who flee persecution from another country and seek refuge in the United States only to find that they are treated as criminals upon arrival. In this chapter, I use ethnographic research with asylum seekers who were detained at the San Pedro Service Processing Center (SPSPC) in San Pedro, California, to show how the experiences of asylum seekers have been impacted by the criminalization of immigration. I draw from in-depth interviews with three asylum seekers who were detained at the SPSPC; an immigration attorney for one of the asylum seekers; two human rights activists, one with Amnesty International and one with Human Rights Watch, each of whom was part of a detention-monitoring team of the facility; and three deportation officers who worked at the SPSPC. I conducted these interviews from 2001 to 2003 and was given a tour of the facility when I interviewed INS staff in 2002. During this time, the SPSPC was controlled by the INS, which was housed under the Department of Justice. On March 1, 2003, the INS was divided into three agencies—the U.S. Citizenship and Immigration Services, the U.S. Immigration and Customs Enforcement (ICE), and the Bureau of Customs and Border Protection—and moved from the Department of Justice to the U.S. Department of Homeland Security (DHS). Immigrant detention facilities are now controlled by ICE. Because these interviews and the time that the asylum seekers spent at the SPSPC occurred before the creation of the DHS, I refer to the government agency that managed detention facilities as the INS when temporally appropriate. All interviewee names are pseudonyms.

### THE SAN PEDRO SERVICE PROCESSING CENTER

The building that housed the SPSPC was erected in 1935. It was built near the San Pedro seaport, because it served initially as a processing center for migrants arriving by ship to the Southern California area. By the late twentieth century, most migrants traveled via air to the United States. Like other U.S. immigration processing centers, the idea behind the SPSPC's creation, and even the name itself—processing center—was that it was intended to be a temporary holding area for migrants to be either accepted, thereby gaining entrance into the United States, or deported. It was not built for the purpose that it came to serve by the end of the twentieth century, which was long-term detainment for many immigrants. The SPSPC operated under the INS from 1990 to 2003. After bureaucratic restructuring resulting from the creation of the DHS, the SPSPC functioned under the ICE, which was overseen by DHS. The SPSPC is no longer an immigrant detention facility and is currently a low-security prison operated by the Federal Bureau of Prisons.

From 2000 to 2002, the years that the three asylum seekers I discuss in this chapter were detained at the SPSPC, there was a population of about 450 immigrants at the facility. José, a deportation officer who worked at the SPSPC, estimated that about 90% of the 450 immigrants were detained as criminals. The remaining 10% of immigrants came to the detention facility directly from the Los Angeles International Airport (LAX), having requested asylum. There were seven pods at the facility, with the first five pods designated for male immigrants and pods six and seven for female immigrants. The approximately 30 employees at the facility included administrative staff, deportation officers, clerks, secretarial support, and detention officers, all of whom were government employees. In addition, there were contract security personnel who worked for private companies such as Lyons or Wackenhut, whose responsibility it was to guard the detainees. One of the consequences of the privatization of immigrant detention facilities is that many personnel are contract laborers rather than federal employees (Dow, 2004).

Since IIRIRA was passed in 1996, a surge in detainment has occurred, because immigrants who commit certain crimes are taken into custody by U.S. immigration officials after they serve their sentences and are then placed in detention, because the crimes prompt a revocation of their current immigration status. David, a deportation officer at the SPSPC, captured how this law increased the number of detained immigrants when he stated that:

> Our bread and butter are the day-to-day jail releases, the state jails and state prisons. They are released nightly. I worked downtown for two years as an investigator before I came here and I did all of the jail releases. In LA County, we will get about 20 to 30 per night. That is a lot.

David's use of the term "bread and butter" reflects the profit-driven mentality of immigrant detention facilities and the role of immigrants who are there to make money for the institution. Although David is an employee of the federal government (rather than a private contract laborer), he has captured the structural shift in immigrant detention of a system that is now defined by the ways in which restrictive immigration laws, prison privatization, and capitalism are inextricably linked.

### DETAINING ASYLUM SEEKERS

I highlight the experiences of three female asylum seekers—Rivka, Mary, and Sahara—to illuminate the lived experiences of asylum seekers and the consequences of immigration policies they face in their quests to live free from persecution. While both men and women who are detained face a range of problems, such as limited access to legal counsel, health care, and language services, women are more likely than men to be traveling with children (from whom they are subsequently separated) and to be targeted for sexual violence while in detention (Women's Commission for Refugee Women and Children, 1997). Moreover, female asylum seekers are at risk of gender-based persecution, such as female genital mutilation, rape, and domestic violence, making their experiences with torture before arriving in the United States compound the suffering they experience in detention (Kassindja & Bashir, 1998).

Rivka fled South Africa after she was attacked and threatened for her antiapartheid activism and criticism of the African National Congress (ANC) tactic of "necklacing," the practice of setting gas-laden tires around the necks of those who did not agree with ANC politics. Like many asylum seekers, Rivka was unfamiliar with the legal terrain of U.S. immigration laws and did not know she could request asylum until after she was detained. She arrived in the United States in 1994 on a student visa and was unaware that she had become a visa overstay, remaining in the United States after her student visa had expired, because her attorney did not file the proper paperwork to extend her legal presence. After being arrested for writing bad checks in 2000, she spent 10 months at the SPSPC.

Rivka's crime is seemingly independent of her asylum case. However, had she been aware of asylum, she would have sought it rather than coming to the United States on a student visa. Once she was forced to live as an undocumented immigrant (through no fault of her own, since her overstay was due to the attorney's oversight), she wrote bad checks in order to survive. Due to the criminal charges associated with writing bad checks, she was only eligible for a form of relief known as "cancellation of removal," which allows her to lawfully remain in the United States. Cancellation of removal replaced "suspension of deportation" in 1996 after the passage of IIRIRA. Cancellation of removal allows migrants to remain in the United States legally by canceling their deportation orders. Cancellation of removal may be granted for an asylum seeker who has committed certain crimes that render the applicant ineligible for asylum. It offers no status adjustment opportunities, such as the ability to petition to become a permanent resident or citizen, that asylum offers. Also, immigrants with cancellation of removal status cannot petition for relatives to join them in the United States.

Mary grew up in a politically active family in Uganda. Her father was involved in anti–Idi Amin politics, and her siblings later became involved in the Democratic Party that resisted the practices of President Yoweri Museveni. Two of her siblings were murdered by Museveni loyalists due to their activism, and Mary left Uganda in 1995 after she was gang-raped. Initially, Mary had intended to live in the United States temporarily and return to her three children when she could safely live in Uganda. In 1999, Mary paid $3,000 to procure a false U.S. passport so she could travel to Uganda to visit her children, who she had not seen in 4 years. After a 1-month stay Mary returned to the United States, because she believed she would be subjected to more violence or even death if she remained in Uganda. Upon her second entry to the United States, this time with the counterfeit U.S. passport and a limited understanding of asylum that she did not have in 1995, she was apprehended at LAX and detained at the SPSPC for 3 months. She chose a U.S. passport for travel documentation because she thought it would ease her ability to return to the United States. Unbeknownst to her, she was committing a federal crime that is a statutory offense and was barred from receiving asylum; instead, like Rivka, she was granted cancellation of removal.

Sahara arrived in the United States in 2002 after she had been jailed, raped, and tortured for being an Eritrean minority living in Ethiopia. Her family paid a smuggler to bring Sahara to the United States after they bribed the Ethiopian prison guards to release her. Unlike Rivka and Mary, Sahara knew about asylum from her cousin and requested it when she arrived at LAX. After her initial interview at the airport, Sahara was taken to the SPSPC for 2 months. Unlike Rivka and Mary, Sahara had not committed a crime and was released from the SPSPC; at her immigration hearing, held in immigration court in downtown Los Angeles, she was granted asylum.

Prior to 2002, asylum seekers in detention at the SPSPC who had not committed a crime were eligible for immediate release and could move their asylum hearings to the Los Angeles immigration court if they had a sponsor. In Sahara's case, her cousin served as her sponsor. After 2002, the policy changed, and nearly all immigrants arriving at a port of entry in the Los Angeles area were detained, at least temporarily, regardless of their criminal records (Dow, 2004). When I inquired with Bob, a deportation officer at the SPSPC, about the change in policy he gave an answer that shows how surveillance of immigrants as well as controlling migration patterns guides policy changes:

> People weren't showing up for their hearing. We never really know where a person is. I discovered once I got here, which I brought to the director's attention, that there were so many counterfeit documentations. They were trying to show an alleged identity to be paroled out of custody. As soon as they started detaining them, they stopped coming. They started to go to other ports.

While Sahara was able to be released from detention and have her asylum hearing in downtown Los Angeles, asylum seekers without criminal records were no longer able to do so after 2002.

## WELCOME TO AMERICA

Rivka, Mary, and Sahara, all articulated how they were treated as criminals while in detention, even though they were seeking asylum. When Mary arrived in the United States in 2000, traveling on a forged U.S. passport, she was immediately made aware of how U.S. immigration officials equate asylum seekers with criminals:

> It was so scary to ask for asylum. When they take you from the airport it's like you are a criminal. In fact, somebody who took a gun and shot somebody, they are treated far better than somebody who is asking for asylum, which is terrible, because it is like you are worse than somebody who killed somebody. And most people when they ask for asylum they are still in fear, you know, and there you are between them taking you back and you know they're taking you back to be killed and even you are not sure if you are going to stay here.

Sahara too was surprised to learn that she was going to be detained when she arrived at LAX. She expressed the following:

> When I was passing the security they knew it was not the right passport. It was my picture but it was a different person's passport. I just started crying because I knew what I was doing was not right but I had to do it. I thought that when I asked for asylum [as her cousin had instructed her to do] at the airport I would be okay. Then they interrogated me and the officer said they're going to send me to detention.

Being placed in detention is confusing for asylum seekers, who do not understand why they are being treated as criminals for fleeing persecution.

Even though detention facilities house both immigrants who are seeking asylum and immigrants who have committed a crime and are in detention due to their changes in immigration status, asylum seekers are keenly aware of how immigration officials do not distinguish the detained populations and instead treat all detainees as criminals. Rivka illustrated this perceived inability to differentiate those detained on the part of the detention officers with the following:

> Some of the officers just thought we were all illegal and criminals and we should all go. They had no idea who was a criminal, who wasn't, who were looking for or wanting to seek asylum. They had no idea, they just

generalized it. They just had this impression that everybody was a criminal and needed to be kicked out of the country.

Mary too was aware of how there was no distinction between criminal and noncriminal detainees.

By the time I was there we are all like mixed up, people who have been taken off the street that had been doing drugs. You know I had been here [in the United States] for four years before and I didn't know anything about drugs. And then you find that it's a different category of people mixed up together.

Several factors affect an immigrant's success in gaining asylum. One such factor is obtaining legal counsel to negotiate the immigration bureaucracy process. Rivka, Mary, and Sahara all had legal representation. Rivka and Mary located their immigration attorneys through the resources, albeit limited, at the SPSPC. Sahara was fortunate to have her cousin assist her in finding an immigration attorney. According to José, when an immigrant arrives at the detention facility, a deportation officer checks the file to see whether the "detainee has representation. If they do, we call their attorney and say that we want to do an asylum orientation." When I asked José what rights migrants have who are destitute and without any family connections in the United States, he said that the procedure is that "they have the right to request a tie to their consulate. If they request in writing that they don't have any money and want to make a phone call to an attorney, we will set them up." Because Rivka, Mary, and Sahara all spoke English, they did not encounter the problems that asylum seekers with limited or no English-language abilities have when trying to locate an attorney. Human Rights reports routinely document the obstacles non-English-speaking immigrants face in detention (Epstein & Acer, 2011).

Mary met her attorney, Martha, at the SPSPC when Martha, an attorney with Catholic Charities, gave a weekly legal presentation. According to Martha, these presentations are a "basic orientation on why they are in INS custody, why they are going to immigration court, who the immigration judge is, what they can do to try to get out of custody, and to seek legal status, or if they wanted to go back to their country quickly, how they can do that." Martha differentiated between the undocumented population that had some knowledge of the U.S. legal system and asylum seekers who are overwhelmingly uninformed:

> I found that the ones with some previous contact with the criminal justice system were a little bit more savvy. They had been to court before. They had been through the American criminal court system, so they had at least some understanding for this is a judge, and this is your lawyer, and those kinds of issues. The shock to them was that they felt that they had already served their time, they were already done dealing with their conviction and they were shocked to learn that now they had to be in jail again for a whole new reason, and a whole new system where they had no idea of when they might be getting out. With the asylum seekers, a lot of them had a bit less understanding. Some of them were not from Western judicial systems. A lot of them really didn't understand how difficult it would be for them to seek asylum if they got here. I remember my first client had this idea in his head that as soon as he got to America it was going to be okay. He was going to be fine, and then he was quite shocked to find himself in San Pedro.

Mary was fortunate to meet Martha, who was able to give her a phone number to contact her so the calls could be charged directly to Catholic Charities, as Mary had no money with her in detention. Migrants with access to money can buy phone cards to call their attorneys.

Rivka located an immigration attorney through the resources at the SPSPC. She described her frustration with the list that was provided:

> If you go to court you'll get a list of legal providers. None of them do any detention work—not one. I called each and every one of them while I was there. Some of them said to me, "Well we do [detention work] but we don't work with aggravated felonies; we do but we only do asylum work and we can't take anymore because we already have enough from other sources. We can refer you to somebody but she only does one case a month or whatever." And a lot of the ones who do pro bono work—a lot of attorneys put their name on the list just to solicit clients. And they will say "Yes, well," and give you maybe five minutes free and after that you've got to pay. I found a lawyer who said that he would help me pro bono but just on my hearing day. And this is almost 6 months later that this had all been going on.

Rivka's experiences mirrored those that Thomas, a human rights activist who worked with Amnesty International's detention-monitoring team found:

> If they didn't have any money, they couldn't call their lawyer. The other problem was that the INS was required to post in the facility places where detainees could call for legal assistance. And we found that the lists that were posted were inaccurate and outdated. Our main concern was that asylum seekers be able to pursue an asylum claim in a reasonable manner and not encounter any unnecessary or unreasonable obstructions in their legitimate pursuit of asylum. And that was our point of interest, was how is the detention impacting the ability of the asylum seeker to go through the system and for a legitimate refugee to go through the system, without, you know, having their legitimate chances damaged by the institution itself. So we found out that there were people who wanted and were able to get representation, legal representation. It was difficult, because of the fact that they were detained that automatically limited their access to legal counsel. For instance, they couldn't go to their lawyer's office. The lawyer would have to come to them, and it's always a problem. Often, they would have hearings scheduled and they wouldn't inform the lawyer, sometimes they would transfer people between facilities and not tell the lawyers where they were.

As Thomas noted, another way detained immigrants are denied legal rights is when they are transferred among facilities with no notification to legal representatives. Rivka was familiar with the INS procedures of transferring detainees:

> I went through four facilities. They just up and move you. The officer will come to you at three o'clock in the morning and wake you up and say you're being moved and you have no idea where you're going. They don't tell you anything. You will be put in this van and sometimes would drive for hours and hours, asking the officer, where am I going; what's going on? And they usually just say, just be quiet; you'll find out when you get there. You have no idea what's going on—it's terrifying to say the least. And of course totally away from their lawyers so all the lawyers freaked out about that. Couldn't counsel with them, couldn't see them. They were away from their families.

INS doesn't care what they do with you. They couldn't give a hoot what they did with you.

In October 2007, five years after Rivka was released from detention, the SPSPC closed the facility temporarily to perform "preventative maintenance" (Gorman, 2007). Not only were the immigrants' attorneys not notified, many were transferred out of state to Texas and Arizona.

In addition to being treated as criminals and overcoming the institutional hurdles in place when trying to secure legal representation as they navigate the legal terrain of the U.S. immigration detention system, women who are detained regularly face sexual violence and harassment (Women's Commission for Refugee Women and Children, 1997). While none of the women I interviewed revealed instances of sexual violence at the SPSPC, Rivka flinched and made faces of disgust as she detailed some of her encounters with the male officers:

There was a guy, a male officer who would stand and look through the window at us. Where the toilets and the walls were this high (holding her arm low to the ground). So 90% of the time he could see anything he wanted to. He can see everything and he would just be at the window like this all the time. They're not even supposed to have male officers in the female pods at all.

Conversely, Sahara, who had been raped after she was jailed in Ethiopia, became tearful as she told me how fearful she was when she learned that she would be detained:

There were so many Eritrean women, young girls just like me in the prison [in Ethiopia] and we were treated so bad. The soldiers were men and it's a tough experience. It's not like here [United States]. When I went to detention, I thought it's going to be the same.

Although the conditions at the SPSPC range from problematic to deplorable, Sahara was ultimately relieved that she was not sexually assaulted in U.S. detention.

In addition to fear of sexual assault and harassment, female immigrants face other problems in detention, such as lack of access to birth control medication and sanitary products. Rivka articulated the frustration she faced during her menstrual cycle:

> You have to go the window every time you shower and ask them for a packet of shampoo or soap or sanitary napkins. One officer refused to give more than one sanitary napkin. Now if you're a heavy bleeder you've got a problem, you've got to go there every five minutes. Stupid, humiliating things that they would do. Anything and everything to harass you.

Barbara, a member of the Young Advocates group of Human Rights Watch, interviewed female immigrants as part of a detention-monitoring project and told me the following:

> One woman had to be on birth control pills, not to prevent pregnancy, but for whatever medical reasons and they would not give them to her. One of the guards was, like, "What do you think you're going to get knocked up in here?"

The refusal to dispense birth control pills for medical reasons is part of a larger violation of basic rights that detained immigrants face when they are denied access to health care (Heeren, 2010). In 2007, Victoria Arellano, a transgender woman from Mexico who was detained at the SPSPC, died just 2 days after finally being hospitalized, despite her pleas for help, because she was refused medical treatment for AIDS (Hernandez, 2008). Arellano was one among many other detained immigrants living with AIDS whose lack of access to health care had dire consequences (Human Rights Watch, 2007).

Asylum seekers are particularly vulnerable to lack of access to health care. During his interview with the medical staff in the early 1990s when he was monitoring the conditions at the SPSPC with Amnesty International, Thomas told how surprised he was to find that the physicians who treat detained migrants had a limited understanding of torture:

> I asked the doctor if he had any training in recognizing signs of physical, well torture of any kind, either mental, emotional or physical, warning signs that the detainee might have been a victim of torture. And not only had he not had any training, he was very dismissive of the idea that that's something that might come up very often. So here [he] is in a facility where if you're

going to run across torture victims anywhere in the United States, it's probably going to be in that kind of environment and here, the head medical person, it was a blind spot. And I think it was a blind spot for him, and probably an institutional blind spot as well. Something they didn't want to deal with.

The physician's indifferent reaction—not acknowledging that asylum seekers might constitute a different population from other detained immigrants—demonstrates the dearth of understanding of the nuances of the lives of detained immigrants.

### CONCLUSION

In many ways, Rivka, Mary, and Sahara each represent a success story in that each was ultimately released from detention and granted a form of relief that allows her to remain lawfully in the United States. Because Rivka was charged with writing bad checks and Mary entered the United States with a counterfeit passport, they received cancellation of removal rather than asylum, which Sahara was granted. This has heartbreaking consequences for Mary, who cannot petition for her children to join her in the United States and is left with the choice of either estrangement or risking illegal travel to Uganda to see them again. All three asylum seekers had several factors that worked to their advantage in being released from detention. They all spoke English, had access to legal counsel, and had either lived in the United States before being placed in detention (Rivka and Mary) or had an advocate (Sahara's cousin). Yet despite the positive outcome in their cases, the interviews with asylum seekers and their advocates in this chapter underscore how the policies and practices of immigrant detention criminalize asylum seekers. Rivka, Mary, and Sahara are among the millions of global migrants who left their countries fleeing persecution only to find themselves jailed in immigrant detention. The growing trend of detaining asylum seekers worldwide has devastating and even catastrophic results for the lives of immigrants seeking freedom from harm. Perhaps what is most problematic is that the practice of detaining asylum seekers consequently equates them with criminal detainees. Immigrant detention in the United States is in dire need of reform so that an asylum seeker can seek freedom from persecution without feeling like a criminal.

## REFERENCES

Dow, M. (2004). *American gulag: Inside U.S. immigration prisons.* Berkeley: University of California Press.

Epstein, R., & Acer, E. (2011). *Jails and jumpsuits: Transforming the U.S. immigration detention system—A two year study.* New York: Human Rights First.

Flynn, M. (2014). *How and why immigration detention crossed the globe* (Global Detention Project Working Paper, No. 8). Retrieved on July 9, 2014, from www.globaldetentionproject.org/publications/working-papers/diffusion.html.

Golash-Boza, T. (2012a). *Due process denied: Detentions and deportations in the United States.* New York: Routledge.

——. (2012b). *Immigration nation: Raids, detentions, and deportations in post 9/11 America.* Boulder, CO: Paradigm.

Gorman, A. (2007, October 27). ICE facility closure causes angst. *Los Angeles Times.* Retrieved on July 21, 2014, from http://articles.latimes.com/2007/oct/24/local/me-immig24.

Heeren, G. (2010). Pulling teeth: The state of mandatory immigration detention. *Harvard Civil Rights–Civil Liberties Law Review, 45*(2), 601–634.

Hernandez, S. (2008, June 8 ). A lethal limbo: Lack of healthcare turns federal detention into a death sentence for some immigrants. *Los Angeles Times.* Retrieved on July 21, 2014, from http://articles.latimes.com/2008/jun/01/opinion/op-hernandez1.

Human Rights Watch. (2007). *Chronic indifference: HIV/AIDS services for immigrants detained by the United States.* New York: Human Rights Watch.

Kassindja, F., & Bashir, L. M. (1998). *Do they hear you when you cry?* New York: Delta.

Mele, C., & Miller, T. (2005). *Civil penalties, social consequences.* New York: Routledge.

PBS. (October 18, 2011). Lost in detention. *Frontline.* Retrieved on June 2, 2014, from www.pbs.org/wgbh/pages/frontline/race-multicultural/lost-in-detention/map-the-u-s-immigration-detention-boom.

Schriro, D. 2009. *Immigration detention: Overview and recommendations.* Washington, DC: U.S. Department of Homeland Security, Immigration and Customs Enforcement. Retrieved from www.ice.gov/doclib/about/offices/odpp/pdf/ice-detention-rpt.pdf.

Welch, M. (2002). *Detained: Immigration laws and the expanding I.N.S. jail complex*. Philadelphia: Temple University Press.

Women's Commission for Refugee Women and Children. (1997). "Protecting the rights of children: The need for U.S. children's asylum guidelines." New York: Author.

# 9

# Hybrid Governance and the Criminalization of Somali Refugees Seeking Social Services in a Midwestern Town

▸ CYNTHIA HOWSON AND ASHLEY DAMP

## INTRODUCTION

IN MANY WAYS THIS CHAPTER documents the challenges faced by a lucky few. The Somali refugees we met were fortunate enough to obtain legal residency in the United States. Many of their family members are still living in unsafe conditions, whether they are in Somalia, in a refugee camp in Kenya or Ethiopia, or in another temporary space. Many of their friends in the United States face detention or deportation. The literature on the criminalization of immigration has established the vulnerability of undocumented migrants and those suspected of crimes that may result in detention or deportation. In particular, the increasing use of criminal law enforcement in the regulation of immigration has been criticized as racist (Esbenshade, 2011; Loyd & Burridge, 2007), sexist (Hartry, 2012), an impediment to the core objectives of social work (Furman, Ackerman, Loya, & Jones, 2012), and a violation of human rights (Fujiwara, 2005). But while the social consequences of "crimmigration" are well documented, particularly for the poor, the simultaneous criminalization of immigration and social welfare remains undertheorized, particularly as it marginalizes migrants regardless of their compliance with the law.

The aim of this chapter is to demonstrate how the criminalization of immigration and poverty interacts with community engagement and service provision in the lives of Somali refugees in a midwestern town. Fortunately, we find that most refugees' concerns were echoed by public and private service providers, and support for cultural competency training was widespread. On the other hand, respondents are highly vulnerable to administrative, logistical, and legal challenges they are underprepared to address. First, we argue that efforts to comply with regulations regarding housing, employment, food, health, and child-care services criminalize vulnerable refugees by placing users at constant risk for accusations of noncompliance and fraud. Second, the obligation of service providers to investigate and prevent fraud is compounded by frequent misunderstandings regarding social as well as administrative rules and expectations. Unfortunately, these tensions are exacerbated by a narrative of suspicion surrounding Somali social networks, such that even sharing food or helping a distant relative can be seen as fraudulent. We argue that the lives of refugee women are marginalized and often criminalized by their obligation to fulfill contradictory moral, legal, and gendered norms.

Data and analysis stem from a 9-month internship and cultural competency evaluation and training undertaken on behalf of a state agency involved in the administration of various public benefits. Somali participants were recruited through the agency, and methods included a focus group (14 attendees) and unstructured individual and small group interviews (more than 20 conducted). Discussions were facilitated by translators, unless the interviewee spoke fluent English. Formal interviews included only women, because they are the vast majority of Somali clients in the agency. Additional qualitative data were gathered from service providers working for public and private agencies. These included a large community focus group (75 attendees), an online survey (47 respondents representing 20 agencies), and individual interviews (more than 20 conducted). Through these encounters, a clear picture of the relationship between the refugee experience and criminalization emerged. Woven into their stories of success, heartache, and struggle was an underlying presence of both perceived and real criminalization of the refugee life. Here, the notion of the "welfare queen" is combined with assumptions about "illegal" immigration in ways that impact the everyday experiences of refugees.

## INHERENTLY SUSPICIOUS: FAMILY STRENGTHS OR A SOPHISTICATED NETWORK OF FRAUD?

We have argued that the criminalization of immigration plays a key role in the construction of immigrant identity regardless of the migrant's legal status. This is particularly evident in providers' efforts to detect and prevent welfare fraud. In many ways the process to determine whether a refugee is eligible to receive public benefits is well intentioned, and providers may well have the ultimate goal of helping clients obtain benefits. On the other hand, the experience can be demeaning, accusatory, and hurtful. First, not all providers see their ultimate objective as helping clients, particularly providers who see fraud prevention as a key component of their job. Second, investigations of immigration and welfare fraud in the Somali community have facilitated a narrative in which several core features of Somali culture are associated with fraud. When one considers the stress and confusion that surrounds efforts to navigate state administration and social services, the narrative of criminalization can become overwhelming. This section will demonstrate how core values of the Somali community have become criminalized in important gendered and racialized ways.

### NORMS OF COOPERATION AND MUTUAL SUPPORT

Social support is among the most important values for the refugees with whom we spoke. Cooperation and mutual assistance are seen as integral parts of Somali identity that are both practically necessary and morally indispensable. In theory, this commitment to community is respected by providers, because it facilitates the success of new arrivals and may even lessen the burden on state resources. There is an extensive literature discussing the importance of family and social support for refugee adaptation and success in a host community (Stewart et al., 2008). In particular, this is viewed as one of the most vital strengths of the Somali refugee community (Busch Nsonwu, Busch-Armendariz, Cook Heffron, Mahapatra, & Fong, 2013; Heitritter, 1999), as a critical tool in successful entrepreneurship (Fong, Busch, Armour, Heffron, & Chanmugam, 2007) and public health (Carroll et al., 2007).

There are a variety of ways in which Somali social networks have enabled the adjustment of struggling newcomers while facilitating the goals of service providers. More established refugees might provide free translation services in meetings with teachers or nurses. They provide insight to facilitate cross-cultural communication. They share food, clothing, and a place to sleep. They help newcomers use the bus, which among our respondents was one of the most frustratingly complex systems newcomers had to navigate. These kinds of assistance are not occasional or when it is convenient. Somali refugees are obligated to provide for their extended family networks in the United States as much as they are required to send money home. Like other immigrant communities, many refugees sought assistance and advice from within the Somali community. Many reported that the support of a good Somali community center or multicultural center had been a key component to their own success or the success of their families in other cities. Without that help, refugees depend more on providers, who may not be equipped to meet their needs. One woman, in reference to public agencies, pointed out, "In Seattle, I was getting help. Here I am not getting help from the community. Not cash, but in general . . . Advice, comfort."

Even when discussing practical interventions that would improve the lives of the people we spoke with, several participants identified the lessons learned in more established Somali communities near Seattle and Minneapolis. In Minneapolis, the Somali Community Center provides child care and a bus service for women taking English-language courses. It also provides basic life skills classes, including lessons for women who want to dress in a way that is appropriate for their faith and classes that help women prepare for the job opportunities that might be available to them. Some of these services are subsidized, but nearly all of them depend on the initiative of more established Somali immigrants and their willingness to volunteer.

Unsurprisingly, social networks are also indispensable for new arrivals learning how to navigate basic services related to housing, food, employment, health care, and life skills training. While community support is critical for people's well-being, it is also an important way in which the state outsources costly public services (Meagher, 2005). Indeed, promotion of African women's commitment to solidarity and voluntary organization has long been a tool to facilitate cutbacks in social services (Tripp, 1997). But, refugees who were able to leave their communities and navigate extraordinary challenges to reach a host country often bring valuable attributes. They are almost necessarily industrious, hard-working, willing to take risks, and willing to sacrifice (Fong et al., 2007), which can make otherwise insurmountable challenges feasible. So, Somali social networks are valuable for refugees, valuable for public and private service providers, and useful for state employees allocating limited resources in a variety of agencies.

On the other hand, the kind of mutual assistance our respondents described comes with a distinct model of family and household that is poorly adapted to the legal definitions embedded in administrative life in the United States. Of course, polygamy is illegal, so any additional wife is unrecognized by U.S. law, but Somali refugees understand this. Since married couples do not pool resources, husbands and wives have very separate budgets and obligations. In many ways Somali women are responsible for their children's basic needs, particularly when a husband lives elsewhere. Meanwhile, many women are in the same situation, so they can help each other with everyday tasks. This is one practice that is likely to feel similar to life in Somalia. Many people live near each other, and they divide chores according to their strengths. Together, tasks like banking, child care, or going to the market are accomplished efficiently, even when men are traveling.

## CRIMINALIZING WOMEN'S SOCIAL SUPPORT SYSTEMS

What complicates these practices is that housing and food benefits are structured according to very strict (and from a Somali perspective, bizarre) notions of family. A woman who lives alone with her children can declare a husband in another state, but she cannot receive money from him, nor can she visit him too regularly, without having her residency questioned. A woman with food stamps can travel to a big city to buy cheaper and better halal groceries, but she must not buy groceries for other women. First, subsidized food cannot be shared. Second, the purchase of large quantities of food in another city may imply fraudulent use of subsidized food as well as fraudulent residency claims.

Even if official residence is unquestioned, refugees must comply with housing regulations that are typical of a nuclear family but difficult to reconcile with Somali values. After all, if a family member (and of course, an aunt's cousin is a family member) comes to visit, one is obligated to receive the guest. But it is not clear how many nights a guest can visit before she becomes a household member. Similarly, it is not clear how many extended family members can come for a meal without violating regulations surrounding food or regulations about use of a rental unit.

Once the rules about food and shelter are overcome, refugees are expected to work. Since welfare regulations require refugees to work or attend classes to become employable, child care is an immediate need, even if cost, transport, and culturally appropriate day care are problematic. That should be manageable. If there is one practice most Americans understand, it's babysitting, and everyone appreciates a family member who will do it for free. But babysitting for more than one friend quickly becomes an illegal day-care center.

What we see is that Somali refugees operate under competing and often contradictory sets of norms. Because women are responsible in many ways for food and child care, they are disproportionately impacted by irreconcilable expectations, wherein the most basic obligations of community may become criminalized. Unfortunately, these are not abstract concerns. While state employees are primarily concerned about more serious violations of welfare rules, most of the women we spoke with have been accused of fraud in multiple sectors. Landlords might call the police, who will notify various agencies responsible for food, housing, and other subsidies. In one focus group, women said they had experienced multiple investigations in which they were suspected of housing fraud. One woman attributed this to discrimination on the part of her landlord. "Dawo" had been living in a first floor apartment for 3 months. "THREE months! And TWICE the police were called because it was loud. Even though [we] were all sleeping. They won't say who turned [us] in . . . The Section 8 people listen to the landlord, not me." The translator further explained, "She's afraid if they think she's a vulture," she will be evicted.

Others saw housing investigations more charitably as frustrating miscommunication, but they lamented what they saw as unfair assumptions on the part of service providers. These women acknowledged that they struggled with compliance but blamed misunderstanding and lack of clarity. As Dawo explained,

> One thing we need to find is an education group to advise and educate women because the less fortunate lack knowledge. If families are educated about the laws, we will have a better understanding. That group needs to be in every part of social life—hospital, schools. That would minimize [the fact that] most don't know the laws of [the state] . . . Every state has its own rules. [The] County needs to designate a person with accurate information . . . someone who does orientation. Video tapes. Do's and Don'ts of the welfare system.

## WHEN QUESTIONS ABOUT COMPLIANCE BECOME
## TRANSNATIONAL WEBS OF CRIME

Although a caseworker's difficulty explaining complicated regulations makes it challenging for refugees to ensure compliance, the presumption of fraudulent behavior is crucial. What further complicates the process of seeking benefits for the refugees we spoke with is that Somali social networks are also thought to facilitate large-scale fraud. In this way, the process of criminalization facing Somali refugees goes far beyond the (already salient) construction of immigrants as fraudulent users of the welfare system (Yoo, 2008). First, providers we spoke with had heard about large-scale investigations of benefit fraud in Somali communities around the country that were thought to cross state lines. Of course, such cases would have involved sums much greater than the housing vouchers and food stamps held by the women we spoke with, but at least one provider was concerned about a nationwide conspiracy among a group of Somalis seeking to defraud the welfare system, a perspective that was fueled by Federal Bureau of Investigation involvement investigating welfare fraud in the Somali community. In this climate, it is less surprising that the local director of the state-run program felt that Somalis were generally out to defraud the system. As a result of the larger investigation and the suspicion of the particular agency, police officers began to attend eligibility meetings for clients seeking certain types of public benefits.

It is worth noting here that many of the providers we met were committed to helping Somali clients and to improving their own cultural competency. In particular, the police officers we spoke with were among the most culturally sensitive participants in our discussions. Equally important, we are not aware of a single prosecution of benefits fraud by a Somali in any of the social service agencies we encountered during our project. By contrast, there was one successful prosecution of several white women involved in a welfare fraud scheme.

This is particularly remarkable, given that Somali refugees reported difficulty maintaining compliance with benefits requirements, strict investigation of their circumstances, and regular interaction with law enforcement. One woman said, "I didn't know what they [the service providers] were looking for. Things are better now that I know what they want. I am happy." But, as Pratt and Valverde (2002) found in Toronto, the discourse surrounding Somali refugees can quickly shift from "deserving victims to 'masters of confusion.'" Here, the cultural strengths of mutual assistance and entrepreneurship quickly form the basis for a narrative in which more established refugees "train" newcomers to obtain benefits fraudulently without getting caught.

Importantly, this narrative is difficult to refute, even for providers who challenge the narrative and advocate on behalf of refugees. It is impossible to prove that undetected fraud is not present. Moreover, even if the perception of widespread fraud is not viewed as a conspiracy of criminalization, it is powerfully connected to broader and more widespread concerns. First, it foments the fear that Somalis who have difficulty adjusting to American life may be recruited by transnational extremist networks. Second, concerns about welfare fraud are highlighted in the context of a widely accepted narrative that any noncompliance diverts scarce resources from more deserving clients.

This is particularly challenging, because although many providers are deeply committed to helping Somali clients, they are not in a position to advocate for refugees in another agency as they face hurtful accusations or full-blown investigations. In this way, refugees' dissatisfaction with social services is intricately bound up with the environment of criminalization and the narrative in which they are inherently suspected of wrongdoing. Indeed, although the women expressed a variety of practical recommendations and concerns, no one expressed concerns about their children's teachers or schools. More than once, women noted that they love the teachers, while one added, "Teachers could teach caseworkers. Kids have equal opportunity. Caseworkers are different from teachers." The difference is striking, because when compared with many social service providers, teachers are not much more deeply trained in cultural competency or unusually embedded in the Somali community. They do, however, view education as an entitlement in which parents are not attempting to access an undeserved resource.

## "A SMILE GOES A LONG WAY": CONFLICTING NORMS AND SOCIAL SERVICES

Making threats when we're applying for services is crossing the line. But what can we do about it? They (providers) hold all the power. A smile goes a long way . . . County caseworkers are rude. You are a public servant. It's not our problem if your day is bad.

(Focus group)

Some of the most common concerns that surfaced in our discussions were not obviously connected to financial resources at all. Common courtesy, politeness, and a willingness to smile were repeatedly included in discussions of opportunities for improvement. Importantly, these concerns emerged in discussions with Somali participants and providers, so accounts of rudeness and hostility were mirrored in surprising ways. Some providers, seeking to articulate difficulties in cross-cultural communication, asked questions like, "Why do many Somalis seem arrogant?" This surprisingly explicit question reveals a variety of tensions that impact immigrants' lives. First, in the context in which all users of public services are suspect, a caseworker might interpret arrogance simply from a client's claim that her family is entitled to particular benefits. But we found that challenges surrounding interpersonal communication were far more complicated and more widespread than tensions attached to subsidized services. One provider explained that women might refuse to leave, being forcibly removed from the building after getting upset about an investigation, poor customer service, or being denied benefits. One example involved a woman in her eighties, weighing approximately 90 pounds. Often, differing norms of communication are exacerbated by refugees' previous experiences with authorities in Somalia and in refugee camps, making it difficult to trust providers. Unfortunately, even simple misunderstandings can foment an environment of mistrust, which leaves little space for benefit of the doubt when there are questions about eligibility and regulatory compliance.

### TRUST AND COMMUNICATION

Somali women may have difficulty trusting providers for a variety of reasons that complicate efforts to improve culturally competent care and communication. In this way basic challenges in culturally appropriate communication are not only important for immigrants' satisfaction but impact directly on the effectiveness of health care, law enforcement, and the provision of basic public services. First, refugee populations are at risk for a variety of physical and mental traumas, including a high incidence of posttraumatic stress disorder and sexual assault (Adams & Assefi, 2002), which can impact the ability to develop a rapport of trust and transparency, particularly in an unfamiliar environment (Upvall, Mohammed, & Dodge, 2009). Moreover, many refugees have learned to negotiate complicated political systems in which the stakes were literally life and death. Assertiveness is vital in "an environment where identity is the main determinant of obtaining access to the structure of the refugee regime, and gaining access depends partly on human agency and the skills and assertiveness to negotiate" (Jansen, 2008, p. 577).

Prior experience with corruption and injustice make it particularly difficult for women to trust providers' accounts of rules and expectations. One woman explained how cross-cultural communication directly impacted not only trust but the criminalization of women's most basic obligations. She explained that in Somalia, written language is rarely used. You are learning, sharing, passing things on orally. A huge part of your identity is how well you can communicate. You have to advocate for yourself, primarily by speaking. Women are not only accustomed to speaking assertively but expect that it is necessary if they want to provide for their families. Meanwhile, their experience with corruption and clan-based favoritism makes it especially difficult to trust state employees. Some refugees were convinced that they had not been given the truth about the rules of particular programs. For example, several were concerned that the whey-free baby formula was of an inferior quality, while others felt that being continually encouraged to breast-feed by a local human service program was disenfranchising. One woman described feeling that being asked to breast-feed was denying her the right to be an independent American woman. These fears can be difficult for providers to understand and alleviate. Unfortunately, the combination of assertiveness and mistrust is often interpreted as arrogance. This, of course, drastically diminishes the likelihood that refugees will be given the benefit of the doubt in the event there are questions of fraud and noncompliance.

The problem is that it is extremely difficult to distinguish between tensions that stem from cross-cultural misunderstandings and situations in which the caseworker actually does intentionally refuse to help a particular client. For example, "Amaani" had been working with a caseworker as she struggled to obtain a small business permit. She wanted to own a store for Somali women to buy clothing and fresh-cooked food, a place where

Somali women could gather the way that men congregate at the local halal. Unfortunately, she could not understand why it seemed so difficult to overcome the regulatory hurdles involved, and she was frustrated because it seemed her caseworker was purposefully refusing to advocate for her. In that case the caseworker in question openly expected her project to fail, so her impression may have been entirely accurate.

### "WHY DID YOU COME HERE?": EXPERIENCES WITH HOSTILITY AND DISCRIMINATION

"We came for freedom."

One of the most important determinants of satisfaction in a new community is the sense that one is welcome. Providers and community members frequently asked refugees why they chose the community. Refugees understandably found the question threatening (since it can imply they should not have) and explicitly suggested that their experience would improve if people stopped asking. Importantly, the question itself is not always hostile or irrelevant. Nor are the answers particularly private. Many women wanted people to understand: "We want to be here for the same reasons they do," good schools, safe neighborhoods, and a good environment to raise a family. One woman added that many had relocated to a smaller town out of fear that their children might be recruited by extremist groups to return to Somalia—a point that highlights women's multiple sources of fear. On one hand, there is the notion that any extremist influence in the community will only foment an environment of fear and prejudice. On the other hand, refugees are rarely completely disconnected from the war they fled, so the effort to build a sense of safety and stability requires a delicate balancing act.

The challenge is that although many refugees were happy to answer questions about their culture and community, questions surrounding refugees' motivations can be hurtful. Occasionally the question is attached to an implication that the immigrant is unwelcome or undeserving. But even when based in genuine curiosity, the implication that there is any other reason to choose the host community is associated with a threatening and accusatory context that the person asking may not understand. In this case, the possibility of economic opportunity for a person on public assistance is inextricably bound up with the assumption that one is "here for a free ride."

Everyday forms of discrimination or hostility appeared in a variety of contexts, many of which were connected to notions of deservingness. Some respondents voiced their experience with being treated as though they came to America to get a "free ride," and many pointed out that most Americans do not realize they had no choice in what host country they were sent to. Here again, refugees are obligated to defend themselves from competing and contradictory expectations. They are expected to be grateful, to love the country (and many do), but they are also marginalized by the perception that their status as a refugee in the host country was entirely a choice, a notion that, as Spitzer (2006) points out, mischaracterizes the refugee experience *by definition*. In discussion of this, one woman shared her humiliation in the simple statement: "I feel like I'm begging."

The "free ride" narrative is exacerbated by the perception that refugees are uneducated, unable to communicate effectively with potential employers, and lacking in the basic life skills they need to adjust successfully in America. One woman lamented that Somalis "seem unintelligent here," because their intellectual strengths are rendered invisible. She pointed out the perseverance and intellectual discipline required of children who memorize the Koran at a young age. She emphasized that Somalis are very intuitive, but without an American education, it is difficult to get a job. And without appropriate child care, it is difficult to attend the required language classes that are necessary for even basic employment. Herein, she explains, lies the vicious circle: if you do not learn English and get a job, you will be seen as a terrorist or as someone trying to cheat the system.

For women, these pressures can be challenging in a variety of gender-specific ways, not only because of the constraints of child care but also because women's communication and mobility are restricted in ways that are particularly persistent. The refusal to shake a male employer's hand can be extremely socially awkward in a midwestern context, making women appear disrespectful and suspicious. More broadly, focus group participants were concerned that Somalis have a hard time keeping a job, since employers "find reasons" to fire them.

Respondents almost never explicitly mentioned racism, but the racial implications of their experiences are important, nonetheless. Interestingly, in a comparison of refugee groups, Hadley and Patil (2009) find that discrimination is significantly more common for Somali refugees than for refugees from Eastern Europe, but only 8% of East African refugees attributed the encounters to racism, while 22% felt they were discriminated against due to their lack of education. This finding, which is consistent with our small sample, "challenges refugee and immigration studies that often focus on the cultural norms and attitudes that migrants bring with them and not on the cultural norms of the receiving country" (Hadley & Patil, 2009, p. 510).

## CONCLUSIONS AND RECOMMENDATIONS

One of the most salient consequences of criminalization is the sense that an immigrant is inherently suspect. The notion in criminal justice that one is innocent until proven guilty emerges with a strong dose of irony, as it is quite distinct from most refugees' experiences seeking social services. We have demonstrated that even migrants who are compliant with the regulations surrounding their immigration as well as their access to state services are profoundly impacted by the broader environment of criminalization. Moreover, we have shown that the criminalization of immigration cannot be separated from the criminalization of poverty or the broader narratives designed to restrict and demonize access to social services. These structural sources of vulnerability interact with and exacerbate the everyday constraints that marginalize refugees. First, refugees' experiences with corruption, violence, and personal trauma make it difficult for them to trust providers, so the basic rules and eligibility requirements seem quite threatening. This is particularly important when regulations vary between states and when compliance seems complicated or, in some cases, incomprehensibly bizarre. These frustrations are compounded by a dominant narrative in which those seeking public assistance, and particularly the entire Somali community, are likely to defraud the state. It comes with a painful dose of irony that precisely those facets of Somali culture that are praised by social workers and health-care providers are also marshaled as evidence of criminal fraud.

One of the most valuable results of this project is that it provided a space for refugees to articulate their own recommendations to service providers. In this way, the cultural competency training was organized around the concerns that refugees identified, and many of their suggestions were both feasible and optimistic. In part, the cultural competency training that formed the basis of the project was itself the most consistently voiced need.

In spite of tensions surrounding discrimination, mistrust, and miscommunication, nearly everyone felt that offering providers a better understanding of refugees' concerns and backgrounds would facilitate much more effective professional and interpersonal relationships. Some public and community service employees had already undergone some cultural competency training and built some trust and good relationships within the Somali community. Positive experiences among some police officers, health-care workers and teachers lent credence to the notion that a little understanding may go a long way.

### REFERENCES

Adams, K., & Assefi, N. (2002). Primary care refugee medicine: General principles in the postimmigration care of Somali women. *Primary Care Update for OB/GYNS, 9*(6), 210–217.

Busch Nsonwu, M., Busch-Armendariz, N., Cook Heffron, L., Mahapatra, N., & Fong, R. (2013). Marital and familial strengths and needs: Refugees speak out. *Journal of Ethnic and Cultural Diversity in Social Work, 22*(2), 129–144. doi:10.1080/15313204.2013.785350

Carroll, J., Epstein, R., Fiscella, K., Volpe, E., Diaz, K., & Omar, S. (2007). Knowledge and beliefs about health promotion and preventive health care among Somali women in the United States. *Health Care for Women International, 28*(4), 360–380.

Esbenshade, Jill. (2011). Discrimination, DNA Testing, and Dispossession: Consequences of US Policy for African Refugees. *SOULS: Journal of Black Politics, Culture and Society* 13(2), 175–196.

Fong, R., Busch, N. B., Armour, M., Heffron, L. C., & Chanmugam, A. (2007). Pathways to self-sufficiency: Successful entrepreneurship for refugees. *Journal of Ethnic and Cultural Diversity in Social Work, 16*(1–2), 127–159. doi:10.1300/J051v16n01_05

Fujiwara. (2005). Immigrant rights are human rights: The reframing of immigrant entitlement and welfare. *Social Problems, 52*(1), 79–101. doi:10.1525/sp.2005.52.1.79

Furman, R., Ackerman, A. R., Loya, M., & Jones, S. (2012). Criminalization of immigration: Value conflicts for the social work profession. *Journal of Sociology and Social Welfare, 39,* 169–185.

Hadley, C., & Patil, C. (2009). Perceived discrimination among three groups of refugees resettled in the USA: Associations with language, time in the USA, and continent of origin. *Journal of Immigrant and Minority Health, 11*(6), 505–512. doi:10.1007/s10903-009-9227-x

Hartry, A. S. (2012). Gendering crimmigration: The intersection of gender, immigration, and the criminal justice system. *Berkeley Journal of Gender, Law & Justice, 27,*(1) 1–27.

Heitritter, D. L. (1999). *Meanings of family strength voiced by Somali immigrants: Reaching an inductive understanding.* Minneapolis: University of Minnesota Press.

Jansen, B. J. (2008). Between vulnerability and assertiveness: Negotiating resettlement in Kakuma refugee camp, Kenya. *African Affairs, 107*(429), 569–587.

Loyd, Jenna M., & Andrew Burridge (2007). La Gran Marcha: Anti-racism and immigrants rights in Southern California. *ACME: An International E-Journal for Critical Geographies, 6*(1), 1–35.

Meagher, K. (2005). Social capital or analytical liability? Social networks and African informal economies. *Global Networks, 5*(3), 217–238.

Pratt, A., & Valverde, M. (2002). From deserving victims to "masters of confusion": Redefining refugees in the 1990s. *Canadian Journal of Sociology/Cahiers Canadiens de Sociologie, 27*(2), 135–161. doi:10.2307/3341708

Spitzer, D. L. (2006). The impact of policy on Somali refugee women in Canada. *Refuge: Canada's Journal on Refugees/Revue Canadienne sur les Réfugiés, 23*(2). Retrieved from http://pi.library.yorku.ca/ojs/index.php/refuge/article/view/21354.

Stewart, M., Anderson, J., Beiser, M., Mwakarimba, E., Neufeld, A., Simich, L., & Spitzer, D. (2008). Multicultural meanings of social support among immigrants and refugees. *International Migration, 46*(3), 123–159.

Tripp, A. M. (1997). Changing the rules: The politics of liberalization and the urban informal economy in Tanzania. Cambridge University Press. Retrieved from http://journals.cambridge.org/production/action/cjoGetFulltext?fulltextid=6272260.

Upvall, M. J., Mohammed, K., & Dodge, P. D. (2009). Perspectives of Somali Bantu refugee women living with circumcision in the United States: A focus group approach. *International Journal of Nursing Studies, 46*(3), 360–368.

Yoo, G. J. (2008). Immigrants and welfare: Policy constructions of deservingness. *Journal of Immigrant & Refugee Studies, 6*(4), 490–507. doi:10.1080/15362940802479920

# Filipina Lives

## TRANSNATIONALISM, MIGRANT LABOR, AND EXPERIENCES OF CRIMINALIZATION IN THE UNITED STATES

▸ VALERIE FRANCISCO, GELEEN ABENOJA,
AND ANGELICA LIM

### INTRODUCTION

ROSE IS A FILIPINA MIGRANT mother living in New York City. Rose, as is the case with the other immigrants we interviewed for this chapter, is not her real name. She was most emotional about her migration story when she recalled the memories of the babies she left behind in the Philippines, and almost equally, when she talked about the trauma in her first years in New York City as a domestic worker for an ambassador. This paper opens with Rose's story both to honor her bravery and courage and to provide the reader with the texture of emotions and insecurity Filipina migrants face as they arrive in the United States. Rose recounts her experience with exploitation at her workplace:

> So two hundred dollars a month, I have to buy shampoo, soap, toothpaste, and everything for myself. How much do I have left? And I send a hundred fifty dollars to my family, plus the remittance charge, how could I make two hundred dollars fit every month? So when I talked to other helpers outside of the school waiting, some ask me "Oh, where do you work?" I say, "With the ambassador." They say, "You must make a lot." I say, "Two hundred dollars." "Two hundred dollars a day?" "No, two hundred dollars a month." They are so shocked. The 10,000 pesos they offered me in the Philippines is huge money to me when I agreed to work for them. It wasn't until I arrived here that it wasn't at all fair. So they all said, you should escape from them. But in the beginning I couldn't find it in myself because I was scared because

they are ambassadors. I know they have power. And who am I? Just a helper compared to them. From when we flew out of the Philippines and when we got here, they held my passport. Later, I realized that that's why they didn't give it to me. They didn't give it to me so we don't escape or leave them.

In Rose's view, being offered a ticket to the United States with a salary of 10,000 pesos a month was a raise from her original domestic helper job in the Philippines, which paid only 7,000 pesos. The opportunity to earn American dollars and the growing needs of her four young children motivated her migration. Rose understood that her new job as a live-in domestic worker in the United States would be difficult, but she did not realize that she would be forced to shoulder her personal expenses out of her salary. She expected that her needs for basic goods would be covered by her employer similarly to her live-in position in the Philippines. She hoped to send the full 10,000 pesos to her family monthly; when she was unable to do so Rose realized the desperation of her situation only through conversation with other Filipina nannies during her downtime. The combination of Rose's lack of knowledge about the living standards in the United States, her rights as a worker, and the retention of her documents resulted in Rose's isolation and feelings of criminality. Her infrequent interactions with other domestic workers and her controlling employers led Rose to doubt herself and the validity of her status in the United States at all times. These conditions and interactions engendered a fear and anxiety within Rose that shaped her self-perception and how she moved in her daily life. When she recognized the extreme exploitation she was enduring with her employer, she made plans for an escape.

On top of cleaning the house, cooking for them, taking care of the kids, I also had to prove myself as a waitress [for the ambassador's parties]. They would yell at both me and the cook if we slip up a bit, yell at us with cuss words and even hold out on food. We had to clean the whole house, up to the third floor, to the kitchen and basement. [When we escaped] I left some of my clothes at another Filipina's house. I didn't have anything when I escaped, just one bag with two pairs of underwear and the jacket on my back. That's it. The cook and me left. I met one Filipina, we only met once, but after she helped me we were close. That's where we ran to the morning after that party. We went with her to work and we hid there at her work that day, sweating and nervous. Then a helper from the ambassador's house called telling us some information that helped us. She was scared too but gained some confidence when we left, she told us to go to this place in Queens. There we met another Filipina for the first time that helped us look for work ... The ambassador's driver really helped us that day to escape, because he knew how the ambassador treated us. He called someone who worked for the ambassador before so that maybe she could help us escape. She agreed to have us come to her house, she talked to her roommates about us staying for a couple of nights to hide us. Then she arranged a more permanent living situation for us somewhere else in Queens.

I was scared for years after that. I couldn't walk around because I thought someone would recognize me, especially because I was exposed to all of the visitors of that residence, whoever I served during my time there. I was so scared, so very, very scared to show my face on the streets of New York. Then I met Ate Virginia and Ate Rita. They were people who were open to helping me even I felt scared.

Rose begins her escape story by qualifying her act through a description of the exploitation she faced as a domestic worker in the ambassador's home. The tremendous amount of work and pressures building in her workplace became a justification for Rose to find a way out. As Rose and her coworker were passed along from safe house to safe house, her self-perception of criminality increased. Although objectively Rose had done nothing illegal by working as a domestic worker, she felt as if *she* was the criminal. Rose reflected on the years she felt as if she was a fugitive from her employer and the U.S. authorities for her ultimate offense: escaping an exploitative situation.

In this chapter, we focus on Filipina migrant workers' adjustment to New York City as new migrants and low-wage workers to explore the nature and emotionality of living under the affective background of xenophobia in the United States. Filipinas contribute to essential domestic industries (nannies, housecleaners, caregivers to the elderly) that allow New Yorkers to work in a global center of commerce and culture. As a migrant domestic worker, Rose gritted her teeth through unusual abuse under her employer because of a Filipino cultural value called *tiis*, or enduring sacrifice, for the golden opportunity to work in the United States. This chance to pursue the American dream ties many Filipinas to their employers, making the simple act of demanding better working conditions feel like a criminal act. This pushes many Filipinas to escape their employers, putting themselves at risk for a range of legal infractions such as falling out of status on their visas. As Rose's story demonstrates, many Filipinas' experiences in public or common interactions are filtered by an understanding that one can get caught any moment by authorities, employers, or passersby. Filipinas' heightened consciousness of immigration status (or lack thereof) is conflated as criminality in their minds, which then shapes their interactions with others. However, many choose to overstay because of their transnational responsibilities to their families and debts incurred for their migration.

We argue that the Filipina experience of immigrant criminalization is unique in that their conception of their migration as debt begins transnationally, which influences their insertion into the American economic order as racialized and gendered subjects. Criminalization for Filipinas is not as easily identified as a reaction to a specific policy or a face-to-face interaction in public. Rather, the neocolonial relationship of the Philippines to the United States shapes Filipinas' logic and incorporation to the United States, wherein the internalization of their subjugation began before they even left the Philippines. Filipina migrant workers are in a precarious situation upon their arrival to the United States, leaving them vulnerable to exploitation and abuse.

Finally, we point to the different contact points of rescue and relief in Rose's story to underscore the expressions of solidarity Filipinas share with one another during times of crisis. Meeting fellow domestic workers Rita and Virginia became a source of strength for Rose despite her fear. A narrative of criminalization in Filipinas' lives would not be complete if we did not address the recurring theme of mutual support across the interviews of Filipina migrants. We argue that the experience of Filipina criminalization also includes a story of *bayanihan*, or collective effort, to assist others who are experiencing great difficulty. We provide evidence that Filipinas, whether they are acquaintances or friends, expend a great deal of effort when they are asked to come to another Filipina migrant worker's aid.

This chapter draws from Valerie Francisco's (2015) larger book project on Filipino transnational families, for which she interviewed Filipino/a migrants working as domestics in New York City and their respective families living in the metro-Manila area in the Philippines. For this chapter, we examine the narratives of six domestic workers out of the 50 interviews conducted by Francisco between 2008 and 2011. Moreover, we contextualize these individual narratives in the macro social forces that have produced the steady stream of Filipina migration to the United States and the meso-level interactions that constrain their mobility and decision-making processes (Deaux, 2006). Thus, the research questions we take up in this chapter are: How do Filipina migrants experience criminalization with regard to their gendered and racialized work as domestics? How do their unstable immigration statuses intersect with their precarious occupations to produce experiences of isolation and marginalization?

We build on the definition of criminality following scholars who have substantiated that experiences of criminalized immigrants are at the nexus of postcolonialism (Das Gupta, 2006), current-day imperialism (San Juan, 2000), neoliberal globalization (Kim, 2008), and racialized economic order in the United States (Diaz, 2011). We define criminality in the lives of Filipinas as tied to transnational responsibilities to families in the Philippines, isolation and exploitation as migrant domestic workers, and solidarity between migrant women.

## STRUCTURES OF CRIMINALIZATION IN THE LIVES
## OF FILIPINA MIGRANTS

Scholars have argued that neoliberal globalization has freed up the flows of capital, goods, information, and people yet simultaneously tightened border restrictions (Bacon, 2008; Harvey, 2001; Sassen, 2006). As migrants are brokered by sending nation-states (Guevarra, 2010; Rodriguez, 2010) to the demands of labor markets across the world, receiving states like the United States enact policies that deny migrants the most basic of rights in low-wage industries such as domestic work and agriculture (Das Gupta, 2006). Scholars have argued that the work of migrant women of color from the global South are policed even if they contribute efficiently to the U.S. national economy. Maggy Lee (2005) suggests that neoliberal immigrant policies perpetuate a state of fear and silence in the lives of migrants by rendering them unable to understand and access the ever-changing bureaucracy of the immigration system. Additionally, the historical record of the U.S. hyperpunitive laws targeting unwanted migrants, both documented and undocumented (Takaki, 1998), attests to the U.S. government's approach to dealing with immigrants without a great deal of concern for their welfare (Furman et al., 2012; Miller, 2008).

The political climate of immigration and nativism influences American conceptions of migrants and perhaps how Filipina migrants understand themselves in their new milieu. Policies that increase the number of deportable migrants while also shifting definitions of criminality from immigration policies to individual immigrants during an uptick in anti-immigrant sentiment defines the social climate Filipinas enter as migrant workers (Furman et al., 2012). The U.S. government places criminality as the responsibility of migrants while taking attention away from the very immigration policies that redraw the boundaries of welcome and unwelcome migrants (Ngai, 2004).

This uncertainty is a particularly heavy burden for migrants who are navigating their daily routines and work while also balancing their trepidation about how their racialized bodies and immigration statuses are read by the general public. Thus, we find that the conceptualization of migrant women as "unruly" (Das Gupta, 2006) or as a "social threat" (Sohoni & Sohoni, 2013) begins at the macro level. This necessarily shapes migrant women's meso interactions and micro experiences. The social imagination of immigrant women as disposable produces an effective background for Filipinas wherein they consider themselves lucky to work in the United States. They feel they must grit their teeth through grueling work conditions to pull their families out of poverty. Filipinas see their migration to the United States as a once in a lifetime chance, a gamble of sorts, as they are expendable commodities in the throes of high deportation rates and rising xenophobia in the United States. For Filipinas, both undocumented and documented, U.S. and Philippine immigration policies are just one piece of larger structural forces that shape their experience of immigration and criminalization. Their stories are anchored to a transnational narrative about the American dream.

## THE FOREVER FILIPINA FOREIGNER

Racial stereotypes coupled with myths about immigration have created a perceived image of Filipino immigrants as "forever foreigners," people who do not and can never fit the definition of a mainstream American (Tuan, 1998). This denigration of the Filipino culture and ethnicity is deeply rooted in U.S. imperialism in the Philippines and took place long before migrants arrived in America (San Juan, 2000). Literature about Filipino migration describes how colonial mentality begins to develop as racial ideologies are embedded in the premigration minds of Filipinos (David & Nadal, 2013; Kim, 2008). The American racial order has been ingrained through years of idolization of American culture and continuous bombardment with inferiorizing messages against Filipino culture.

Filipino immigrants unknowingly enter an established racial hierarchy in which they face discrimination, prejudiced attitudes, and further ethnic and cultural denigration. According to Tiongson, Gutierrez, and Gutierrez, "Racialized as foreigners, Filipino Americans are subject to both private discrimination and government policies that limit full participation in U.S. life because of the ascription of foreignness" (2006, p. 104). Through historic and institutional barriers, Filipino immigrants are often viewed as foreigners who come to America with no intention of staying permanently, taking American jobs and driving down wages, only to send a majority of those wages back to the Philippines as remittances (Bonus, 2000). Thus Filipino immigrants consider themselves outside of the American social rubric, forever foreign to a country that they, ironically, have been tied to since the early twentieth century. This dislocation or nonbelongingness shapes Filipinos' deference to American employers, institutions, and the American dream.

In recent decades, the gender composition of transnational labor migration from the Philippines has shifted. Sixty percent of emigrants are now women working in industries described as women's work such as nursing and domestic labor (Guevarra, 2010; Tadiar, 1997), with a majority of Filipina migrant labor directed toward North America among other global regions. Receiving countries benefit greatly, as Filipinas take up essential social reproductive occupations (Tyner, 1999). Filipina migrant workers coming to accept these jobs often leave as disposable and expendable labor, thus adding to their experiences of precarity and eventual criminality when they assert their rights and welfare as migrants and workers.

### DISCUSSION

Many Filipinas leave behind husbands and children when they migrate, redefining their role of mothering through their transnational participation in the family, encouraged by their hopes for better futures for not only themselves but their children (Francisco, 2015). We use the cultural value of *tiis* to explore how Filipinas interpret and absorb a range of exploitation and mistreatment by their employees upon their arrival in the United States in honor of their families. Filipinas understand their harsh work conditions through *tiis*, which normalizes exploitation and ultimately contributes to an overall climate of fear in their lives. Finally, we discuss the recurrent theme of *bayanihan*, or collective unity and solidarity, as a marker of the relationships built between Filipino/a migrants through their shared experiences of isolation and marginalization. Many of the women express the importance of solidarity within the Filipino migrant community, thus we argue that these networks act as resources for rescue and critical healing as a response to criminalization in the lives of Filipina migrants.

## TRANSNATIONAL NARRATIVE OF *TIIS* AND ENDURANCE

Many Filipinas' experiences of criminalization begin with their stories of migration as a necessity. Sharon was 53 years old when she migrated. She had an established career as a businesswoman and her four children were in their teens. Her decision to migrate came at a time when her husband lost his job and her children were all looking to go to college. She deemed her migration as a necessity to be able to support her ailing husband and children. Sharon states:

> For me I have no choice. I can't go back. If didn't got a job here, I was not able to support my husband there when he needs it. We would have been bankrupt. All the money that we had would have been gone. Luckily I was able to look for a job. Although it was not a high-paying job. I was able to support my family, my husband, and everything turned out good. With my sacrifice, good enough, I cannot ask for more. It is easier for you to go and work in America and do a little sacrifice to end up better. Actually it was acknowledged by my children. That my decision was right at the time when we were very much in need with money. Even though I was a businesswoman, I can't give them what they need, especially when their father was already in the hospital. I paid a lot of bills.

Sharon described her migration from the Philippines as her only option and her support from abroad as being the lifeline of her family. This reasoning undergirds Sharon's perseverance in finding and maintaining a job in New York City. Like many Filipinas, she is not in a position to fail any of her family members in the Philippines. Sharon also acknowledges that she is the only member of her family who could have gone abroad and achieved the financial goals set out for her because of her gender, the global demand for women domestic workers, and the cultural value of *tiis* that she believes Filipinas possess inherently:

> It's because women have better opportunity than men. Because women works whatever jobs available, whereas men, they're very limited. Men cannot be nannies, men cannot be housekeepers. It's easier for mothers to adjust. The feelings of women especially *sa pagtitiis* [in enduring hardship]. Men don't have that or only little. *Tiis* is women's language but men no.

In Sharon's explanation of feminization of migration (Castles & Miller, 2009) she has an innate understanding of why it is easier for women to find work in domestic spheres. Belief in traditional gender roles and gendered work—women are the nurturers, mothers, caretakers, nurses—plays into increasingly gendered migrant labor, both in demand and in the migrants who answer that call. She mentioned that "*tiis* is women's language," which therefore leads women to make larger sacrifices and endure more difficulties than men. The reasoning of transnational families and lasting transnational cultural values are the mentality of many Filipinas premigration.

Marisol's story exemplifies the recurrent theme of transnational responsibility taking primacy for whatever hardships may come in migration and work in the United States. Marisol, a migrant mother of three, left the Philippines, even though she was college educated and had a career as an accountant, because she was not fully able to support her family. Upon her arrival in the United States, she was in debt because of the many fees for her visa and travel arrangements and, additionally, two of her three children were starting their university educations soon. With these pressures weighing on her, Marisol described her experience in the United States:

> When I came, I went to New Hampshire [because] a job was already waiting for me. I didn't like my boss, they were just not nice. For example, I was cleaning the kitchen countertops and because I was cleaning the countertops with the Windex and paper towel. The lady boss when she saw me was upset. "Why are you cleaning the countertops with Windex? Don't you know that this is granite? It's very expensive! Why are you cleaning this with Windex?"

Little things like that I got reprimanded. The last straw was at *one o'clock in the morning,* the lady boss wake me up just to scold me because I forgot something for the baby, something I should have done. But actually I didn't forget, I didn't know how, and the other nanny Michelle said "I'll take care of it." So, she woke me up one o'clock in the morning just to say, "You can't always blame Michelle." I was being scolded wrongly. So, I was crying the whole day, they were not paying me a lot, just $400 a week. We didn't have day offs.

In recounting her experience with exploitation, Marisol endured much of the verbal abuse, working overtime, and underpaid labor because she put her familial responsibilities before standing up for herself. Her reference to her employer as "lady boss" points to the unequal power relations between employee and employer that paralyzed Marisol for the time she worked at this job. We want to highlight that this experience of exploitation coupled with the transnational responsibilities and the cultural value of *tiis* places Filipinas in a vulnerable situation wherein they lack the voice and ability to push back on such situations. Another example is Janessa's experience as a domestic worker:

When I got there, I arrived to work, I only slept for 2 hours. I didn't rest, they just put me to work. Guess what, I didn't even notice, but I fell asleep because I was so tired and I still had to cook for them so they could eat. Even if they did treat me fine, they paid me so little. Three hundred dollars a month. No off. Without time off, because you work to until they don't need something from you. It's not like a 9 to 5. Like you're off at 5 o'clock, no. They'll even say that if I'm doing laundry at 9:30 pm, that it's still early in the day, I could still fit in ironing. But you can't do anything because they are your boss. You have no right to say *no,* because you feel that they'll get mad at you or something right? It's like that. It's hard when you are the victim of your employer. Because you have to be thankful that you are here.

In Janessa's case we found that Filipinas use *tiis* to grit their teeth through hardship because of their huge sacrifices to migrate to the United States. The idea of demanding better working conditions or pay raises was out of the question for Filipina migrants; the mere suggestion of action in and of itself feels like a criminal offense to their employers who gave them jobs, the families who went into debt to help them migrate, the networks who helped them find jobs, and so on. Further, Filipinas described that the treatment from their employers signaled to them that they were expendable and could be easily replaced. With their transnational responsibilities, Filipinas expressed the importance of keeping their employers happy, which constrains their mobility and ability to advocate for themselves.

### BAYANIHAN: RESOURCE BUILDING
### AND SHARED EXPERIENCES

Filipinas saliently interpret their experiences of migration as criminalized when they decide to assert their right to well-being and safety. Many Filipinas emerged out of their exploitative situations using escape and relying on other Filipino/a migrants to come to their aid. Janessa explains her escape after she developed a condition and had surgery from the amount of work she did for her employers:

> I escaped from them. I escaped because my woman employer knew I was operated on but she wanted me to go back to work. Little by little, I took my belongings away [to] where an acquaintance lives. When I leave the house, I take my clothes and they don't know it. I left on Friday because if it didn't leave that day or the next I wouldn't know when the next time I would have the opportunity that they'd be away. I have to escape now. When I left, I took a taxi and I hid on the floor of the taxi. Because I didn't want them to see where I was going, because it was sort of close to where they live. I didn't want to take a bus or train, because they might see me. So I took a taxi to where my friend works, just a few blocks over. When I escaped, I can't tell you. I was always looking over my shoulder, looking at who is next to me. One time my new boss asked me if I could meet him by 46th Street or 55th Street. But shit, it's so close to the Philippine consulate. I was so so scared to get out of the cab. I really hid, because I was so scared that someone would see me and catch me. You know, it's like you have a phobia. I'm so fearful, so you do whatever you can to survive.

Janessa's escape from her employer made her hyperaware of her precarious status as an immigrant in the United States. Even after some time, she still felt haunted by her abusive employer. Janessa's life post-escape was mired with feelings of insecurity and surveillance that haunted her every move in New York City. More importantly, although Janessa had overwhelming feelings of fear living in New York City, it was with the help of a Filipina migrant who sheltered her after her escape that she survived. Parallel to this moment of solidarity, we remind you of Rose's opening story, in which she related that she also relied on migrant domestic workers to help her knit a network of rescue and solidarity to facilitate her escape. In these moments of tremendous fear, we find that Filipinas also express thick solidarity with other migrants who may have similar experiences. Carmie expounds on why Filipinas may take up this type of solidarity:

> We just see each other and talk, talk, talk as if we know each other for a long time. Even in stations I can see some nannies and some caregivers they invite you if you're a Filipino. That's because of our special bonding, it's our nature. It's a Filipino custom. *Bayanihan.* You know the *bayanihan*, when you put up a hut even if you don't know each other. It's a sign of respect, sympathy and help.

*Bayanihan* is a Filipino cultural value of collective effort for those in a community who may need assistance. This value is translated to migrant communities abroad; even if migrants do not know one another, they are able to express solidarity and provide what resources they can in times of crisis. For Filipina migrants, the experience of leaving their families and adjusting to exploitative employers and relentless work becomes the basis for helping out Filipinas in need. Many of the accounts talk about Filipinas who have helped complete strangers because of an understanding of the conditions of hardship and drawing on the cultural value of *bayanihan*.

### CONCLUSION

In this chapter, we demonstrated that the experience of criminality for Filipinas is moored to their subjectivities as migrants and domestic workers in the United States. First, we trace the transnational linkages between filial obligations in the Philippines to Filipina criminalization in the United States. We argue that even before Filipinas leave the Philippines, they migrate with a colonial mentality that informs the way they perceive their incorporation into American society. Stemming from U.S. imperialism and the ongoing neocolonial relationship between the United States and the Philippines, Filipinas come to the United States as racialized and gendered workers who are often incorporated as subjugated, disposable migrant workers. This shapes how Filipinas interpret their own work and how employers in the United States view them. We find that this arrangement puts Filipina migrants in vulnerable positions as domestic workers, and their experience of criminalization begins with the treatment they receive from exploitative employers, which pushes them to find avenues of escape. As migrants in a new country with the burden of transnational responsibility and guilt from leaving employers to whom they feel indebted, the experience of criminalization for Filipinas heightens as they try to survive on their own. Despite these desperate conditions, we highlight that Filipinas express solidarity with one another through times of crisis by providing avenues of relief and resources. We believe it is important to punctuate these criminalized experiences with the resilience fostered in Filipino/a migrant communities, because it is in these moments of critical hope and healing that conditions of despair are negotiated with spirits of resistance.

### REFERENCES

Bacon, D. (2008). *Illegal people: How globalization creates migration and criminalizes immigrants*. Boston: Beacon.

Bonus, R. (2000). *Locating Filipino Americans: Ethnicity & the cultural politics of space*. Philadelphia: Temple University Press.

Castles, S., & Miller M. (2009). *The age of migration: International population movements in the modern world*. New York: Palgrave Macmillan.

Das Gupta, M. (2006). *Unruly immigrants: Rights, activism, and transnational South Asian politics in the United States*. London: Duke University Press.

David, E., & Nadal, K. (2013). The colonial context of Filipino American immigrants' psychological experiences. *Cultural Diversity and Ethnic Minority Psychology, 19*(3), 298–307.

Deaux, K. (2006). *To be an immigrant*. New York: Russell.

Diaz, J. (2011). Immigration policy, criminalization and the growth of the immigration industrial complex: restriction, expulsion, and eradication of undocumented in the U.S. *Western Criminology Review, 12*(2), 35–54.

Francisco, V. (2015). Multidirectionality of care: Transnational Filipino families and care work. In G. Man & R. Cohen (Eds.), *Engendering transnational voices: Studies in families, work and identities* (pp. 86–114). Waterloo, ON: Wilfried Laurier University Press.

Furman, R., Ackerman, A., Loya, M., Jones, S., & Negi, N. (2012). The criminalization of immigration: Value conflicts for the social work profession. *Journal of Sociology & Social Welfare, 29*(1), 169–185.

Guevarra, A. (2010). *Marketing dreams, manufacturing heroes: The transnational labor brokering of Filipino workers.* New Brunswick, NJ: Rutgers University Press.

Harvey, D. (2001). *Spaces of capital: Towards a critical geography.* New York: Routledge.

Kim, N. (2008). *Imperial citizens: Koreans and race from Seoul to LA.* Stanford, CA: Stanford University Press.

Lee, M. (2005). Human trade and the criminalization of irregular migration. *International Journal of the Sociology of Law, 33*(1), 1–15.

Miller, D. (2008). Immigrants, nations, and citizenship. *Journal of Political Philosophy, 16*(4), 371–390.

Ngai, M. (2004). *Impossible subjects: Illegal aliens and the making of modern America.* Princeton, NJ: Princeton University Press.

Rodriguez, C. (2010). *Migrants for export.* Minneapolis: University of Minnesota Press.

San Juan, E. (2000). *After post-colonialism: Remapping Philippines–United States confrontations.* New York: Rowman & Littlefield.

Sassen, S. (2006). *Territory, authority, rights: From medieval to global assemblages.* Princeton, NJ: Princeton University Press.

Sohoni, D., & Sohoni, T. (2013). Perceptions of immigrant criminality: Crime and social boundaries. *Sociological Quarterly, 55,* 49–71.

Tadiar, N. (1997). Domestic bodies of the Philippines. *SOUJOURN, 12*(2), 153–191.

Takaki, R. (1998). *Strangers from a different shore: A history of Asian Americans.* Boston: Little, Brown.

Tiongson, A., Gutierrez, E., & Gutierrez, R. (Eds.). (2006). *Positively no Filipinos allowed.* Philadelphia: Temple University Press.

Tuan, M. (1998). *Forever foreigners or honorary whites? The Asian ethnic experience today.* New Brunswick, NJ: Rutgers University Press.

Tyner, J. (1999). The global context of gendered labor migration from the Philippines to the United States. *American Behavioral Scientist, 42*(4), 671–689.

# The Criminalization of Brazilian Immigrants

▸ *KARA CEBULKO AND HELOÍSA MARIA GALVÃO*

## INTRODUCTION

ELEVEN DAYS BEFORE CHRISTMAS IN 2012, Daniela, a Brazilian immigrant living in Boston since 2005, faced an impossible decision. Earlier that day, her husband, Juan, and their 4-year-old daughter, Vanessa, had gone to the Burlington immigration office. Having been told by his lawyer that he had more than a 100% chance of winning his case, Juan, a Guatemalan immigrant, was hopeful this meeting was an important step to becoming a lawful permanent resident. He had worked for the same family for 15 years, had been issued a work permit and social security number, and had paid his taxes. Instead, on that December day, Juan was detained. For 6 hours, 4-year old Vanessa was held by officials as they refused to release her to anyone but her mother.

Daniela had no choice but to rescue her daughter. Yet she did so with fear. After all, as an unauthorized immigrant, she too risked detention and deportation by picking up her little girl.

On that day, Daniela's worst fears came to fruition. Instead of releasing her daughter without incident, officials determined that Daniela must also leave the country. While Juan was detained, Daniela was released that day but scheduled to return for further processing. At the next meeting, Daniela was ordered to voluntarily deport by mid-March. If she failed to do so, she would be arrested, and Vanessa would be placed in foster care.

As Daniela met with agents, Vanessa waited with a lawyer's assistant. Last time the young child was at the office, her father had not returned. Inevitably, little Vanessa worried about a similar fate for her mother. She turned to the lawyer's assistant and asked "Who will take care of me if she doesn't come back? Will you take care of me?"

Being unauthorized in the United States is a civil not a criminal offense. Yet the lived experiences of immigrants contradict this legal designation (Golash-Boza, 2010). Today, not only unauthorized immigrants like Juan and Daniela but even lawfully present immigrants and U.S. citizens—like Vanessa, a U.S. citizen by birth—can *feel* very much like criminals. No one had committed a crime, but detention and eventual deportation—to two different countries—was devastating for the family. Separated for more than a year, the family members miss one another terribly and face a precarious economic position, as Juan has been unable to find work in Guatemala.

Stories of family separation and the resulting economic hardships have become increasingly common. Since the 1990s, and especially since 9/11, exclusionary laws targeting immigrants have expanded from the borders to the interior of the United States. With this expansion there has been a dramatic increase in the arrest, detention, and deportation of immigrants with deep and long-established ties in the United States (Kanstroom, 2007). While the U.S. Department of Homeland Security (DHS) claims that enforcement measures target "criminal aliens," the reality is that many immigrants are arrested, detained, and deported for immigration violations—civil offenses. Moreover, it is Latin American immigrants who are disproportionately targeted by anti-immigrant measures (Golash-Boza, 2012), as "Latino" and "illegal" are conflated in the public imagination, propagated by a discourse that constructs all immigrants from Latin America as threatening others (Chavez, 2013).

In this chapter we examine the consequences of criminalization for Brazilians in Massachusetts—the group with the greatest proportion of removals for civil offenses between 2010 and 2012 (Simanski & Sapp, 2013). We examine both the first generation of immigrants and the 1.5 generation, those immigrants born abroad but raised in the United States. We delve into the ways in which these immigrants have experienced *acts* of arrest, detention, and deportation to themselves or loved ones, and we pay particular attention to how they navigate their lives against the constant *threat* of deportation. Our findings reveal their resilience in adapting to new realities, adjusting routines, concealing identities, and adjusting plans for the future, but also demonstrate the ways these adaptations carry costs for them and their families. Further, we find that even partially inclusionary policies such as Deferred Action for Childhood Arrivals (DACA), a discretionary initiative announced by the Obama administration on June 15, 2012, which granted temporary reprieve from deportation for certain eligible immigrants who migrated as children, have only limited impact in the broader context of criminalization.

### BRAZILIANS AND THE MASSACHUSETTS CONTEXT

The stories in this chapter come from the authors' experiences as scholars and activists. Cebulko draws primarily upon in-depth interviews conducted between 2006 and 2014 with forty-seven 1.5-generation young Brazilian adults, 20 of whom participated in longitudinal interviews. A snowball sample was used, with Brazilian leaders serving as initial contacts. Galvão, the current executive director of the Brazilian Women's Group (BWG), draws primarily upon her 19 years of grassroots organizing in the Brazilian community. The authors met in the summer of 2006, and for the past 8 years Cebulko has served as the periodic grant consultant for the BWG. Both authors are active in advocating for immigrants' rights in New England.

While Brazilians are not officially considered "Latino" by the U.S. government, and often not by Brazilians themselves, Brazilians are often racialized as Latino (Beserra, 2005). Thus, it is not surprising that Brazilians, like other immigrants from Latin America, are disproportionately arrested and targeted for removal (Golash-Boza, 2012). While the absolute number of deportations to Brazil is much lower than deportations to other Latin American countries (i.e., Mexico, Guatemala, and Honduras), a higher percentage of Brazilians than any other group were deported for immigrant violations between 2010 and 2012. Just 15.9% of all deportations to Brazil during those years were for criminal offenses (Simanski & Sapp, 2013).

We focus on Massachusetts, as it has the highest concentration of Brazilians of any U.S. state. After Chinese and possibly Dominican immigrants, they were the second- or third-largest immigrant group in Massachusetts by 2007 (Marcelli et al., 2009). Following an economic collapse in Brazil in the 1980s, Brazilian migration increased (Goza, 1994). Many Brazilians, especially before the turn of the century, entered the United States on tourist visas and overstayed, but after 2000 more came via Mexico (Margolis, 1994). While some in Massachusetts were able to adjust their legal status to lawful permanent resident, most often through employer and family sponsorships under Section 245(i) of the Immigration and Nationality Act, many others have been unable to adjust their status and/or became stuck in liminal legality, a gray area of legal limbo in which they had access to social security numbers and work permits but not a guaranteed path to citizenship (Cebulko, 2013, 2014).

Importantly, the lived experiences of immigrants are context specific, as no systematic nationwide approach to immigration enforcement exists. The expansion of interior enforcement measures has been coupled with the devolution of immigration policing powers. In other words, state and localities have increased powers to enforce civil violations of immigration laws. States and localities, however, often pursue policies that are contradictory or even conflicting in nature, resulting in a "multilayered jurisdictional patchwork of immigration enforcement" (Varsanyi, Lewis, Provine, & Decker, 2012, p. 138). These contradictions and conflicts are apparent in Massachusetts, where new administrations have reversed policies and localities have pursued conflicting measures.

For example, in 2006, then-governor Mitt Romney signed an executive order on 287(g), authorizing an agreement between the Massachusetts State Police and the DHS. This agreement effectively permitted designated police officers to enforce civil violations of immigration laws. Just a few months later, however, newly elected Governor Deval Patrick rescinded Romney's executive order on 287(g).

Until 2012, Governor Patrick also resisted statewide implementation of Secure Communities, a program that allows state and local police to check the fingerprints of individuals they are booking into jail against DHS immigration databases. Yet while Governor Patrick resisted statewide implementation, the program was simultaneously pursued in Boston, as Mayor Thomas Menino agreed to pilot Secure Communities in 2006. Thus, despite some progressive moves by Governor Patrick, the state's largest city, where many immigrants are concentrated, moved in a more oppressive direction.

Moreover, a federal raid just 60 miles southeast of Boston in March 2007 exacerbated fear. Three hundred heavily armed Immigration and Customs (ICE) agents raided Michael Bianco, a leather factory in New Bedford, Massachusetts, and arrested 361 workers. The aftermath of the raid was, in the words of Governor Deval Patrick, a "humanitarian crisis," as children were stranded at day-care facilities and schools. Detainees later reported mistreatment by ICE officers (Golash-Boza, 2012). While only eight Brazilian women were arrested in the raid, the spectacle magnified fear throughout the community.

Large worksite raids have seemingly disappeared since 2008, but annual deportations remain at a record high, and other enforcement measures have expanded. Further, much to the chagrin of immigrants' rights advocates, Governor Patrick eventually resigned himself to the federally mandated implementation of Secure Communities in 2012. As immigrants rights' groups anticipated, this program has not targeted immigrants with criminal records. A 2013 *Boston Globe* analysis found that "45.6 percent of the 768 immigrants deported through Secure Communities since 2008 had criminal records, far below the national average of 76 percent and lower than states such as Arizona, New York, and Texas" (Sachetti, 2013).

There have been, however, two positive developments for immigrants in recent years. First, Massachusetts has responded to President Obama's announcement of DACA in more inclusive ways than other states (i.e., North Carolina). As previously mentioned, DACA, a federal action, grants certain eligible unauthorized immigrants who migrated as children a temporary reprieve from deportation and allows them to work in the United States for up to 2 years. While some states have been reluctant and/or outright hostile to granting driver's licenses and access to in-state tuition for DACA beneficiaries, Governor Patrick affirmed just a few months after DACA was announced that beneficiaries would be eligible for in-state tuition (because they now possessed work permits), signaling a more welcoming state environment, at least for a subset of immigrants. Second, in August 2014, recently elected Boston mayor Marty Walsh signed the Trust Act, which prohibits city police from detaining unauthorized immigrants for possible deportation, unless they were convicted of a serious crime. At the time of this writing, however, the program had not been fully implemented.

Thus, while the Patrick administration has been more immigrant-friendly than administrations in other states, anti-immigrant measures, especially at the federal and local levels, have created an overall hostile context for immigrants, their families, and communities. In the following sections, we examine the consequences of criminalization measures for Brazilians and highlight the strategies they develop for navigating their new realities.

## THE AFTERMATH OF ARRESTS, DETENTIONS, AND
## DEPORTATIONS: FEAR, ANXIETY, AND PAINFUL DECISIONS

As detailed in the opening story, detentions and deportations cause pain, pain that is exacerbated by dehumanizing treatment at the hands of government authorities and via surveillance measures. For example, Gisele, one of the eight Brazilian women arrested in the New Bedford raid, reported that immigration officials threw away her medication, disregarding her serious health conditions.

While Gisele was eventually released because she was the primary care-taker of her children, she was fitted with a GPS monitor, a surveillance mechanism often considered a humane alternative to detention. The experience of wearing the monitor, however, is stressful and debilitating for immigrants. Gisele was forced to "check in" via weekly telephone recordings. The recordings, however, were in Spanish, not Portuguese, and Gisele's accent often sounded off an alarm, as the recording did not "read" her accent. Each time this happened, Gisele panicked.

Ultimately, the stress took a toll on Gisele's already precarious health. Per agreement of her release, Gisele could not leave her home between 7 p.m. and 7 a.m. But these rules are impractical, especially during medical emergencies. One night, Gisele's health deteriorated to the point that she was crying out in excruciating pain. Yet out of fear, she refused to seek medical care. It was only after Galvão intervened and pleaded with dispatchers to send an ambulance to her home that Gisele received the medical attention she needed.

The pain of forced removals can also strain family relationships, as family members of deportees must make painful decisions about whether or not to stay in the United States. This was the case for Victoria, an unauthorized 1.5-generation Brazilian immigrant who moved to the United States at age six. One day, when she was 18, immigration officials raided her home while she was at work. Authorities detained her brother and seized her mother's passport. Her mother, Maria Fernanda, a homeowner who had lived and worked in the United States for 12 years, was ordered to leave the country.

Maria Fernanda wanted Victoria to return to Brazil, but Victoria refused. She was active in the immigrants' rights movement and committed to its cause. Her decision, however, led to fights with her mom. "We never got into more serious arguments then at that time—when I first told her that I was not going back with her." Thus, her mother's forced removal—and Victoria's decision to not return to Brazil—put pressure on their relationship.

Seven years later, the separation from her mother is still devastating. A recent DACA beneficiary, Victoria now has a valid work permit and social security number. But without a green card, which DACA did not grant, Victoria could not be guaranteed safe reentry into the United States if she visited her mother in Brazil. For this reason, Victoria called DACA a major "disappointment." Its limited inclusionary benefits could not rectify the painful separation from her mother.

Victoria's family's story is not unique. Other Brazilians face similar difficult decisions following deportations of a loved one. Luana, who was unauthorized, stressed about where to live following the deportation of her husband, her children's stepfather. On the one hand, her husband, Marcelo, was depressed and lonely in Brazil. On the other hand, her children, Gabriella and Jonas, who had been raised in the United States since they were young children, were firmly rooted in the United States. Speaking of her mother's dilemma during an interview, Gabriella, now 28, said:

> [My stepfather is] the best thing that ever happened to my mom. It's sad because now hecan't come back, you know? And I want her to go [to Brazil], but then that's the thing . . . she's here because . . . can you imagine if something happens to my brother? If [my brother or I] get sick or someone's in the hospital, she's going, she's going to die. She's going to go nuts. So she has to be [in the United States].

For Gabriella, whose own life seemed to be moving in a positive direction since receiving a green card in her early twenties, the deportation of her stepfather highlighted her family's continued exclusion in the United States. As the only authorized member of her family, she was the only one who could visit Marcelo in detention. She was appalled how he and other detainees were treated like criminals.

> I would have to take money [for him to buy food at the cantina]. Because can you imagine? You're used to eating this much food [gestured a large amount], and then you get—you're treated like a criminal. You get this amount of food [gestured a small amount with her hands], and that's it. Six o'clock, you're not going to get food until the next day.
>
> (Gabriella, age 28)

Gabriella was not only horrified by the detention conditions, but she was also furious that when Marcelo finally was deported, there was no advance warning to her family and no opportunity for a final goodbye.

The world of detentions and deportations is far from transparent. As Gabriella detailed, her family received no warning when Marcelo was finally deported. For family members abroad, the experience of trying to track a loved one can be particularly harrowing. For example, one night while working late at the BWG, Galvão received a panicked phone call from Rafael in Brazil. His son, Erasmo, had been arrested. In the wake of the arrest, Rafael and his wife had sent nearly all their savings to Erasmo's wife to help her bail Erasmo out of jail. But since that time, Rafael had lost communication with Erasmo's wife, and he was in a panic about his son's whereabouts and well-being.

Galvão promised Erasmo she would do her best to locate his son. After making some phone calls, she eventually discovered the name of the detention center holding him. When Galvão spoke with Rafael the next morning, his words drove her to tears, "This was the first night we slept in over a week. Thank you and God bless you." Even though Galvão had been unable to speak of Erasmo's well-being, Rafael had found comfort in having an ally in the United States.

### Adjusting Lives in the Face of the Constant Threat of Deportation: Avoiding the Police

As De Genova (2002) has argued, it is not just the act of deportation that matters but also the constant threat of deportation that penetrates the lives of immigrants. In particular, immigrants fear interaction with the police, who increasingly act as immigration agents. As Mayra, age 23, who had lived in the United States since age eight, describes:

> For the longest time I feared . . . like, if I saw a cop, I would have this fear in me. It's ridiculous. It sounds ridiculous, because cops are supposed to protect you. But you're like, you're running away, because you don't want to have anything to do with them.

Some Brazilians take extra precautions in their daily routines to avoid interacting with police. For example, Jesica, age 23, raised in the United States since age 12, explains how carefully she drives. "There's never a light on my car that is not working. Never over the speed limit. Never run through a yellow light. Nothing wrong."

Rodrigo, 24, spoke of how unauthorized immigrants purposefully "lose" arguments to avoid contact with police:

> There are times where you end up losing in an argument—and something that is of monetary value—for losing. Let's say you are driving and you end up—somebody hits your car or something like that . . . Sometimes I see it at bars and places where somebody puts their coat down or something and somebody else picks it up and it's like—it's an argument over whose it is. And it's like "keep it," you know? "Would rather not finish this argument. Whatever, I'll lose it. I'll lose the jacket—you keep it."

As Rodrigo underscores, avoiding interaction with police can come with monetary costs. But avoiding interaction has other costs, including the safety of immigrants.

The BWG receives calls from many women who experience domestic violence but are fearful of reporting it to the police. For example, one January evening, the BWG received a phone call from Claudia, who was worried about her missing mother, Leticia. After a horrible argument with her husband, Leticia, fearing for her safety, had fled her home in her nightgown, with no other protection to keep warm in the frigid January air. When Leticia reappeared a few days later, she and her daughters refused to call the police for fear of detention and/or deportation. Thus, as other scholars have shown, uncertain legal status can make immigrant women particularly vulnerable to domestic violence (Menjívar & Salcido, 2002).

Ultimately, there are a number of unintended consequences when police act as immigration agents. Immigrants not only suffer monetary and psychological costs, the well-being of families and communities are compromised as immigrants and their family members, including victims of domestic violence, become fearful of reporting crimes and seeking protection.

### Hiding Illegality: Strategies of Concealment

In an era of criminalization, immigrants are not only distrustful of police but also attempt to conceal their "illegality" from anyone they do not know well. Sometimes this includes concealment from other Brazilians.

One day while shopping, Galvão told the store manager, Renata, that she was dressed nicely. Renata smiled and said that she was wearing the same dress she had worn to her green card interview. But months later, after breaking down in tears, Renata admitted to Galvão that the green card story was an invention, a story to deflect people's questions. In truth, she was unauthorized. Moreover, she was fearful for her future. Her partner, who was authorized, had a new job opportunity out west, and they were moving. For Renata, who was a manager of a successful business, the prospect of starting over in a new city was incredibly scary due to her legal status.

While some Brazilians like Renata conceal unauthorized status from other Brazilians, most are fairly open with community members. Indeed, 1.5-generation Brazilians reported to Cebulko that most Brazilians know their status. They were much less willing, however, to share their status with non-Brazilians, especially nonimmigrants. Yet concealing "illegality" became more difficult as they aged into late adolescence.

As children, 1.5-generation immigrants are relatively protected, legally entitled to public school education because of the 1982 Supreme Court Decision, *Plyler v. Doe*. But as age, they are excluded from driver's licenses (in most states) and meet barriers to higher education (Ábrego, 2006; Gonzales, 2011; Silver, 2012). Thus, they face more circumstances in which questions arise about why they are not engaging in traditional life course rituals such as driving, going to college, or traveling on trips abroad (Cebulko, 2014).

In order to keep their "illegality" hidden, many 1.5-generation Brazilians adopt strategies to conceal their status, including developing stories, like Renata did. For example, Leila, age 30, carefully crafted the telling of her immigration story:

> My answer [about how we can to the United States] was always "through my aunts." My aunts had been here for a long time. "We came through my aunts." Because [my aunts] actually had petition[ed] for my mom and I think a petition had been in place for like a good 10 years or something. And it was just not coming through. My mom was like "Screw it, let's just do, you know?" So that's always been my story to kids who ask, "Oh, like, why did you come here? How did you come here?" So, "Oh, you know, I have aunts who live here and they petitioned for her, and that's how we came." The end.

Leila's story was crafted from true events. Her aunts *did* petition for her mom. She left out the detail, however, that the petition was never granted. For Leila, telling this story caused her enormous anxiety.

> [Telling this story is] always bothersome. It's always bothersome. It sucks. Like it's a topic that if I start talking about a lot, it makes me want to cry, you know what I mean? I don' t like it at all.
>
> (Leila, age 30)

Concealing an identity is stressful for immigrants. Indeed, throughout the interview, Leila did cry, especially as she spoke of her hope that other young children would not have to fear the police or lie to protect themselves like she did. "It's not a good way to live!" she exclaimed through tears.

Ana Maria, another 1.5-generation immigrant, also reported concealing her unauthorized identity throughout her life, including from school mentors, gatekeepers who may have been able to help her navigate the college application process had she disclosed her status. At the time, however, she did not trust them.

Years later, concealing her status became very problematic when she met John, a white American. In order for the relationship to progress, Ana Maria knew she would have to disclose her status. Yet she found it easier to tell John that she had been date-raped than to tell him she was unauthorized. Ana Maria was fearful the relationship would end and John would alert immigration officials:

> He told me he was a Republican. I'm like, "Oh my God, he's going to announce me to immigration! And this, like, perfect, like, little relationship that I'm building in my head is all going to disappear. In a blink of an eye." So I started bawling.

Ana Maria eventually did tell him her status, and today they are married. But her fear at the time was pronounced, causing major anxiety and tears.

Thus, criminalization creates fear and leads to generalized distrust. In order to navigate unknown relationships, some Brazilians develop strategies to conceal their "illegality." But concealment carries psychological and material costs, as many Brazilians feel they are living a lie and/or closing off potential relationships and opportunities.

### Uncertainty in Planning for the Future

Some Brazilians report navigating their criminalized context by adjusting their life plans to the realities of precarious futures. For example, Claudia was so fearful of what might happen to her children if she were detained/ deported that she contacted the BWG for help in drawing up a legal document, a type of "will" that would detail who would take care of her children. She wanted the peace of mind that they would be left with someone she trusted rather than placed in foster care. Her worry is well founded, as more than 5,100 children of deported parents were living in foster care in 2011 (Applied Research Center, 2011).

For 1.5-generation immigrants, adjusting plans is particularly painful due to their early socialization experiences in the United States. Often, the United States is the only home they know. Yet, many 1.5-generation Brazilians, including several DACA beneficiaries, talked about how they were hesitant to plant roots.

Roberta, age 26, a DACA beneficiary who was married to an undocumented Brazilian, had been living in the United States since age 12. While most of her family had returned to Brazil following her younger brother's deportation, she and her husband had decided to remain in the United States. Yet Roberta was hesitant to "settle down," saying:

> Without a legal status, you can't really truly settle down. Like, I would never buy a house . . . without having documentation, you know what I mean? And maybe even have kids, because you don't know what tomorrow is going to bring. If we're going to have to pack up and leave.

Alexia, age 26, also a DACA beneficiary, echoed Roberta's concerns over buying a home or having children:

> I can't buy a house. I can't. I mean, I think the first step to the American dream is buying a house. And being your own person here and not, you know? Right now, I can't. I would be able to buy a house after I build credit, but what if I'm deported? . . . Why invest someplace that is not going to give me the opportunity to stay? . . . Why have children so that they can be in limbo too? 'Cause even though they are going to be born here, they have to go where I go.

Although Alexia was concerned about her precarious future, she was even more concerned for her husband, who was ineligible for DACA. A few times throughout the interview she mentioned that her own sense of relief from DACA was tempered by the fact that he could be deported at a moment's notice. For, as she said, "If he has to go, I have to go."

Like Victoria, who was disappointed that DACA did not reunite her with her mother, the stories of Roberta and Alexia highlight that inclusionary policies like DACA are limited in a broader context of harsh immigration enforcement. While DACA expanded these women's work opportunities and permitted them valid driver's licenses, their husbands were not safe from deportation and they themselves were not guaranteed a permanent future in the United States.

### CONCLUSION

While Massachusetts has a reputation as a progressive state, the lived experiences of Brazilians suggest that increased interior enforcement measures have led to widespread fear and anxiety not only for unauthorized immigrants but for their family members in the United States and abroad. Thus, as other scholars argue, the convergence of immigration and criminal laws has had a devastating impact on immigrants and their families (Dreby, 2012; Golash-Boza, 2012; Hagan, Castor, & Rodriguez, 2010; Menjívar & Ábrego, 2012).

Immigrants are not passive, however, and they learn to adapt their daily routines, navigate uncharted relationships, and adjust their future plans. These adaptations, however, come with costs to their well-being. Being forced to choose between husbands and children when making decisions on where to live, drawing up "wills" in case of detentions and/or deportations, fabricating stories to conceal identities, and delaying life course milestones are not, as Leila said, "a good way to live."

While administrative policies such as DACA that grant temporary reprieve from deportation move immigrants in a more inclusive direction, they are limited. DACA is only temporary, does not fully grant membership to beneficiaries, and is ultimately, exclusive—that is, it benefits a limited number of people, excluding beneficiaries' loved ones. Of course, in the face of congressional inaction on comprehensive immigration reform, further administrative policies should be utilized by the executive branch, as temporary measures such as DACA do provide some sense of security and increased opportunities. But immigrants ultimately need policies that grant pathways to citizenship for themselves and their loved ones.

### REFERENCES

Ábrego, L. J. (2006). I can't go to college because I don't have papers: Incorporation patterns of Latino undocumented youth. *Latino Studies, 4*(3), 212–231.

Applied Research Center. (2011). Shattered families: The perilous intersection of immigration enforcement and the child welfare system. *Research Reports*. Retrieved on May 26, 2014, from http://arc.org/shatteredfamilies.

Beserra, B. (2005). From Brazilians to Latinos? Racialization and Latinidad in the making of Brazilian carnival in Los Angeles. *Latino Studies, 3*(1), 53–75.

Cebulko, K. B. (2013). *Documented, undocumented and something else: The incorporation of children of Brazilian immigrants.* El Paso, TX: LFB Scholarly Publishing.

——. (2014). Documented, undocumented, and liminally legal: Legal status during the transition to adulthood for 1.5-generation Brazilian immigrants. *Sociological Quarterly, 55*(1), 143–167.

Chavez, L. (2013). *The Latino threat narrative: Constructing immigrants, citizens and the nation* (2nd ed.). Stanford, CA: Stanford University Press.

De Genova, N. (2002). Migrant "illegality" and deportability in everyday life. *Annual Review of Anthropology, 31,* 419–437.

Dreby, J. (2012). The burden of deportation on children in Mexican immigrant families. *Journal of Marriage and Family, 74*(4), 829–854.

Golash-Boza, T. (2010). The criminalization of undocumented migrants: Legalities and realities. *Societies Without Borders, 5*(1), 81–90.

——. (2012). *Immigration nation: Raids, detentions and deportations in post-9/11 America.* Boulder, CO: Paradigm.

Gonzales, R. G. (2011). Learning to be illegal: undocumented youth and shifting legal contexts in the transition to adulthood. *American Sociological Review, 76,* 602–619.

Goza, Franklin. (1994). Brazilian immigration to North America. *International Migration Review, 28,*136–152.

Hagan, J., Castor, B., & Rodriguez, N. (2010). The effects of U.S. deportation policies on immigrant families and communities: Cross-border perspectives. *North Carolina Law Review, 88,* 1799–1824.

Kanstroom, D. (2007). *Deportation nation: Outsiders in American history.* Cambridge: Harvard University Press.

Marcelli, E., Holmes, L., Estella, D., Da Rocha, F., Granberry, P., & Buxton, O. (2009). *(In)visible (im)migrants: The health and socioeconomic integration of Brazilians in metropolitan Boston.* San Diego: Center for Behavioral and Community Health Studies, San Diego State University.

Margolis, M. (1994). *Little Brazil: An Ethnography of Brazilian immigrants in New York City.* Princeton, NJ: Princeton University Press.

Menjívar, C., & Ábrego, L. J. (2012). Legal violence: Immigration law and the lives of Central American immigrants. *American Journal of Sociology, 117*(5), 1380–1421.

Menjívar, C., & Salcido, O. (2002). Immigrant women and domestic violence: Common experiences in different countries. *Gender & Society, 16,* 898–920.

Sachetti, M. (2013, February 17). Program deports many with no criminal record. *Boston Globe.* Retrieved on June 29, 2014, from www.bostonglobe.com /metro/2013/02/17/ seccomm/5T1u8iv24z48Yl9t4UHmTJ/story.html.

Silver, A. (2012). Aging into exclusion and social transparency: Undocumented immigrant youth and the transition to adulthood. *Latino Studies, 10,* 499–522.

Simanski, J. F., & Sapp, L. M. (2013). *Immigration enforcement actions: 2012.* Washington, DC: U.S. Department of Homeland Security, Office of Immigration Statistics. Retrieved on June 29, 2014, from www.dhs.gov/sites/default/files /publications/ois_enforcement_ar_2012_1.pdf.

Varsanyi, M. W., Lewis, P. G., Provine, D. M., & Decker, S. (2012). A multi-layered jurisdictional patchwork: Immigration federalism in the United States. *Law & Policy, 34*(2), 138–158.

# Living with Drug Lords and Mules in New York

*CONTRASTING COLOMBIAN CRIMINALITY AND TRANSNATIONAL BELONGING*

▸ ARIANA OCHOA CAMACHO

GOING AS FAR BACK AS *Miami Vice,* contemporary media portrayals depict Colombians as drug lords and mules with sadistic propensities for violence. The widespread infamy of Pablo Escobar and other narcotraffickers preoccupies U.S. perspectives on Colombia and Colombians. The Colombian narcotrafficker and his Colombian mule (a beautiful woman who unwittingly or unwillingly participates in drug smuggling) are featured regularly in prime-time TV in shows of police drug enforcement escapades through urban spaces. Although Colombians as a group are rarely featured as protagonists in mainstream media, the association of Colombians with drugs and drug mules on prime-time TV is commonplace. The inhumane violence of drug lords and drug syndicates or cartels is routinely connected with a Colombian boss running a global operation that wreaks havoc and terrorizes innocents in U.S. cities already plagued by poverty and drugs. The movement of drugs and people across the border remains critical in establishing the spectacle of narcotraffickers. That is, Colombians are associated with widespread criminal organizations and "illegal" border crossings. These double discourses of criminality shape Colombian experiences of migration to the United States. This chapter explores the counterclaims and negotiations of three Colombian migrants in the New York metro region to explore the impact of criminality.

## CHARACTERISTICS OF COLOMBIAN MIGRATION

First, though, I would like to provide some context regarding the scale of Colombian migration and some of the basic characteristics of the migration to clarify the case of Colombian migration itself. There is a paucity of information about and few have documented Colombian migration to the United States. This section reviews some of the pertinent demographic information for Colombians in the United States to contextualize Colombian migrants. Accurate population estimates on just how many Colombians are in the United States have been elusive in the last few decades. The University of Albany's Mumford Center for Comparative Urban and Regional Research notes that "Within ten years, we need to become as aware of Dominicans, Salvadorans, and Colombians—people with very different backgrounds and trajectories—as we are of Puerto Ricans and Cubans" (Logan, 2001). Some of the most significant characteristics of Colombian migration to the United States are its scale and growth and the documentation status of Colombian migrants, among other demographic factors.

According to the International Organization for Migration (2010), Colombia has the second-highest emigration rate in Latin America, second only to Mexico. Approximately 10% of the national population of the Republic of Colombia (4.7 million people; Bérube, 2005) lives outside the national territory, according to the Colombian Ministry of External Relations (2008). Due to the difficulties of reaching Colombians after they migrate and to their distrust of government, these figures likely represent undercounted totals. Some migration is regional, the most significant being to Venezuela, with a much smaller secondary flow to Ecuador— together accounting for roughly a quarter of emigration from Colombia. The main destinations for migrants outside of Latin America, though, are to the United States (34%) and Spain (23%), according to the Colombian Ministry of External Relations (2013).

The 2010 U.S. Census places this population number much lower at 972,000. However, the U.S. Census has impressively undercounted groups of Hispanic origin—the 1990 census undercounted Dominicans and Colombians at a rate of over 50% according to the Mumford reports (Logan, 2001). In this case, the most recent Colombian census (DANE) seems to provide the most reliable and systematic source of information on the total population. The DANE reports that Colombian populations in the United States doubled between 2000 and 2010 (Ramírez & Mendoza, 2013). Using earlier Colombian Ministry of External Relations estimates that 1.7 million Colombians live in the United States; combined with the Mumford estimates of Colombians present in the United States in 2000 (Gaviria, 2004), these growth patterns and statistics indicate there could be as many as 2.2 million Colombians in the United States by 2020. Even so, the DANE and the Pew Centers both report between 900,000 and 980,000 Colombians in the United States today (Ramírez & Mendoza, 2013).

Like other Latino groups, Colombian migrants to the United States are caught up in a crisis on the meaning of citizenship with the proliferation of levels of citizenship and the perils made manifest by the politics of immigration (Chavez, 2008). The changes in immigration policy have shaped experiences of criminality for Colombian migrants in a way similar to those of other Latin American migrant groups to the United States. That is, the revisions of the 1965 immigration law that replaced a race-based system of quotas from the 1920s into a system based on national origin as a proxy for race (Ngai, 2004) narrowed the possibilities for entry to a very limited number of visas for Colombians and other Latin Americans (Valderrama-Echavarria, 2014). This quota system did not impact the factors stimulating migration such as investment and destabilization of national economic systems by multinational corporations (Sassen, 1990), but at different moments there was a diasporic flow due to ongoing the civil conflict (Cepeda, 2010). As a result many Colombian migrants to the United States overstayed tourist visas, and a smaller minority entered without inspection.

Colombians face struggles with documentation status. They have been identified by Immigration and Naturalization Service/ U.S. Department of Homeland Security (Chaney, 1977) as a significant undocumented population and in 2000 were identified as the top estimated undocumented immigrant population in the United States in 1977. Among Colombian migrants are significant numbers of well-educated professionals (Ramírez & Mendoza, 2013) as well as those traveling without legal documents (Stavans & Augenbraum, 2005). RCN, a national radio network in Columbia, reported that at least 40% of Colombians living abroad are undocumented immigrants, according to data from the Colombian government (Radio Cadena Nacional, 2010). Changes in quotas also caused the number of legal entries by Colombians to the United States to plateau after tightened restrictions in the 1990s made authorized migration more difficult (Ramírez & Mendoza, 2013). Colombian migration did not shift after these immigration policy changes but continued to increase—peaking in 2001 with a sustained level until the great economic recession of 2008, when immigration more generally slowed significantly for most groups. Today, Colombians continue to migrate, and the motivations for migrating include economic opportunity, "personal security," professional opportunity, and family reunification. Many Colombians continue to struggle with navigating life as undocumented or "out of status" and also reformulating their lives in response to changes in their documentation status.

These two factors intersect to create unique experiences for Colombian migrants and shape their response to their criminalization. With a significant portion of Colombians experiencing life as undocumented at one point or another, Colombian migrants in the United States should be understood as operating in relation to two different notions of criminality—that of the undocumented migration based on a racialized system of immigration (Ngai, 2004) and that of the narcotrafficker (Guarnizo, Sanchez, & Roach, 2001). The intersection of these two forms of criminality are then explored in cases from my ethnographic work that illuminate migrants' experiences shaped by this double criminalization of "illegal" migrant and drug trafficking.

The various cultural representations of the war on drugs circulate in a wide variety of cultural products in both English and Spanish, collectively referenced as "narcocultures" (Cabañas, 2014). As a group inextricably tied to drug trafficking, Colombians find that these representations shape their experiences in the United States. The Colombian government has dedicated significant material resources to rebrand the image of Colombia and distance Colombia from narcotrafficking. "The Colombian government, its citizens, as well as informed foreigners are increasingly founding, funding, participating in, and supporting programs that present an image of them as peaceful and peace loving people in stark contrast to the violence represented by the media" (Nasser, 2008, p. 15). Colombia es Pasión used millions of taxpayer dollars to create the image of Colombia as ready for investment and tourist-friendly (Rojas-Sotelo, 2014).

Programs to counter the representations of narcotrafficking and endemic violence are funded through branding or marketing efforts by the Colombian government. Even so, the reach of programs like Colombian es Pasión are limited and did not get taken up more widely in U.S. media, and the notions of Colombians being involved in drug trafficking and drug-related violence continue to mark Colombians living in the United States as migrants who threaten the nation.

Many Colombians also respond to these perceptions of criminal association with the drug trade portrayed in U.S. popular culture by advancing contrasting positive discourses or representations. This governmental effort to change the close association of Colombia with drugs and narcoviolence is accompanied by the deep investments by both elite and working-class Colombians to change these associations, a project in which diasporic Colombians also invest heavily. During my interviews, most Colombian migrants wanted to convey to others their images of their country by highlighting what they saw as its best representatives.

Alejandro Quintero is a 62-year-old man who has lived in Jackson Heights and Brooklyn for more than 25 years since arriving to New York City in 1984. After discussing his life experiences leaving the Cauca Valley, living in another country, and then arriving in the United States, he felt it was urgent to discuss the perception of Colombians. In response to my question "What do you think others should know about the Colombians here in Queens?," he replied:

> In the United States, and in the whole world, they have to know that most, almost all of the Colombians are good, are honest, are hard workers and peaceful people. They have to understand about the good things, of the great personalities that exist in Colombia and, similarly, here in the United States, people who are a part of NASA, people who have demanding jobs that require guts to do them, people . . . I think that the head of security for Bloomberg or of the police here who are Colombian. There are so many people, they are smart, Colombian scientists, businesspeople, good people, noble people, clean people, right? We need to erase the stereotypes that all Colombians are *narcotraficantes*, nor are we criminals [*malhechores*], and not all our women are prostitutes.

In a similar vein, Maria Marin, a 67-year-old woman who has lived in the New York metro region since 1973, noted that:

> I have been able to see the Latino community grow and the Colombian community which had many different businesses . . . but at the same time it

began changing the *ambiente* [atmosphere] of the neighborhood of Queens. There were lots of conflicts because of the narcotrafficking for many different reasons. But things changed, the economy changed significantly, and it became more difficult to acquire a property, the business[es] changed the social groups they served.

Maria notes the way in which Queens changed during the years of the narcoboom economy in the 1980s and laments some of the changes. Narcotrafficking changed the economy, property values, and relationships with other Latino groups but also was notable for its decadence. During this time, though, the Colombian community was also more visible through businesses bearing names like "El Cali Viejo" that were obviously references to particular Colombian regions or cities or to Colombian culture.

These changes, for Maria, were significant in changing the character of the entire neighborhood. On one hand, Maria was happy to see Colombians visible on the landscape and having opportunities to work in local businesses, but she was concerned about the stigma of narcotrafficking that unfavorably marked the entire area and its Colombian residents. She wanted others to know what it meant to be Colombian. She defined this as:

> Well . . . it's the demonstration that we are a group of people who have many abilities and energy to do them, but something we are missing a lot is unity. And to be Colombian is to demonstrate that we have everyone in every camp who we develop and that we feel proud of who we are, but doing things well. Educating ourselves, showing that we can, because our cause is deteriorating, the image that we have of Colombia, has been very badly exploited.

Maria calls out for unity and for others to counter the exploitation of narcotrafficking associated with Colombians. She does this out of a concern for the neighborhood and in the hope of creating unity within the Colombian community.

The project of countering this criminalization as a drug trafficker or as being associated with drugs shapes the way in which many Colombians interpret their experiences of migration, present themselves, and narrate their experiences in the United States as migrants. Maria's call for unity, however, is unusual in that Colombians as a group are very fragmented and exhibit less unity than other groups. The isolation and fragmentation produced in response to the stigma and shame of narcotrafficking produces a particular strategy in some cases.

## ASPIRATIONAL WHITENESS

Colombian migrants respond to these pressures in different ways—but consistent with Guarnizo's work is an attempt to create distance. "How newcomers imagine themselves and are imagined by the larger society in relation to the nation is mediated through representations of immigrants lives in media coverage" (Chavez, 2008, p. 6). Guarnizo, Sanchez, and Roach (2001) note that the stigma associated with drug trafficking shapes Colombian social formations in the United States, where Colombians tend to isolate and distance themselves from other Colombians with a persistent mistrust for other Colombians and government. In Colombia, certain topics such as drug trafficking and politics are avoided in everyday discussion, but the impact of distancing from topics does not translate into an intensely isolated society—this isolation, though, is one quality of migrant life reported by many Colombians. In the United States this avoidance of the stigma extends to distancing from other Colombians. This turning away from Colombians, and other Latinos, results in "aspirational whiteness," which entails the embrace of Anglo-American cultural norms and ideas without the material benefits of propertied whiteness. The case of Flor provides an excellent example. For Flor, a Columbian from a small town near Medellin in Antioquia currently living in northern New Jersey, this strategy creates a deep sense of isolation from other groups but offers her the "safety" of being removed from the stigma of narcoculture.

Flor works in building maintenance for a local nonprofit that offers social services to low-income women. Flor, who is in her fifties, is very light-skinned with light eyes and graying salt-and-pepper hair. Despite having lived in areas with large numbers of other Latinos and African American residents, Flor presently lives in an all-white area with many second- and third-generation Italian and Polish immigrants. When I inquired about why she chose that area, she noted that other Latinos were noisy with their music and African Americans were loud. In our less structured exchanges she would share blatantly racist remarks. In the 2008 U.S. presidential election in which Barack Obama ran as a candidate for the Democratic Party, she voted for the Republican candidate,

John McCain, because of her dislike for Obama. She also admitted that she did not vote for Obama the second time around because he was African American but could not bring herself to vote for Romney due to his "self-deportation" comments.

Although Flor is a naturalized citizen, she knows many undocumented migrants and is very sympathetic to politicians who can address the needs of the Latino community. Her own experiences as a Latina in the United States for many years are also marked by a lack of class mobility and marginalization. She had a markedly unprivileged background in Colombia and has improved her economic situation greatly through migration. Even so, being a Spanish-dominant Latina has proved to present many challenges.

Flor migrated to the United States in 1982 to marry her husband, who was a technical worker during the 1970s and 1980s. In Colombia, she worked in lamp and textile factories and also bought and resold household products. Soon after arriving in the United States Flor began working again. The death of her husband was traumatic for her, as she was thrown into having to fend for herself. She had relied principally on her husband for economic stability, even though she always worked. Her limited English capability has posed a special challenge for her in her life in the United States. However, her lack of familiarity with different policies and legal systems is the deeper challenge. She has difficulty using these systems to advocate for her needs. For example, Flor was unable to keep their home due to pressure from her husband's relatives and decided not to assert her rights as his spouse. She asserts, "I could have kept it, but I didn't want to have to fight his family." However, she was left, in her terms, "floating" and "without direction," with no home. She ended up living in housing for low-income women, where she was able to access support and social services. Flor did not speak extensively about this experience. Now Flor has a relatively stable full-time job with good benefits. She works three jobs in building maintenance or cleaning—one full-time job, a contract job, and a couple of regular clients for housecleaning. Her health suffers, and she has serious injuries from the physical strain of her work.

This work, however, is easier than many of her previous jobs in factories, and her current work in building maintenance also secures her a very modest basement apartment in her desired all-white neighborhood. She is a marginal member of these communities in many senses due to being a Spanish-dominant speaker and of limited economic means. I would like to note that Flor is very proud of her accomplishments as a product of her work and ingenuity. With relatively more material and financial stability than would be accessible to her in Colombia as a widow/single woman, she has been very successful at saving and buying an apartment in a more desirable middle-class area back in Medellin, where she hopes to retire. Her financial situation is greatly aided by her late husband's pension from working in telecommunications for more than 20 years, but even so she has modest means and has accumulated little for retirement here in the United States. Like many migrants Flor has sent most her of earnings back to Colombia, investing in a few small properties. Many of these enterprises tend to be more complicated, because her business dealings there require her to rely heavily on family members in Medellin—many of whom are more interested in their own dealings than with her concerns.

In addition, Flor and her family have experienced firsthand some of the trauma of the violence in Colombia. Two of Flor's family members were shot and killed while visiting the countryside. This experience changed her profoundly and polarized her against the guerrillas in Colombia. She rarely speaks about politics or the state of civil conflict in Colombia but attributes the problems to narcotraffickers and guerrillas. Flor is aware of her extreme position, stating that she is friends with anyone who is against the people who executed two of her family members at their country house. Flor is suspicious of other Colombians and tends to associate with a very limited, mostly Anglo-American group of people in her daily life.

Her work requires little English or contact with others, and her social relationships are almost exclusively with other Colombians or members of the local ethnic Italian or Polish communities who she has come into contact with doing housecleaning work on the side. Light-skinned, she is often able to "pass" for Polish or Italian if she does not speak. Although Flor is exceedingly resourceful, she also laments not having stronger English abilities or studying when she was younger. She describes her English as "*muy malo*," because she never achieved more advanced levels of reading or writing in English and has limited comfort speaking with strangers. Despite this, she insists that the only way in which English presents a barrier is that she cannot conduct some routine occasional tasks, particularly over the phone, without assistance. For these sorts of activities, she relies heavily on her two social networks for information and support. Even so, Flor is very isolated, with little daily contact with others.

However, tensions with an African American manager at her full-time job were very telling. This employee works in a horizontal supervisory capacity, sharing responsibilities for the operation of an area for which Flor is charged with providing basic maintenance. Flor refuses to accept any authority that this employee manager might have over her in the work setting. She asserts that the manager is lazy, stupid, and "doesn't know what she is doing," because she has been transitioning into the position from a welfare-to-work program. In passing conversation Flor takes every opportunity to disparage this woman. In addition, it is also clear to Flor that the woman expresses clear anti-immigrant sentiments. Flor believes that this woman intentionally tries not to understand Flor's English and attempts to make her feel stupid by making her repeat her words multiple times, saying that she does not understand. There are clear tensions between the two women in the workplace, aggravated by competition, cultural differences, and lack of communication.

In an interview, though, Flor was extremely evasive about race, saying she knew "those kind of people" and thought everyone was equal. She readily reiterated a color-blind discourse, literally saying, "I don't look at skin color, just the person." At the same time, Flor will express blatantly racist ideas. One day I accompanied Flor to the airport to drop off a friend. The American Airlines Airport luggage handler, an older African American man, was nearly systemic in taking his time to process the suitcase. The three of us waited a long time on the curb for the man to attend to us while a long line formed behind us. He did not make eye contact with us, asked the passenger who spoke with a slight accent to repeat herself multiple times, and clearly was disinterested in further engagement with us, his customers. Flor was visibly impatient, pacing, sighing, and making faces to communicate that she was very annoyed. As we pulled away, sharing our frustrations at the amount of time the whole process took, she interjected, "That's why they were slaves." Her blatantly racist remarks were shocking. I engaged her in a debate in which she revealed that "I am not like those people, who are lazy and stupid." Again, Flor turned to mobilizing and reiterating stereotypes because she felt discriminated against by African Americans. Her racial hatred was over the top and provoked a strong response from me in clarifying what she meant. The logic she revealed was indefensible, but she also compared how hard she worked to please customers and clients in her maintenance role.

What motivates her to make such statements? Her exclamations do mobilize white supremacy, but to what end? What does it result in for Flor? The tension that provokes her statements often has to do with her own experience of subjugation as an immigrant. In the case of her coworker, she nearly quit, and the situation nearly resulted in some disciplinary action against her. While she mobilizes these discourses, they are also discourses that can work against her as an immigrant, and they are often in response to nativism as it is deployed against her—particularly around language. In her interview, Flor recounts that the most difficult thing about her experience as a migrant is the language. In both cases, her responses are provoked by a defense of her efforts to communicate.

It is easy to dismiss her inflammatory racist remarks as problematic because she is deploying the logics of white supremacy uncritically. Even so, Flor's exclamations are petitions for inclusion into whiteness, and her inclusion into such structures is marginal at best. She is a service worker in white environments—she is neither empowered in these circumstances nor is she able to reap many of the benefits in this status. She does not control the terms of her engagement, and her limited English skills make them challenging to navigate. Her experience is not even honorary whiteness, because she has little to no economic mobility in her engagement with whites. Rather, as her embodied capacities change, she experiences more exclusion, because she is unable to work in physical jobs as she did when she was younger. Her whiteness is marginal at best—one that I characterize as aspirational and not material. Flor is marked by her status as a racialized immigrant who is Spanish dominant. This, though, she prefers to immersing herself in nearby Union City among other Colombians, Cubans, or other Latino groups.

This distancing strategy resonates with the findings on social fragmentation among Colombians by (Guarnizo et al., 2001). While Flor looks to distance herself from other Latinos, Colombians, and other groups of color, her intense isolation is produced in relation to the double bind of criminality she faces as a Colombian immigrant in the United States.

As a Colombian woman her ability to embrace other Colombians and Latinos is circumscribed by the suspicion, shame, and trauma of the stigma of narcotrafficking violence. By distancing herself from the "bad immigrants," she offers herself as a "good immigrant" and a "good Colombian" in contrast to the bad immigrants and bad Colombians. This racial performance of aspirational whiteness, however, is provoked by the double bind in which she finds herself. Rather, it is produced in response to the terms offered by the deep racial investments of migrant criminalization discourses.

### CONCLUSION

Colombians are perceived to not only pose a double threat to the nation as morally corrupt, contaminating outsiders connected to a wide drug cartel network that threatens to "infect" U.S. society with indiscriminate terror and violence but also as part of the homogenous "Latino" group threatening to overrun the southern border of the United States. As carriers of Latin American culture and the Spanish language, Colombians blend into the homogeneous grouping of "Hispanic." This grouping, details Chavez (2008), posits that all Latinos, including U.S.-born groups like Chicanos, are invaders and outside the imagined national community waiting to reconquer the country. This imaginary scenario of Latinos taking over the country creates a false distinction between American and Latino by creating a boundary of whiteness synonymous with American-ness. Following this social imaginary, when present inside the nation, then, Latinos are perceived as a threat to the larger community, where Latino belonging is always illegitimate and inassimilable.

Within the experience of Colombian migration to the United States, migrant criminality creates a set of experiences heavily invested in decency, goodness, and assimilation. Some strategies used by Colombian migrants include social distancing, aspirational whiteness, and efforts to celebrate and document the "good Colombians" in the United States. The heavy investments in projecting "goodness" over "badness" impacts undocumented immigrants even more so. For Colombian migrants there is intense secrecy around anyone who has an undocumented status. This shame and secrecy may prevent them from seeking necessary services, engaging in local communities, and building a strong support network. Even documented migrant or citizens continue to live some of the profound impacts of this stigma—as seen in the case of Flor.

The many small Colombian-run businesses thriving in the Jackson Heights commercial landscape make the Colombian presence visible in Queens, New York. This visibility in the urban landscape, though, is not matched by visibility of or unity among individuals within the Colombian community. Colombian migrants in New York experience the distress of migration and fight high levels of isolation and invisibility that characterize life in the United States as marked by solitude. In particular, undocumented Colombians live experiences of intense isolation. The challenge for Colombians in the United States to come together to create and address solutions to overcome this extreme economic and social marginalization is significant. In this respect, there is important work for community leaders, service providers, and policy makers to address the trauma of this fragmentation and social isolation for Colombian migrants.

### REFERENCES

Bérube, M. (2005). Colombia: In the crossfire. Washington, DC: Migration Information Service, Migration Policy Institute. Retrieved from http://www.migrationpolicy.org/article/colombia-crossfire.

Cabañas, M. A. (2014). Imagined Narcoscapes: Narcoculture and the Politics of Representation. *Latin American Perspectives, 41*(2), 3–17.

Cepeda, M. E. (2010). *Musical imagiNation U.S.-Colombian identity and the Latin music boom*. New York: New York University Press.

Chaney, E. (1977). Colombian outpost in New York City. *Society, 14*(6), 60–64.

Chavez, L. R. (2008). *The Latino threat: Constructing immigrants, citizens, and the nation*. Stanford, CA: Stanford University Press.

Colombian Ministry of External Relations. (2008). "Colombians in the exterior: Cuantos son y dónde estan?" Retrieved from www.minrelext.gov.co.

Colombian Ministry of External Relations. (2013). "Fortalecimiento de Políticas Públicas para la atención y vinculación de colombianos en el Exterior: Resumen Ejecutivo Proyecto de Inversión 2013." Retrieved from https://www.cancilleria.gov.co/sites/default/files/informe-ejecutivo-2013-vinculacion-colombianos-exterior.pdf.

Gaviria, A. (2004). *Visa USA: Fortunas y estravios de los migrantes Colombianos en los Estados Unidos* (Vol. 17). Bogota: University of Los Andes.

Guarnizo, L. E., Sanchez, A. I., & Roach, E. (2001). Mistrust, fragmented solidarity, and transnational migration: Colombians in New York City and Los Angeles. *Ethnic and Racial Studies, 22*(2), 367–396.

International Organization for Migration. (2010). The future of migration: Building Capacities for Change. In K. Koser & F. Laczko (Eds.), *World Migration Report 2010*.

Geneva, Switzerland: International Organization for Migration (IOM). Retrieved from http://publications.iom.int/bookstore/free/WMR_2010_ENGLISH.pdf.

Logan, J. (2001). *Immigrant enclaves in the American metropolis, 1990–2000*. Albany, NY: Lewis Mumford Center for Comparative Urban and Regional Research.

Nasser, M. R. (2008). *Tra(n)zando identidades: Colombian neighborhoods, images, and narratives from narco-trafficking to beauty queens*. Tulane University.

Ngai, M. M. (2004). *Impossible subjects: Illegal aliens and the making of modern America*. Princeton, NJ: Princeton University Press.

Radio Cadena Nacional. (2010). El 40 de los Colombianos vive en el Exterior Illegalmente. *RADIO CADENA NACIONAL*. Retrieved from http://www.rcnradio.com/noticias/nacional/01-09-10/el-40-de-los-colombianos-vive-en-el-exterior-ilegalmente.

Ramírez H., C., & Mendoza S., L. (2013). Perfil Migratorio de Colombia (pp. 44–47). Bogota, COL: Organización Internacional para las Migraciones.

Rojas-Sotelo, M. L. (2014). Narcoaesthetics in Colombia, Mexico, and the United States Death Narco, Narco Nations, Border States, Narcochingadazo? *Latin American Perspectives, 41*(2), 215–231.

Sassen, S. (1990). *The mobility of labor and capital: A study in international investment and labor flow*. West Nyack, NY: Cambridge University Press.

Stavans, I., & Augenbraum, H. (2005). *Encyclopedia Latina: history, culture, and society in the United States* (Vol. 4). Danbury, CT: Grolier Academic Reference.

Valderrama-Echavarria, C. (2014). *Fragmented ties: Colombian immigrant experiences*. Boise, ID: Boise State University.

# 13

# Mexico's Transmigrants

## BETWEEN LOS ZETAS AND THE IRON FIST OF THE STATE

▸ SONJA WOLF

### INTRODUCTION

MEXICO IS HOME TO DIFFERENT migration dynamics, but the flow of undocumented migrants is the most intense of these. Each year an estimated 140,000 individuals of all ages enter Mexico irregularly (Comisión Interamericana de Derechos Humanos [CIDH], 2013, p. 31), mostly in the hope of crossing into its northern neighbor. Most hail from northern Central America (Honduras, El Salvador, and Guatemala), sometimes pulled by a desire for family reunification but chiefly expelled by deep-seated marginalization and generalized violence. The clandestine journey through Mexico—entailing long walks, interminable bus trips, or hazardous rides on top of cargo trains—exposes them to crimes and horrific abuses at the hands of delinquent groups and corrupt state agents, notably police and migration authorities.

Mexico's focus on the welfare of its own nationals abroad traditionally displaced any concern with the fate of undocumented foreigners within its borders. This situation began to change with the increase in and, thanks to migrant shelters, heightened visibility of migrant rights violations, including kidnappings and extortion. The watershed, however, proved to be the massacre of 72 undocumented migrants in San Fernando, Tamaulipas, in August 2010, perpetrated by the former Gulf cartel *sicarios* Los Zetas to remind *coyotes* of their obligation to pay a quota for each migrant smuggled through their territory (Martínez, 2014a). The tragedy provoked widespread criticism of the government's lax response to what had long been considered a humanitarian crisis.

A 2008 decree had already decriminalized irregular entry into Mexico. But it was in reaction to the now vociferous calls for a more effective and humane migration policy that the Calderón administration (2006–2012) decided to overhaul the applicable normative framework. The 2011 Migration Law and its 2012 regulations constitute an improvement on earlier legislation. Even so, they contain structural flaws, among them adherence to a national security perspective and the detention of undocumented migrants for what is an administrative violation, that continue to make the protection of migrant rights an unfulfilled promise.

More important, perhaps, these reforms have left untouched the policies and practices of the relevant state institutions, particularly but not exclusively, the National Migration Institute (Instituto Nacional de Migración, or INM). A decentralized body within the Secretariat of the Interior, the INM, is tasked with migration management and has privileged the detection, detention, and deportation of undocumented migrants over their rights. U.S. pressure on Mexico to stem these irregular flows underlies this priority, but institutional management shortcomings, especially regarding recruitment and training, supervision and control, sanctions for misconduct, and transparency and accountability, contribute to continued corruption and abuse of migrants.

This chapter explores the experiences of transmigrants in Mexico, including their motivations for abandoning their homelands, the dangers and uncertainties of their voyages, and the difficulties of building new lives in their host nations. It centers on the author's in-depth interviews with two young men, Rudy and Alex, who escaped their native Honduras for different reasons, but whose encounters with Mexico's reality has been equally mixed. The chapter argues that the country has adjusted its legislation and rhetoric on migrant rights, but institutional incapacities permit the continued criminalization of undocumented migrants.

### FLEEING HOME

Some of the children and adolescents who travel north seek to reunite with relatives in the United States. Others cite abuse in the home as a reason for navigating their way through unknown territory (United Nations High Commissioner for Refugees, 2014). More often, however, the dearth of decent education and job opportunities drives youths and adults across frontiers. The overriding factor for the mass exodus from Central America, though, is the stunning level of social and criminal violence. The situation has been especially serious in the northern states, where repressive Mano Dura ("iron fist") policies launched in 2002–2003, ostensibly to crack down on street gangs, have contributed to a sharp rise in murders. In 2013 the national per capita murder rate stood at 34 per 100,000 inhabitants in Guatemala, while the same indicator reached 43 in El Salvador and a staggering 79 in Honduras (Central American Business Intelligence, 2014).

Much of the generalized violence is associated with street gangs, particularly the Los Angeles–born Calle Dieciocho and Mara Salvatrucha. Both groups were formed by Latino youth, including civil war refugees, in response to the discrimination and exclusion they encountered in their host country. Mass deportations of noncitizens imported the gangs into northern Central America, where they absorbed local marginalized youth desperate for respect and social status. Gradually, they developed into more brutal and operationally sophisticated groups, largely due to law enforcement offensives that led to mass detentions of gang members and leaders in segregated prisons (Wolf, 2012). Today they are based in impoverished neighborhoods throughout the affected countries, with an estimated 60,000 affiliates in El Salvador alone (Valencia & Alvarado, 2014).

The two groups are involved chiefly in homicides, extortion, disappearances, and drug sales, although a gang truce announced in El Salvador in March 2012 halved the daily murder rate before its collapse 2 years later. Throughout its lifespan, the ceasefire, in reality a government-sponsored pact designed to cut homicide levels in return for prison privileges, had no discernible impact on disappearances, extortion, and gang harassment (Valencia, 2013). In gang-controlled barrios male youths are targeted for forced recruitment, but females often go through more disturbing experiences. Cliques may choose a girl as a birthday present for one of its members, resulting in the victim's rape by a dozen or more testosterone-charged adolescents (Valencia, 2011). Worse yet, gang members may compel young women to become their spouses, bear their children, and, if necessary, smuggle illicit objects into the prisons and provide inmates with sexual services. Refusals earn the victims and their families certain death (Valencia & Alvarado, 2014).

A growing phenomenon is the forced displacement of entire families. Whereas in some localities, especially rural areas, drug-trafficking groups have turned to land-grabbing (Cantor, 2014), many urban zones have seen the street gangs snatch houses from their rightful owners (Valencia, 2012b). Often, internal relocation is insufficient, and repeated threats push people to abandon their countries entirely. The situation is exacerbated by pervasive corruption and collusion with gangs and organized crime by those tasked with protecting citizens. Many police agents are bribed or coerced into turning a blind eye to illicit pursuits, filtering information, or otherwise collaborating with those they are meant to put behind bars. In Honduras, police corruption has reached critical levels (Valencia, 2012a). Unsurprisingly, Central Americans have little trust in authorities that are ineffective at best and dishonest at worst. In addition to actual victimization, perceptions of insecurity feed intentions to migrate (Hiskey, Malone, & Orcés, 2014).

Twenty-nine year-old Rudy and his seven siblings grew up in Choluteca, a colonial town 83 miles south of the Honduran capital Tegucigalpa. At the age of 13, the loss of his mother constituted an emotional blow that prompted him to drop out of school and leave the family home for a job in construction. However, Rudy never gave up on his hope of one day joining the police force himself and as a 16-year-old entered the academy. When asked how, in light of extensive sleaze in the law enforcement sector, he could have nourished such a dream, Rudy admits: "There is a lot of corruption, and many police die because of bad people or the fight against corruption. But you can be a good police officer." His recollections of his time at the academy, from which he graduated at age 17, oscillate between sadness and nostalgia. "During the training I suffered mistreatment. The rights of the police are not respected. But," Rudy adds proudly, "I was one of the best in my class!"

Since Honduras has no career prison guards, the police exercise this function, and Rudy was soon dispatched to the Tamara Central Prison outside Tegucigalpa. Tasked with making the roll calls, he was in frequent contact with the Dieciocho members held there. After 10 months, they asked for weapons and drugs to be smuggled into the premises in return for a financial compensation. Rudy declined, and the bribes were substituted with threats. After a while, these were followed by warnings that his family would come to harm if his stubbornness continued. In order not to jeopardize the safety of his relatives, Rudy ceased all contact with his family, stopped going out, and started sleeping in the barracks.

For nine years, these were the circumstances of his life. Rudy's efforts to avoid a premature death worsened when a fellow police officer was killed. In late 2011, senior officers ordered that firearms be unlawfully removed from police headquarters. Rudy's friend worked the shift and noted down the irregularities in the police log. His integrity cost him his life, as those behind the theft subsequently orchestrated his murder. When the threats to Rudy himself intensified, he concluded that his departure from Honduras had become inevitable. His hope to find shelter led him to Mexico, but his attempt to open a new chapter in his life would be fraught with unexpected difficulties and frustrations.

### TRANSITING MEXICO

Each year thousands of transmigrants see their plans foiled when INM agents detain them for deportation. Like Alex, many who were unsuccessful in reaching the United States try again. For those who are held in an INM detention center, the experience constitutes a reminder of Mexico's contemptuous attitude toward unwelcome foreigners. The internment can turn into a prolonged ordeal, especially for certain nationals who file appeals against deportation, such as Cubans who fear imprisonment if returned to the island or individuals who present asylum applications or criminal complaints.

In 2005 the institute was incorporated into the national security system, a designation that has shaped migration agents' training and limited access to information and installations (Wolf, 2013). Although actual prisons must no longer be used for migrant detention, the current facilities nonetheless have a prison-like character. Surrounded by sturdy, high walls and fences that are meant to prevent breakouts, the buildings contain cells and surveillance corridors to control the population. As for independent observers seeking admission, journalists are forbidden access, and nongovernmental organizations (NGOs) wishing to conduct human rights monitoring or provide legal services face serious difficulties in obtaining the necessary authorization. This lack of transparency permits abuse and misconduct to go largely unnoticed. INM detention centers are more modern and offer improved conditions than used to be the case. Even so, frequent overcrowding requires many migrants to sleep on cement floors and affects hygiene.

The treatment of migrants, however, is of greater concern and entails systematic human rights violations. These include the denial of detention-related information; limited telephone communication; the discouragement of complaints, appeals, or asylum applications; unsatisfactory food standards; inadequate medical services; and a lack of specialized care for vulnerable groups (Wolf, 2013). Agents also resort to verbal and physical mistreatment as well as illicit activities such as extortion, drug sales, and sexual exploitation (Observatorio de Migración, 2014). All of this is possible due to poor oversight and ineffective sanctions for misconduct.

Twenty-three year-old Alex hails from the Honduran town of Choloma, situated some 11 miles north of San Pedro Sula, the most violent city on earth (Consejo Ciudadano para la Seguridad Pública y Justicia Penal, 2014). Born into a campesino family, he and his seven siblings lost their mother during childhood. His life remained uneventful until another family in the area, operating as a criminal gang, murdered two of his brothers and injured a third. In August 2012, when the violence had begun to affect him directly, Alex left his country with the intention of reaching the United States. His journey, however, only took him as far as the southern Mexican state of Chiapas. There he was stopped by INM agents and transferred to the Siglo XXI detention center in Tapachula to await his deportation.

Alex remembers his short stay in the installation with abhorrence. "The center was overcrowded, and people had to sleep on the floor, some without mattresses. Not only were we given little food, but the showers were clogged, and there was no privacy in the bathrooms." But what Alex recalls most clearly is a demonstration of the disproportionate use of force against unarmed individuals. "The center was congested. Many migrants had been there for weeks, because the INM argued that no transport was available. Some people got desperate and started to burn mattresses. One guy wanted to climb over the fence. A security guard threatened to shoot him, but some migration agents intervened to control the situation. Generally, though, people's complaints aren't heard." Alex's expulsion from Mexico occurred after only four days. Like everyone else on the bus, he was dropped at the Guatemala/Honduras border, but the danger awaiting him in his hometown made his return impossible. And so, like most deportees that day, he immediately embarked on his next trip north.

Undocumented migrants experience ill-treatment in detention, yet those who manage to traverse parts or all of Mexico often suffer unimagined horrors. The existence of this road lined with cruelty and corruption says much about the country's respect for the rights and dignity of defenseless individuals. Regardless of their means of travel, irregular migrants are susceptible to robberies, sexual violence, kidnappings, extortion, torture, homicides, and disappearances (CIDH, 2013). The magnitude of the problem is impossible to ascertain, as most of these crimes go unreported, but abductions alone are estimated to exceed 20,000 a year (Comisión Nacional de los Derechos Humanos, 2011, p. 12). The abuse occurs with impunity, because the state human rights commissions are ineffective in defending migrant rights, and the justice system is largely inadequate in investigating and successfully prosecuting offenses. Victims can apply for a free, 1-year humanitarian visa that allows them to remain in the country legally while pursuing criminal complaints. However, it is difficult to obtain for those unfamiliar with the procedure and is often denied, as the INM worries that migrants may fake a crime in order to obtain the authorization and continue traveling to the United States (Wolf, 2013).

The actors responsible for the harm that comes to irregular foreigners include criminal networks and corrupt state agents, notably police and migration officers, who extort migrants, accept bribes at checkpoints, or collaborate with kidnappers. It is impossible to ignore, however, the role that organized crime has come to play in the contemporary migrant industry. *Coyotes* used to accompany their paying clients to the final destination, but the business irrevocably changed when drug-trafficking groups responded to President Calderón's drug war by diversifying their criminal portfolio. Los Zetas, in particular, has established control over smuggling routes and requires *coyotes* to pay a quota for each migrant crossing their territory. A migrant traveling from El Salvador to the United States is charged at least $7,000 for the entire trip, including transportation, accommodation, food, and the inevitable bribes and quotas (Martínez, 2014b). Many smugglers turn out to be swindlers who violate the agreements and may abandon their customers along the way or relinquish them to Los Zetas. The latter torture their victims in "safe houses" to extract telephone numbers and demand a ransom or force them to move drugs across the border (Martínez, 2014b).

On the first occasion Alex traveled with a Mexican *coyote* who absconded after an installment of the $5,000 fee that was meant to get him to Houston did not come through. He initiated his second trip alone, but in Chiapas happened upon a friend who made the passage with a Honduran *coyote*. Alex joined the group in Palenque and made a down payment of $1,000. In the center of Mexico he persuaded his relatives to wire another payment, but their reluctance to keep disbursing large sums of money grew as the journey progressed. On the way north to Celaya, in the mining state of Guanajuato, the group of three Hondurans and four Salvadorans was stopped at two federal police checkpoints but was waved through after providing the officers with the code word *el tío* ("the uncle") the *coyote* had given them. In Celaya another $1,000 had to be wired to a Western Union branch for transportation to Piedras Negras. After a brief stop at a ranch, it was in this border town in the Zetas-dominated state of Coahuila where Alex's nightmare began.

In Piedras Negras, taxis took them to a safe house that was already holding some 15 Mexican and Central American migrants. The victims, visibly beaten, had spent the past three weeks awaiting the fulfillment of extortion demands. In the jam-packed, sweltering edifice the new arrivals had their hands bound and had to supply telephone numbers amid warnings that nonpayment would cost the migrants their lives. As his next of kin arduously made wire transfers totaling $1,800, Alex spent 27 days with little food and water and no shower, sleeping on the floor. When more migrants were brought to a place that was already filled beyond capacity, his group was dumped at the banks of the Río Bravo. Alex and his companions crossed the river at night but got lost in the desert and returned to Piedras Negras. A local migrant shelter received them, and at the insistence of its director, they reported the kidnappings to the attorney general's office.

The attorney's staff relocated the complainants to Mexico City, where they spent the first 4 months at a migrant shelter while they waited for their humanitarian visas to be issued. Sin Fronteras, a Mexico City–based NGO working on migration and refugee issues, supported them financially during this time. The authorities opened investigations, but these eventually stalled. In July 2013, Alex was summoned to identify one of the presumed kidnappers, but he was only permitted to make a voice recognition and could not positively identify the suspect. Alex remains eager to obtain justice and recover his money, but he was never contacted again by the attorney general's office and is unsure how to follow up on his complaint. Although the case remains open, the INM refused to renew his humanitarian visa. Unable to obtain any other form of authorization, Alex lost his legal status in the country but decided to remain in Mexico City.

## LIVING IN MEXICO

The 2011 Law on Refugees and Complementary Protection and its 2012 regulations constitute the legal basis for asylum claims. The recent legislation established a more formal and detailed procedure and introduced a human rights perspective into asylum eligibility and refugee assistance. Importantly, an exclusion clause allows the authorities to reject asylum applications if the claimant provides insufficient supporting evidence or has committed serious crimes, such as homicide or firearms and drug trafficking. The agency tasked with resolving asylum cases, the Mexican Commission for Refugee Assistance (Comisión Mexicana de Ayuda a Refugiados, or COMAR), was created in 1980 to deal with the influx of Central American civil war refugees. Once these refugees had returned home or settled in Mexico, the COMAR shrank in size and resources. An autonomous entity within the Secretariat of the Interior, it has about 40 staff and maintains only three offices in Mexico City, Tapachula at the Mexico-Guatemala border, and Acayucan at the Gulf Coast (B. Pérez, personal communication, July 11, 2014).

Asylum seekers can approach either a COMAR office or, if detained, channel the application through the INM. Often, migration agents discourage such requests or claimants abandon these after tiring of the confinement and the abuse it entails (A. Nigenda, personal communication, July 11, 2014). After receiving the claimant's initial declaration, the agency issues a certificate that grants legal status in Mexico, prepares its investigations and interviews, and finally issues a resolution that, if negative, can be appealed. For applicants the process is challenging, as the certificate bars them from engaging in remunerated work and, silenced by fear or detention, they often find it difficult to gather the necessary evidence. The COMAR insists that it undertakes scrupulous investigations (B. Pérez, personal communication, July 11, 2014), but according to NGOs its resolutions are mostly based on Mexican consulates' Wikipedia-style reports (A. Nigenda, personal communication, June 12, 2014).

Many asylum seekers, given their limited education and difficulty in understanding the technical nature of the procedure, require legal representation but struggle to obtain it (M. García, personal communication, June 12, 2014). In INM detention centers, access to legal practitioners is complicated. Furthermore, few lawyers specialize in migration and asylum law, much less work on a pro bono basis. Currently, only Sin Fronteras in Mexico City and the Fray Matías de Córdova Human Rights Center in Tapachula offer legal aid to asylum seekers. Since the volume of applications exceeds their capacity to respond, the NGOs are selective in choosing their cases and when assigning inexperienced volunteers or law students, may do their clients a disservice (B. Pérez, personal communication, July 11, 2014). The COMAR, for its part, has been accused of doctoring individuals' declarations in order to deny them asylum (A. Nigenda, personal communication, June 12, 2014), a charge that the agency itself has strongly rejected (B. Pérez, personal communication, July 11, 2014). It is hard to determine how and why this might occur, since access to case files is restricted so as not to jeopardize asylum seekers' safety. But the ensuing lack of transparency certainly facilitates procedural defects and human rights violations.

Since 2008 Mexico has seen an increase in asylum claims, particularly by Central Americans fleeing street gangs, organized crime, and domestic violence (B. Pérez, personal communication, July 11, 2014). Between 2009 and 2013 the number of applications grew by 90.5%, mostly by nationals from Honduras (27.5%), El Salvador, and Guatemala. During the same period, only 1,134 requests, less than 25% of a total of 4,589 requests, were granted (Montalvo, 2014). It is open to conjecture why few responses are favorable. Can the individuals not provide convincing evidence of the danger they face at home? Are the Mexican authorities concerned that the beneficiaries might travel onward to the United States or that a rise in successful applications by a certain profile of asylum seeker might open the floodgates to refugees, including Central Americans escaping generalized violence?

Armed with survival skills but otherwise limited education and experience, Rudy crossed from Guatemala into Tenosique, a Zetas stronghold in the state of Tabasco, and rode on the cargo train to the center of the country. Once he got to Mexico City, he spent 3 days living on the streets before finding temporary lodging with the Salvation Army. Staff helped him locate the offices of Sin Fronteras, and the NGO's lawyers agreed to help him prepare his asylum application. The process before the COMAR took almost three months, during which time Rudy received a one-off financial support of 470 pesos and was housed in a migrant shelter. The agency sought evidence of the threats against him, some of which, such as bullet scars, he was unable to provide, and eventually the application was rejected on grounds of nonsubstantiation. Rudy found that the wording and content of his declaration had been amended, but Sin Fronteras deemed it too difficult to prove the text had been tampered with and decided against an appeal. Subsequently, he set out to renew his visa, a process that would take many months with no certain outcome, and as time went by his frustration and loneliness intensified. For Rudy, as for Alex, the disappointments multiplied as integration into the job market and Mexican society proved more challenging than expected.

For much of Mexico's population the labor outlook is mixed. Since formal jobs grow insufficiently, many people are required to toil in the informal sector, which is characterized by precarious working conditions, low wages, and no benefits. The situation is more taxing for refugees and undocumented migrants, who are more susceptible to discrimination and exploitation than Mexican citizens. Many refugees, particularly more recent arrivals, have access to basic services but can afford only basic, rented housing in insecure areas. One of the chief obstacles they face in building a new life is access to stable and well-remunerated employment. Often, they find themselves performing semiskilled manual labor with an average monthly income of 7,000 pesos or less (Cobo & Fuerte, 2012). Many report discrimination at the workplace, such as differential wages based on gender and nationality, overtime without extra pay, no benefits, and sexual harassment (Alto Comisionado de las Naciones Unidas para los Refugiados, 2013).

His attempts to support himself financially during his asylum process led Rudy to several jobs, all of which were poorly compensated and entailed no small measure of bigotry and abuse. Initially, he spent several months at a wholesale food market where he was supposed to work 9-hour shifts selecting potatoes for sale in return for 1,000 pesos a week without benefits. However, he ended up regularly working 15 hours or more a day, had to clean up the waste water, and was permitted few meal and bathroom breaks. Whereas the Mexican helpers earned up to 1,500 pesos per week with benefits, the Central Americans were advised that foreigners had to expect a lower pay. Subsequently, Rudy was hired by a woman judge to wash her car, do repair work in the house, and assist in the kitchen. Initially promised a weekly wage of 1,000 pesos, he had to work 15-hour stints and deal with growing verbal abuse and ill-treatment. When the job ended after three weeks, he was rewarded with a total of only 600 pesos. As he pondered his circumstances, Rudy burst into tears. "It's not just the pay that matters, but also the treatment. I can't stand the abuse and lack of respect. But migrants have to live like that, because they don't have a choice. I came to Mexico with the intention of studying, because I don't know much besides handling guns. But now I'm thinking of risking everything, of going to the United States. I don't have a life here."

Upon arrival in Mexico City, Alex searched unsuccessfully for stable employment. Time and again he secured odd jobs in construction, removals, and newspaper delivery that earned him 100 pesos a day. On other occasions, however, he was unable to claim his promised wage. Alex still remembers the disappointment he felt at the time. "As a foreigner, you can't defend yourself. If you complain, they threaten to notify the migration authorities." Meanwhile, Alex moved in with his Mexican girlfriend, a change that provided him with an important degree of moral and financial support. As his job situation remained bleak, he teamed up with three other migrants to start a food business. A one-off government aid permitted them to launch the venture, but the group is unsure how to make it sustainable and expand it. Alex tried once more to legalize his status in Mexico but could not meet the onerous visa requirements. In these testing circumstances, Alex can neither visit or financially support his family in Honduras nor repay the debt he incurred for the *coyotes'* services.

### CONCLUSION

The victimization of undocumented migrants begins in their home countries, nations, like in Central America, where opportunities for advancement are sparse, generalized violence displaces entire families, and street gangs forcibly recruit youths. The abuse continues during the transit through Mexico, where irregular foreigners fall prey to both criminal networks and corrupt state agents. Migrant shelters and human rights defenders play an invaluable role in providing humanitarian assistance and publicizing the barbarism that stains the migrant trail. Even so, Mexico has proved unable or unwilling to break the chain of complicities that allows the greed and terror to continue. Rather than translating the rhetorical commitment to migrant rights into policy and institutional practice, the authorities keep prioritizing curbs on undocumented migrant flows.

Given Mexico's geographical position and the United States' overbearing influence over the region, the search for a more effective and humane migration policy is necessarily complicated. Nonetheless, the country cannot avoid embarking on a fresh approach to the subject both domestically and in its relations with its neighbors. Viewing migration through a national security lens unhelpfully depicts irregular migrants as a threat to the integrity of the state. Instead of implementing harsh controls that endanger people's lives, Mexico needs to move toward adequate border controls and respect for the rights of migrants irrespective of their legal status.

The institutions tasked with migration and refugee affairs, notably the INM and COMAR, require more effective, and ideally, external oversight so that corruption and human rights violations can be reduced. Public servants who are found guilty of misconduct need to face sanctions so that impunity does not fester and the detected practices do not recur. In the case of the COMAR this may require the segmentation of the asylum procedure so that the agency, currently judge and jury, is not solely responsible for receiving and assessing applications as well as resolving appeals.

Mexico and its partners will need to agree on a regional migration policy that manages to balance labor demands with individuals' rights to education, work, and a life free from harm. Migrant-sending nations, for their part, have yet to find a sustainable way of transforming communities and diminishing social and criminal violence so that people are not forced to leave their homes. Donor assistance could usefully support local development and institutional strengthening, rather than border security. Achieving only small advances in any of these areas will take time. The question remains whether governments can muster the political will to begin confronting these challenges in earnest or whether they will continue to administer them and leave their successors with an intractable problem.

### REFERENCES

Alto Comisionado de las Naciones Unidas para los Refugiados. (2013). *Ser una persona refugiada en México*. Mexico City, Mexico: Author.

Cantor, D. J. (2014). The new wave: Forced displacement caused by organized crime in Central America and Mexico. *Refugee Survey Quarterly, 33*(3), 34–68.

Central American Business Intelligence. (2014). Violencia homicida en El Salvador, Guatemala y Honduras. Retrieved on July 10, 2014, from http://ca-bi.com/blackbox.

Cobo, S., & Fuerte, P. (2012). *Refugiados en México*. Mexico City, Mexico: Secretaría de Gobernación & Alto Comisionado de las Naciones Unidas para los Refugiados.

Comisión Interamericana de Derechos Humanos (CIDH). (2013). *Derechos humanos de los migrantes y otras personas en el contexto de la movilidad humana*. Washington, DC: Author.

Comisión Nacional de los Derechos Humanos. (2011). *Informe especial sobre secuestro de migrantes en México*. Mexico City, Mexico: Author.

Consejo Ciudadano para la Seguridad Pública y Justicia Penal. (2014). *Las 50 ciudades más violentas del mundo en 2013*. Mexico City, Mexico: Author.

Hiskey, J., Malone, M., & Orcés, D. (2014). *Violence and migration in Central America* (AmericasBarometer Insights, Number 101). Retrieved on July 15, 2014, from www.vanderbilt.edu/lapop/insights/IO901en.pdf.

Martínez, Ó. (2014a, March 24). Los coyotes domados. *El Faro*. Retrieved on March 24, 2014, from www.salanegra.elfaro.net/es/201403/cronicas/15101.

——. (2014b, April 7). La desafortunada historia de un hombre indocumentado, vendido, extorsionado y deportado. *El Faro*. Retrieved on April 7, 2014, from www.salanegra.elfaro.net/es/201404/cronicas/15196.

Montalvo, T. L. (2014, June 20). Refugiados en México, en el olvido y marginados. *Animal Político*. Retrieved on June 20, 2014, from www.animalpolitico.com/2014/06/refugiados-en-mexico-en-el-olvido-y-marginados.

Observatorio de Migración. (2014). *Informe sobre estaciones migratorias del Instituto Nacional de Migración en Iztapalapa, Puebla y Saltillo, 2013*. Mexico City, Mexico: Instituto para la Seguridad y la Democracia.

United Nations High Commissioner for Refugees. (2014). *Children on the run*. Washington, DC: Author.

Valencia, D. (2012a, March 19). Así es la policía del país más violento del mundo. *El Faro*. Retrieved on March 19, 2014, from www.salanegra.elfaro.net /es/201203 /cronicas/7982.

——. (2012b, October 1). La legión de los desplazados. *El Faro*. Retrieved from www.especiales.elfaro.net/es/salanegra_desplazados.

——. (2013, January 21). Los desaparecidos que no importan. *El Faro*. Retrieved on January 21, 2013, from www.salanegra.elfaro.net/es/201301/cronicas/10773.

Valencia, D., & Alvarado, J. (2014, August 17). La región de los que huyen. *El Faro*. Retrieved on August 17, 2014, from www.salanegra.elfaro.net/es/201408 /cronicas/15827.

Valencia, R. (2011, July 24). Yo violada. *El Faro*. Retrieved on July 24, 2014, from www.salanegra.elfaro.net/es/201107/cronicas/4922.

Wolf, S. (2012). Mara Salvatrucha: The most dangerous street gang in the Americas? *Latin American Politics & Society, 54*(1), 65–99.

——. (2013). *Diagnóstico del Instituto Nacional de Migración*. Mexico City, Mexico: Instituto para la Seguridad y la Democracia.

# Stigmatized, Segregated, Essential

*THE POSITION OF IMMIGRANT LIVE-IN CARE WORKERS
VIS-À-VIS FORMAL SOCIAL WORK PROVISION IN ITALY*

▸ PAOLO BOCCAGNI

## INTRODUCTION

IMMIGRANT WORKERS EMPLOYED IN HOME care—most of them women, sometimes in live-in arrangements with dependent elderly as typical clients—play a unique role at the intersection of immigration and social welfare as fields of discourse and practice, in Italy and elsewhere (Williams, 2010). As a result of their pervasive contribution to domiciliary care provision, immigrant women are simultaneously "alien" and "intimate" to the everyday social functioning of a number of Italian households. While their centrality to the social welfare regime is well recognized, immigrant care workers are little if at all recognized as far as *their* welfare needs and claims are concerned. Revisiting their mixed position vis-à-vis professional social work, then, opens up an original and singularly neglected research perspective.

Women from abroad employed in live-in care in Italy have even been given a label of their own: *badanti*—those who "look after," although their work is essentially "care," with strong relational and emotional implications. Generally speaking, their lived experience does not bear the signs of an overt criminalization or not, at least, as compared with several other immigrant categories in the country. However, in the public discourse they are subject to social representations that oscillate between patronizing, orientalizing, and openly stigmatizing tones. At the very least, *badanti* are essentialized as docile, servant-like care workers "naturally" inclined to care for the elderly by virtue of their gender, age, and ethnic traits. As long as they fill a widening niche in social welfare provision, all the aspects of their lives that exceed labor are basically invisibilized. Besides, the processes of criminalization that periodically affect the political discourse on immigration in Italy—as traceable in a number of (often symbolically) xenophobic legal measures and in several instances of hatred speech, but also in immigrants' overexposure to detention (e.g., Cere, 2010; Colombo, 2013; Palidda, 2014)—are likely to affect interethnic relations even when it comes to relatively less "threatening" immigrant profiles, such as the care worker one. Even *badanti* are unlikely to avoid the long-term consequences exerted, at the very least, on commonsense categorizations by a political climate that combines "explicit fanaticism, implicit moderation, and poisoned fruits" (Colombo & Sciortino, 2003).

Against these external categorizations, how migrant care workers frame their conditions, how such conditions interrogate social work practice, and how the latter can be refined along more inclusive and anti-oppressive lines are the questions I address in this chapter. To do so, I build on two sets of life stories of immigrant care workers. The first consists of 165 in-depth interviews—out of a national archive of almost 700—conducted all over Italy between 2005 and 2007 (Catanzaro & Colombo, 2009). For my purposes, the subset of respondents was delimited on the basis of nationality (including those with greater prevalence in domestic work—namely Ukrainians, Romanians, Moldovans, Peruvians, Ecuadorians, and Filipinos); working arrangements (only live-in workers); gender (only women). On average these interviewees were 46 years old and had stayed in Italy for 7 years. The second source is an archive of 30 in-depth life stories of immigrant women employed in live-in care in the local area of Trento and interviewed between 2010 and 2011. Most of them were from Ukraine and Moldova, with an average age of 52 and a length of stay of 8 years (Boccagni & Ambrosini, 2012).

The two archives provide an extended collection of written life stories that touch upon, among other subjects, the interviewees' perceptions of their life conditions and their reported interactions with welfare agencies. Importantly, such topics can be appreciated against the background of respondents' work and migration trajectories. This makes for a rich analysis of issues such as migrants' transnational ties, their family arrangements, the social networks they build upon, their relationships with employers, and so forth.

While obviously not statistically representative, these archives are a valuable source of insights on migrants' perceived conditions, whose implications in the social work area are still understudied. As a way of fueling this debate, I first provide an overview of immigrants' gendered and ethnicized concentration in domestic care work in Italy. I then revisit their narratives to reconstruct the prevalent views of their jobs and of themselves as care workers. The underlying constructions of their own social needs, claims, and rights are also explored. Finally, I briefly discuss the implications of this case study for the care migration–social work nexus.

## IMMIGRANT LIVE-IN CARE WORKERS IN ITALY: THE "HOMELY FACE" OF A STUBBORNLY "IMMIGRANT OTHER"

Migrants' increasing participation in domestic and care work has been a key marker of the growth of immigrants' employment across the Italian labor market over the last decades. While figures about the labor force in this sector are often tricky, current estimates point to about 800,000 foreign-born workers employed in domiciliary care jobs (Pasquinelli & Rusmini, 2013), out of an immigrant population of 4.4 million (Istituto Nazionale di Statistica [ISTAT], 2014). Domestic work at large makes for one immigrant employee out of five and even for one out of two, in the case of female workers. Indeed, while foreign workers correspond to 10.6% of the country's labor force, they make up the majority of the labor force in the domestic sector (ISTAT, 2014). This is a major indicator of the transition from a "family model of care" to a "migrant-in-the-family model of care" in southern Europe (Bettio, Simonazzi, & Villa, 2006). In Italy, in particular, increasing resort to live-in immigrant assistants is the milestone of an "invisible welfare" arrangement in home care to dependent elderly (Ambrosini, 2013). This has been a sort of privatized, low-cost strategy of family conciliation between contrasting demographic, household, and labor market pressures, all of them being poorly addressed by a typically familist welfare regime (Da Roit, 2007).

As the literature suggests (e.g., Catanzaro & Colombo, 2009; Di Rosa, Melchiorre, Lucchetti, & Lamura, 2012), the prototypical live-in care worker is a first-generation, middle-aged immigrant woman who has been left alone. Strong intergenerational ties and obligations (but often weaker conjugal ones), short-term return expectations, and little interest in and capability for family reunification are communal traits of this population. Their occupational careers tend to be fragmented and discontinuous with very limited scope for upward mobility—unless as a transition from live-in to jobs paid by the hour. At the same time, the stereotypical label of *badanti* conceals strong internal variations along lines of legal status, nationality, length of stay, and gender (with a relative increase in male participation during the current recession). The differential accessibility of circular migration patterns, depending on the country of origin (whether a European Union member or not), is also a major axis of internal stratification.

Compared with other immigrant profiles, those of home care workers have been the subject of an ambiguous and contradictory political construction. Although they are often employed as undocumented workers, they are seldom expelled or deported. Even under the periodical "repressive turns" that mark immigrant policies in Italy, *badanti* are hardly ever the target of xenophobic measures. At the same time, the anti-immigrant discourse that has been systematically advanced by right-wing parties, most notoriously by the Lega Nord, has negatively affected the mainstream social representations of immigrants altogether, including care workers. This is particularly the case for the ranks of the less educated and privileged natives, who may indeed perceive the foreign born as welfare and labor market competitors. That said, political closure, whether symbolic or real, has ironically gone hand-in-hand with a number of (economy-led) openings. Over the last decade, all legal measures that tended to criminalize migrants in general, possibly as an attempt to discourage their long-term settlement, were paralleled with amnesties to which care workers had large access (Ambrosini, 2013). More recently, *badanti* have even been the declared beneficiaries of such provisions, although the attendant labor demand seems less urgent than in the past. This does not mean, though, that the welfare needs and claims of *badanti* are specifically recognized, let alone addressed.

In a country such as Italy, with its relatively weak immigration and welfare policies, immigrant domestic care work has developed out of a constellation of micro work practices embedded in private household economies. Despite public recognition of the structural contribution of *badanti* to long-term care, these workers' living and working conditions are underdebated and uncontentious. While being subject to specific national regulations, live-in care work is a politically marginal phenomenon—even for the yardstick of Italy, with its limited tradition of immigrant mobilization and political participation (Pilati, 2010). Domestic work is arguably the most spectacular instance of the gap between the number of workers involved, or the socioeconomic weight of the work itself, and the modest impact of their claims-making in the public sphere—unless through the mediation of the mainstream civil society, as care workers' special access to amnesty policies has shown. The traditional marginality of domestic work from trade unionism and its embeddedness in a private and intimate life domain also contribute to its failure to inform public policy—including social work practice.

Altogether, the social position of these immigrant workers is generally one of widespread vulnerability and marginality, as is the bulk of immigrant labor in Italy, or possibly worse, given the feminization of this labor market niche. Especially telling are the figures on immigrants' rate of poverty as three times higher compared with natives against a background of general deterioration of living standards under the persisting recession (ISTAT, 2011).

Having said this, overt discrimination is not the central marker of the narratives I analyzed, although, unsurprisingly, episodes of discrimination are far from infrequent in migrants' everyday lives. More in-depth, such narratives are marked by a sense of systematic stigmatization for the kind of work interviewees do, both as depicted by the receiving society and, more important, as perceived by the workers themselves, with their past work experience as a term of comparison. Likewise, migrants' self-narratives include a number of tacit indicators of their structurally disadvantaged condition. This has to do with the physically and emotionally intensive nature of their jobs, their restricted scope for negotiating better employment conditions, and the few (if any) opportunities of access to less devalued jobs. In all of these respects, gender intersects with ethnicity and legal status in making for still higher risks of systematic oppression (Anderson, 2000; Lutz, 2011).

### THE BLURRED TERRAIN OF SOCIAL RIGHTS, NEEDS, AND CLAIMS: ALL FOR CLIENTS, NOTHING FOR THEMSELVES?

No specific data are available in Italy, interestingly, on the access to local welfare provision of immigrant care workers. Several case studies, though, indicate strong fragmentation and territorial variations in the (mostly residual) provisions available to immigrants in general as service clients. This seems to depend not only on their formal entitlements (i.e., the set of rights associated to their legal status) but also on the preexisting welfare cultures and arrangements. The latter includes the reach and intensity of collaborative networks among public and private welfare agencies, or between social care, health, and educational services. Strong discretion in social work practice, lack of expertise in helping relationships with migrants, and limited investments in dedicated training and supervision are also reported (Barberis & Boccagni, 2014). Having said this, of primary interest here is immigrants' construction of their own needs and entitlements, as well as of their role as care providers. This will result in a dual focus of analysis—on the subjective perceptions of their living/working conditions and on the personal motivations, feelings, and needs emerging from them.

### The Work Setting and Conditions

Judging from my case studies, significant variations can be found in the relational balances underlying the *badante* job on a contextual basis. This primarily depends on the attitudes of their employers, on the severity of the clients' conditions, and on the resources available to each worker. Importantly, I found several instances of what immigrant workers frame as good coexistence with their clients. Most interviewees report some instance of a work setting in which they were treated respectfully or even felt themselves to be "one of the family"—a relational and emotional condition that, in turn, is not without ambivalence (Ambrosini, 2013; Stacey, 2011). That said, less favorable cases, besides being often more widespread, can helpfully exemplify the downside of this work experience and its structural constraints and contradictions.

Live-in care work is, in essence, a labor market niche with low barriers to entry and high ones to exit. Immigrant women in their middle age—especially those of a white and Christian background—are relatively facilitated in finding a *badante* job in Italy, mostly through informal word of mouth. They typically struggle and are far less supported, though, in finding any way forward out of it. Perhaps unsurprisingly, the word "segregation" does not belong to their everyday language. Nonetheless, their narratives point to this existential condition in a number of ways: not only the overlapping between work and life milieus, or the attendant risks of social isolation, but also the weight of the expectation that they "be there" at any moment, whenever necessary, irrespective of any formal boundary between work and private life (DeGiuli, 2007). In revisiting her career as paid home caregiver, K. provides a particularly reflexive account of this prison-like condition—including the delicate family balances she and her peers have to navigate.

> Now I have a room of mine [close to the one of her elderly client], but when you sleep you must always prick up your ears, like a rabbit, and you hear everything. She [the old woman] does not want to disturb her daughter, and the daughter says: "Mum sleeps all night." Wish it was like that! . . . If I had an ordinary job, I work eight hours, then I'm free. Here, you're like a bird out of the wood: you've got something to eat, you've got some water, and that's all. This is a prison—you can't go in or out when you like, you can't—as I'm working, I can't leave madam alone even one minute. Can't go anywhere while she's having a rest. No way . . . and it was even worse when I worked with a madam with Alzheimer's—I thought I would fall ill too: when you're close to a person who's out of her mind, all the time, you lose your mind too—can't think like a normal person any more.
>
> (K., Ukrainian, 61 years old, in Italy for 9 years)

It bears repeating that this is not necessarily a discriminatory work setting in a strict sense. It is, however, an often oppressive one, as living segregation is combined with another source of vulnerability: extended exposure to deep human suffering (often as a result of dementia or even of terminal disease), with limited coping resources, whether in terms of professional skills, personal and institutional support and supervision, collaboration with other domiciliary aides and health staff, and so on. While this is the subtext of many of the narratives I collected, instances of work with exploitative or violent "clients" can also be found. Leaving aside the specificities of each work setting, however, what makes the *badanti's* condition a structurally vulnerable one is still another point—as reminded, for instance, by S.: the power asymmetries between workers and the families of their clients and the precarious, short-term (of often undefined tenure) nature of their jobs. This makes for a sort of vicious dependency on the dependency of the elderly they care for and about.

S.: This kind of work is heavy for your mind, when an old woman is—how do you all this disease, when she's all . . . ?
Interviewer: Alzheimer's.

S.: Alzheimer. Yeah, it's so heavy—I've worked with a woman with Alzheimer's, where she's beaten me, she's beaten me. I've never talked with her daughter [about this], not at all.

Interviewer: Never?

S.: Never.

Interviewer: Never indeed?

S.: Never indeed.

Interviewer: Why is that?

S.: Don't know, don't know. After that, after she died, I did talk with her daughter: "How was it with our mother, S.?" And I tell her: "Okay, everything okay . . . she's beaten me three times." "Really? Why haven't you ever said that, S.?"—No, no, she was sick—I know what she was like. After just five minutes . . . she'd forgotten all of it.

Interviewer: Didn't you even tell her that the old woman used to cry all night?

S.: No.

Interviewer: I mean, you thought there was nothing they could do about that?

S.: No, I thought I was afraid—if they take her to a nursing home . . .

Interviewer: You would have lost your job.

S.: Yeah . . . everything is okay like that—that's all.

(S., Ukrainian, 51 years old, in Italy for 8 years)

The job experience reported below, from the narrative of J., may well be extreme for its brevity. It is, however, telling of a background of human suffering, with the attendant emotional and psychological costs, that cuts across the narratives of immigrant women employed in live-in care work. Getting emotionally attached to a dying person, as sometimes is the case, exacerbates further the consequences of the abrupt end of a personal relationship—and for that matter, of one's job.

That volunteer from Caritas helped me find another job. This man was 75 years old. I was glad I went to his home. I stayed 15 days but he was very ill. He'd got some stomach surgery. He could eat only raw food. I felt sorry to see him like that. Then a nurse tells me, you know, granpa will die soon. Your job will last 10 days, no more—I can't believe it, I tell her. And then granpa died right in my arms, true. Every time I carried him to his bed I made a prayer, as I saw he was suffering so hard. One day he tells me: I feel very bad. I feel very bad, go and call my daughter—poor guy, he died that day.

I worked just few days there. And then I had to look for another job once again! I say, enough with that, don't want (to care for) the elderly any more, I want (to care for) a family.

(J., Peruvian, 43 years old, in Italy for 12 years)

While the these work conditions are shared across the interviews, the more subjective side of the matter—how immigrant women themselves make sense of and feel about them—requires more elaboration. This was a critical if sometimes painful transition that most interviewees went through.

### The Workers' Feelings and Constructions of Themselves and Their Jobs

"Italians just need us as labor—nobody cares about our lives," is a remark from O., a Ukrainian woman of 50, that sums up the primary perception of most interviewees. Against this background, common to all of their narratives is a strong motivation to work, save, and remit money home. This identification with a transnational breadwinner role, however, is often paralleled with ambiguous emotional stances about job position. Feelings of oppression, stigmatization, and marginality may well coexist with some emotional attachment to their clients, the members of the households, or even their dwelling places. Ironically, some respondents frame as their worst job experiences those in which clients display no emotional involvement, thus disappointing their implicit expectations.

The interviewees' prevalent relational isolation and the mixed weight of their emotional engagement are compounded by the extended separation from children and other kin left behind. While these migrant women enact, unsurprisingly, a variety of forms of transnational parenting (Bonizzoni & Boccagni, 2013), distance over space and time does matter. A tacit and elusive tension cuts across their narratives as the hands-on, somehow intimate care they provide to a stranger, on a paid and everyday basis, is paralleled with the impossibility to care likewise—at least in terms of physical copresence—for their dear ones in their home communities. Among other things, the processes of fictitious kin-making that emerge in several narratives—whereby the dependent old client is renamed as "granma" or "granpa"—mirror an attempt to cope with this tension. In the words of L., an Ecuadorian woman of 47, "Whenever I look after an old man, or an old woman, I think they are my own grandparents." It remains to be seen whether the need for emotional work and the workers' emotional overinvolvement, both of them part and parcel of live-in care, can be turned into a resource to improve their living conditions—for instance, through some form of psychosocial or relational support from social work or other helping agencies.

Leaving emotional issues aside, the workers' construction of their own needs and the resources available to address them is another subject to be further investigated. The easier way to do so, during the interviews, was to probe into respondents' access to and awareness about the social and health-care resources available at a local level. The network map that stems from their responses is a very loose and low-intensity one. Their access to health-care provisions has been shown to be weak and unsystematic, unless for emergencies or other circumstances related to the clients' care needs (Tognetti, 2010). Even weaker are, in general terms, the interviewees' ties with formal social work agencies. This is consistent with the renunciative construction of their health and social care needs that emerges from these narratives. "Whenever I work I'm fine—now I'm not," is the blunt conclusion of E., a 48-year-old Moldovan who was unemployed at the time of the interview. It is as if, as long as a migrant has a job and is not ill or does not seem to be so, everything else is less of an issue—including social rights and all sorts of less than basic needs. This attitudinal combination of self-sacrifice, altruism, and short-termism is exemplified by the remarks of N. and R., among others.

N.: I do want . . . to help my daughter. As I always say, concerning myself . . . what do I need for myself? Nothing! I just need money to help my daughter and my grandchildren.
Interviewer: But do you feel that you are well?
N.: You mean—in terms of health?
Interviewer: Well—in terms of everything.
N.: Don't know—Yeah, I guess so . . . when you've got a job, a good and a right job, which you like, I'm glad—even more as I earn money, 'cause I've come here to earn money.
(R., Ecuadorian, 45 years old, in Italy for 6 years)

Interviewer: What is it that one needs to live well here?

R.: Health—good health, that's the fundamental thing for me. If you're in good health, you don't need to ask for more, you know what I mean?

Interviewer: Just that?

R.: That's enough—I just need to keep in good health.

Interviewer: As for all the rest . . . ?

R.: Well, for me, the rest—don't need anything else, you know? If I'm in good health, then I've everything I need.

> (N., Ukrainian, 52 years old, in Italy for 6 years)

Across the narratives of these immigrant women, caring about oneself is tacitly constructed as an unaffordable luxury. A sort of "procrastination" and "externalization of well-being" is at work (Boccagni & Ambrosini, 2012). Hard living conditions here and now are rationalized as necessary to the well-being of someone else—the recipients of their remittances back home—and possibly to migrants' own well-being in some undefined future, once they return to their homelands. How, if at all, their faceted needs and rights are addressed in the meantime is left in the shadows.

It was not infrequent, across the interviews, to encounter cases of women who intentionally gave up their days and times off, looking rather for some extra job—apparently to accelerate the timeline of gaining (or saving) "enough" to meet the money demand of their left-behind kin, and then return home. Similar instances, together with the astonishing weight of their remittances, invite a counterintuitive reading of migrants' transnational engagement as an irremediably mixed phenomenon. There is no predefined balance in migrants' transnational relationships between what they send and what is further demanded and expected from those left behind; what they can consume for themselves and what they should rather save or remit; what needs/interests of their own they can legitimately address "here," and what needs and interests they are expected to transnationally foster "there." What is clear from these interviews, however, is that they often have to cope with an overburden of home-related obligations and expectations. What if, ironically, migrants' transnational obligations exacerbate further their marginality in the countries of settlement? While this is a thorny and delicate question, it is not irrelevant to social work practice, even more so in a transnational perspective.

## THE CHALLENGES FOR PROFESSIONAL SOCIAL WORK

With limited exceptions, formal social work provision is conspicuous by its absence across the narratives of these care workers. To some extent the absence is due to the relatively early stage of their migration trajectories. This makes their needs and claims easier to be met, basically at least, by grassroots nongovernmental organizations and charities, mostly with religious or political left-wing backgrounds (Ambrosini, 2013). The limited access of *badanti* to family reunification also makes their profile less than salient to the eyes of social work agencies. However, there is more than that.

Leaving aside undocumented workers (who are not entitled to formal take-up), even long-settled interviewees report sporadic contact with social work agencies, primarily for issues of "ordinary" immigrant marginality, such as requests for benefits, housing support, or school/vocational orientation for their children. Migrants' distinctive needs and vulnerabilities *as home care workers* tend instead to remain invisible to social work agencies (and often to migrants themselves).

"*Badanti* mostly have a job, even after the crisis—why should they [come] get here?" This was the typical reply I received from social workers in local authority agencies anytime I asked about immigrant caretakers as potentially relevant clients. As long as they are gainfully employed—so the subtext reads—there is not much point in social work agencies taking them up; even less so in a regime of decreasing welfare budgets and little investment in community development. This commonsensical understanding from the side of practitioners makes for a double-edged sword. In principle it reflects an inclusive and "progressive" view of immigrant workers as active welfare providers or as emerging actors for the integration of social and health assistance in long-term care. Nonetheless, the mainstream social work discourse frames *badanti* as simply a cheap and taken for granted resource, rather than subjects with unattended social rights and needs— themselves eligible for more systematic and qualified support. It is only once (if at all) they explicitly ask for support, or experience some very visible distress, that their everyday overexposure to oppression is really tracked by social workers.

Even in the field of social welfare, then, immigration exerts a "mirror effect" about the structural contradictions and inequalities of the receiving society. Apart from everything else, the predominant ways of employing and framing migrant care workers tell much of the poor and unequal provision of domiciliary care in Italy (Di Rosa et al., 2012). In paid care, as much as in several other labor market domains, immigrants are basically instrumental in containing the costs of system maintenance, irrespective of their skills and qualifications. Over time, this is unlikely to enhance the quality or contrast the systematic inequalities of welfare arrangements—not to mention the short- and long-term costs for migrant workers themselves (Saraceno, Sartor, & Sciortino, 2013).

As far as social work practice is concerned, addressing the invisibilized needs and claims of *badanti* would first require deeper understanding of their life conditions and prospects. This is the case, to repeat, in a professional context marked by service retrenchment, lack of a strong antidiscrimination culture, and limited institutional competence in social work with immigrant clients (Barberis & Boccagni, 2014). That said, the challenge does not lie only in enhancing workers' skills along anti-oppressive (rather than simply culturally competent) lines. This is clearly a future challenge for social work training—a field in which, interestingly, students with immigrant backgrounds are severely underrepresented; in stark contrast, once again, with migrants' overrepresentation on the lowest rungs of care work. Aside from that, the challenge lies in enhancing the advocacy, outreach, and community work bases of social work practice against all incentives to "desk work" accelerated by the trends toward bureaucratization and managerialization in Italy as much as elsewhere (Lorenz, 2005).

Another field open for development lies, of course, in transnational social work (Furman, Negi, & Salvador, 2010). In principle, facilitating migrants' ties with home societies is a promising strategy for coping with the social downsides of extended migration. In practice, as the limited evidence available in Italy suggests, this option is expensive and uncommon. When some interagency transnational initiative does occur, this is primarily related to highly vulnerable populations, such as asylum seekers or victims of trafficking; or possibly, and more contentiously, to the facilitation of "voluntary" return programs. As far as migrant women employed in care work are concerned, supporting transnational interactions with homelands, and most notably with left-behind kin, is for sure an option. It does bring in itself, though, the risk of legitimizing and advancing further the gendered and racialized hierarchies on which care work is based and the deeply unequal family balances reproduced by this pattern of employment and migration (Boccagni, 2014).

### CONCLUSION

*Stigmatized, segregated,* and still *essential* are the attributes through which I have mapped the marginal and ambiguous position of immigrant care workers vis-à-vis professional social work. Common across these attributes is an implicit way of framing immigrants as "naturally" vocated to do a number of (bad) jobs, including those at the lowest rungs of personal care provision. This cognitive subtext is not absent from social work discourse and practices. The pervasive recruitment of immigrants in intimate and emotionally rich settings does little to undermine their gendered and ethnicized framing as "others," however helpful, provided they maintain a docile, servant-like stance. That their structural vulnerability and overexposure to oppression are little recognized is no surprise, given these premises. Unless this subtext is explicitly questioned from within social work practice and education, the profession is unlikely to achieve much in terms of advocacy against the ebbs and flows of immigrants' criminalization and against the everyday tacit and unnoticed "inferiorization" that surrounds them.

That said, the invisibilization of migrant care workers' needs and claims illuminates two issues of broader relevance for social work. The first is the transition from private concerns to public questions, which has involved a number of social and health "problems" over time, as quintessential to the development of professional social work (and of the welfare state more broadly). As far as personal care is concerned, in Italy at least, this transition is far from complete. And as long as care is conceived as a merely private need, belonging only to family-based intimate economies, it is difficult to advance the debate on its public relevance and on the risks associated to immigrants being recruited only as a low-cost solution.

The second issue involves the transnational side of social work practice with migrant clients, which would require further reflection—up to finding out that it also holds an "invisible" dimension. Migrants' transnational engagement is a complex and faceted phenomenon. Cross-border relationships and obligations are a major reservoir of affection, morality, and emotion for care workers like the ones studied here. However, they may also be a channel to reproduce overly burdensome obligations, as a part of asymmetric, oppressive, and gendered relationships. Factoring the transnational into social work practice is potentially a way to better address migrants' needs and aspirations. Yet this should be done in a critical and sensitive way, lest one falls into one more "naturalizing" pitfall—exactly like the one of equating migrant women with submissive and motherly care workers while losing track of the systemic oppression that affects their life trajectories.

## REFERENCES

Ambrosini, M. (2013). *Irregular migration and invisible welfare.* Basingstoke, UK: Palgrave.

Anderson, B. (2000). *Doing the dirty work? The global politics of domestic labor.* London: Zed.

Barberis, E., & Boccagni, P. (2014). Blurred rights, local practices: Social work and immigration in Italy. *British Journal of Social Work, 44*(s1), i70–i87.

Bettio, F., Simonazzi, A., & Villa, P. (2006). Change in care regimes and female migration. *Journal of European Social Policy, 16*(3), 271–285.

Boccagni, P. (2014). Caring about migrant care workers. *Critical Social Policy, 34*(2), 221–40.

Boccagni, P., & Ambrosini, M. (2012). *Cercando il benessere nelle migrazioni.* Milan: Angeli.

Bonizzoni, P., & Boccagni, P. (2013). Care (and) circulation revisited: A conceptual map of diversity in transnational parenting. In L. Baldassar & L. Merla (Eds.), *Transnational families, migration and the circulation of care* (pp. 78–93). London: Routledge.

Catanzaro, R., & Colombo, A. (Eds.). (2009). *Badanti & Co.* Bologna: Mulino.

Cere, R. (2010). Globalization vs. localization: Anti-immigrant and hate discourses in Italy. In M. Ardizzoni & C. Ferrari (Eds.), *Beyond monopoly: Globalization and contemporary Italian media* (pp. 225–244). Plymouth, UK: Lexington.

Colombo, A. (2013). Foreigners and immigrants in Italy's penal and administrative detention systems. *European Journal of Criminology, 10*(6), 746–759.

Colombo, A., & Sciortino, G. (2003). The Bossi-Fini law. *Italian Politics, 18*, 162–179.

Da Roit, B. (2007). Changing intergenerational solidarities within families in a Mediterranean welfare state. *Current Sociology, 55*(2), 251–269.

De Giuli, F. (2007). A job with no boundaries. *European Journal of Women's Studies, 14*(3), 193–207.

Di Rosa, M., Melchiorre, M., Lucchetti, M., & Lamura, G. (2012). The impact of migrant work in the elder care sector. *European Journal of Social Work, 15*(1), 9–27.

Furman, R., Negi, N. J., & Salvador, R. (2010). An introduction to transnational social work. In N. J. Negi & R. Furman (Eds.), *Transnational Social Work Practice* (pp. 1–21). New York: Columbia University Press.

Istituto Nazionale di Statistica (ISTAT). (2011). *I redditi delle famiglie con stranieri*. Rome: Author.

——. (2014). *Noi-Italia*. Rome: Author.

Lorenz, W. (2005). Social work and a new order. *Social Work & Society, 3*(1), 93–100.

Lutz, H. (2011). *The new maids*. New York: Zed.

Palidda, S. (2014). *Racial criminalization of migrants in the 21st century*. Aldershot, UK: Ashgate.

Pasquinelli, S., & Rusmini, G. (2013). Il punto sulle badanti. In Network Non Autosufficienza (Ed.), *L'assistenza agli anziani non autosufficienti in Italia* (pp. 93–111). Rimini, Italy: Maggioli.

Pilati, K. (2010). *La partecipazione politica degli immigrati*. Rome: Armando.

Saraceno, C., Sartor, N., & Sciortino, G. (Eds.). (2013). *Stranieri e disuguali*. Bologna: Mulino.

Stacey, C. (2011). *The caring self*. Ithaca, NY: Cornell University Press.

Tognetti, M. (2010). Le badanti e la rete delle risorse di cura. *Autonomie Locali e Servizi Sociali, 25*(1), 61–77.

Williams, F. (2010). Migration and care. *Social Policy & Society, 9*(3), 385–396.

# 15

# Immigrants' Experiences with Law Enforcement Authorities in Spain

THE TERRORIST ATTACKS IN THE United States on September 11, 2001, were followed by bombings in Madrid on March 11, 2004, and in London on July 7, 2005. These events triggered the emergence of national discourses centered on national security in the United States and Europe. The discourse produced by conservative politicians and the media have generated the rejection by governments and their law enforcement agencies of anything considered unfamiliar and threatening, including immigrants. Border enforcement activities and permanent police surveillance on unauthorized immigrants and the detention and expulsion of unauthorized immigrants from host communities have increased the criminalization of immigrants. In this chapter, I center on recent trends on immigrant criminalization in Spain.

## EXCEPTIONAL IMMIGRATION TRENDS AND IMMIGRATION POLICY IN SPAIN

Immigration in Spain can be considered exceptional in two ways. First, Spain went very rapidly from traditionally being a country of emigrants to becoming a net recipient of migration. In the late 1980s and in the mid-2000s, Spain became the largest receiver of immigrants in Europe. For example, in the period 2004–2006, net migration to Spain accounted for 1,857,781 persons, equivalent to 36% of the total net migration to the 27 countries in the European Union (EU; Eurostat, 2007). Figure 15.1 shows the exceptional growth of immigration in Spain between 2001 and 2011. Three main reasons explain this rapid growth: (1) sustained growth of the Spanish economy; (2) a demand for unskilled workers in construction, agriculture, and domestic services, among others areas; and (3) the mismatch between the Spanish labor force and the characteristics of the workers needed (Martin, 2009). However, the negative impact of the Great Recession on the labor market has been so deep that a substantial number of immigrants have returned to their countries of origin. In 2012 Spain registered for the first time a negative net migration. In 2013 this trend accelerated, and Spain's net loss of immigrants ascended to 111,153 persons (Instituto Nacional de Estadistica, 2014).

The second feature of Spanish international immigration is its institutionalization. In 2000 the Spanish state recognized the magnitude and impact of immigration and created government agencies and laws and regulations based on a multicultural approach to incorporate immigrants and their families into the Spanish economy and society (Cachón, 2002). The development of a multicultural framework and the institutionalization of immigration in Spain evolved over time. The current law is based on Organic Law 4/2000, which is considered the most influential legal framework in Spain regarding international immigrants and one of the most progressive legislations in Europe. The development of the Spanish immigration framework,

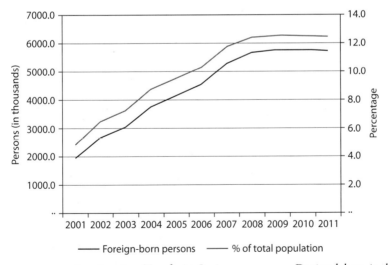

FIGURE 15.1.    **Immigration Trends in Spain, 2000–2011.** Depicted here is the growth of immigration in Spain between 2001 and 2011 followed by a downward trend of net losses starting in 2012.

laws, and policies took place at an uncrossed point: Spain needed to have a system to order the large number of immigrants it was receiving, and at the same time it needed to comply with the newly designed directives on immigration from the EU.

According to Joppke (2007), the prevailing model of "repressive liberalism" on immigrant integration in Europe is based on standards that relied on migrants' "self-sufficiency" and "autonomy," making migrants independent of the state. The Spanish immigration framework is different. It is based on a multicultural approach (Cachón, 2009). In 2004, during the discussions for the definition of the EU Common Basic Principles on International Migration, the Spanish socialist government advocated for the protection of immigrant languages and cultures and advocated for an active role by the state in immigrant integration (Joppke, 2007). In 2007 the Spanish government approved the Strategic Plans for Citizenship and Integration. The 2007 program included recommendations on 10 areas deemed strategic for immigrant integration: education, social services, housing, reception, employment, equality of treatment, gender perspective, immigrants' participation in the process, and sensitization of the Spanish society toward the immigration phenomenon, and codevelopment by the sending countries (Gobierno de España, 2007).

During the evolution of its immigration legislation the Spanish government conducted six extraordinary regularization processes. Between 1985 and 2005, 1,162,979 regularizations were granted to unauthorized immigrants. During the last and largest regularization process in 2005, there were more than a half-million residence permits granted (Cachón, 2009). As a result, between 2002 and 2011, the Spanish government issued 665,761 citizenships through naturalization (Ministry of Labor and Social Security, 2013).

Moreover, the Spanish legislation includes provisions for the regularization of unauthorized immigrants through labor and length of residence (*arraigo*). For example, all residents, including unauthorized immigrants, can register on municipal population records (*padron municipal*) to have access to health-care services and education and proof of length of residence in the country. Unauthorized immigrants can apply for their individual regularization after 3 years of continuous residence in Spain if they have no criminal record and a job contract for at least a year. The Spanish immigrant legislation establishes that being in Spanish territory without a work or residence permit is a serious civil offense. If an authorized immigrant is detained, and an order or expulsion is issued, the immigrant can appeal the order, pay a fine, and if his or her appellation is approved in court and all other previously mentioned criteria are met, apply for his or her regularization (Ilustre Colegio de Abogados de Madrid, 2014). However, many immigrants do not know about the Spanish legislation, do not have access to legal counsel, and are unable to use the established legal channels to become authorized immigrants (Servicio Jesuita a Migrantes España, 2014).

Although a few changes have been made to Spain's immigration policy during the current recession, these changes have primarily affected unauthorized immigrants' access to health-care services (Royal Decree-Law 16/2012).

### IMMIGRATION AND THE NEGATIVE EFFECTS
### OF THE GREAT RECESSION

The current practices on immigrant persecutions and detentions in Spain have been carried out in a context of economic crisis. Since 2008 Spain has faced a deep and long economic crisis coupled with a high proportion of immigrants. In 2013 there were 6.74 million foreign-born persons living in Spain, accounting for 14.6% of the total population (Organization for Economic Co-operation and Development [OECD], 2013).

Spain has experienced one of the highest increases in unemployment during the crisis (OECD, 2010). The unemployment rate during the recession reached its highest point (26.1%) in the first quarter of 2013. The rate of long-term unemployment reached 62.1% in the second quarter of 2014. The social consequences of the unemployment crisis are reflected in the proportion of households living in poverty, which at 6.4% is a relatively high figure compared with the 3.5% in 2007 (Malgesini & Candalija, 2014). The social crisis has been exacerbated by the conservative fiscal policies imposed by the EU. Although there are signs of economic recovery, many countries, including Spain have had jobless recoveries (Coibion, Gorodnichenko, & Koustas, 2013).

The incorporation of immigrants in sectors in the labor market in which unskilled workers were needed in vast numbers during the economic boom and the return of many migrants during the crisis have had positive effects in maintaining a favorable social environment toward immigrants, and particularly Latin American immigrants. However, there are still a number of instances in which the discrimination and rejection of immigrants, particularly immigrants from Africa or those belonging to stigmatized groups, is palpable.

### ECONOMIC DOWNTURN AND OPINIONS TOWARD IMMIGRANTS

As noted by many scholars, periods in which large numbers of immigrants arrive are marked by resistance from the receiving communities, who see the newcomers as a threat to their way of life (Massey & Sanchez, 2010; Portes & Rumbaut, 2006). According Cea D'Ancona and Valles (2008, 2013, 2014), the greatest increase in opposition toward immigration in Spain coincided with a larger presence of immigrants. However, there were variations in the perceptions toward immigrants depending on their regions of origin. Latin American immigrants are perceived as closer culturally to Spaniards and more able to integrate in Spain than other groups of immigrants (e.g., only 29% of Spaniards responded in 2011 that Muslims were well integrated).

The trends on rejection of immigration in Spain are linked to public perception of the growth of immigration. This is explained by two structural trends. First, the crisis in Spain has been so deep that a substantial number of migrants have returned to their countries of origin. Second, the aging structure of the Spanish population and the relatively high level of education of the Spanish youth looking for "desirable" jobs might not consider immigrants as competitors in the job market but as needed workers to support the aging population.

During the economic crisis, the perception by natives of immigration as a problem dropped from 58% in 2009 to 44% in 2013 (Transatlantic Trends, 2013). In addition, Spaniards' opinions on the question of whether "immigrants take jobs away" (from natives), has been declining every year from the start of the crisis. Even when asked about whether "immigrants are a burden on social services," respondents in Spain were less worried in 2013 (41%) than in 2011 (55%).

Overall, the data suggest that natives' perceptions toward immigrants in Spain on average did not deteriorate significantly during the recession but were linked to the rapid growth of immigration in the 2000s.

## A DIVERSE IMMIGRANT POPULATION

In the last decade, the racial and ethnic immigrant composition in Spain has changed due to the diversification of immigrants' countries of origin. According to the distribution of immigrants by region of origin, it can be said that there are three groups: citizens from the EU, among whom Romanian immigrants are many; Latin American immigrants, among whom there are large populations of Ecuadorans and Colombians; and Moroccans and immigrants from other African countries. There are also relatively small but still growing immigrant groups from China and other countries in Asia.

Citizens from the EU member states have the right to free circulation in the Schengen zone. Therefore, European citizens, including Roma populations from Romania, of which Spain is a large receiver, have the same labor and social rights as any other Spanish citizen.

For non-European immigrants the routes and modes of arrival vary depending on the region of origin. Most immigrants from Latin America arrive by air, and those who are undocumented tend to overstay their temporary permits as visitors (90 days) or visas. Spanish law provides preferential treatment to Latin American immigrants, and once granted permanent residence, they only need to maintain this status 2 years before they can apply for citizenship. Immigrants from other countries must wait at least 10 years as residents before they can apply for citizenship. Preferential treatment given to Latin American immigrants, their integration into the workforce and social structure, and their voluntary return has generated a more positive view toward them than toward other immigrant groups coming primarily from Morocco and other African countries.

The arrival of immigrants from northern Africa in rafts (*pateras*) to the coast of Cadiz or the Canary Islands or by jumping the walls (*saltos de la valla*) surrounding Ceuta and Melilla has received considerable attention from the Spanish and international media. The Spanish government has implemented controversial strategies to deter immigrants from entering and traveling to the Spanish territory (e.g., installing blades on the walls and shooting balls at immigrants trying to jump the wall). These strategies have only changed the routes that migrants use but has not stopped their migration efforts (e.g., instead of traveling to Cadiz, they use a longer and more dangerous route to the Canary Islands and currently sail to Lampedusa along the Italian coast).

Spain has signed agreements with many Africa countries to return nationals upon arrival (e.g., Morocco) or migrants who departed from a territory (e.g., Senegal). Even if these binational agreements facilitate the return of unauthorized immigrants, Spanish legislation states they are entitled to due process once they are in Spanish territory. A recent report on "express expulsions" (*expulsiones en caliente*) describes how state agents are violating Spanish law, expelling immigrants who have crossed the walls into Ceuta and Melilla without an order of expulsion from a judge (Escamilla et al., 2014).

## IMMIGRANTS' LIVED EXPERIENCES WITH LAW ENFORCEMENT AUTHORITIES

To describe the lived experiences of immigrants with law enforcement authorities in Spain, I gathered data from three sources. First, I interviewed immigrants about their experiences. Second, I collected information about the conditions of immigrants at internment immigrant centers, known as CIEs (Centro de Internamiento de Extranjeros). Third, I explored court cases in which immigrants have been criminalized due to their physical features or cultures. The cases presented in the next paragraphs represent not only the experience of undocumented immigrants with law enforcement officers but also of those who have being stigmatized by law enforcement officers.

The first informant is a French citizen, who came to Spain to learn Spanish but could not understand Spaniards (in his words: "Spaniards talk too fast"). He ended up learning Spanish in a community of Colombian immigrants and consequently speaks Spanish with a Colombian accent and socializes with Colombians. Among Latin Americans, Colombians have been stigmatized in connection to drug-trafficking activities, and Spanish police officers have developed strategies to target this national group (Barbero, 2012). This French informant, who has the same rights as any other Spanish or European citizen, has been stopped several times by the police in clubs visited by Latino immigrants, in parks, and in metro stations. He described his last experience with the police during the interview. He was stopped in a park by an undercover officer, who asked a series of questions that used Colombian slang references to drugs, for example, "Y tu traes baretico?" ("Do you have pot?"), and also queried the meaning of a religious image he had hanging around his neck (*escapulario*). Then he was asked about his nationality, but since the police officers did not believe him, given his French-Colombian accent, he was put in a police car and driven to his home, where his Colombian neighbors were interviewed by the police. He was asked to show his passport as proof of his French nationality and was then taken to the police station to verify the authenticity of the document. This case shows how the profiles constructed by law enforcement bodies and strategies used to "capture" unauthorized immigrants, preferably in relation to serious offenses (e.g., drug trafficking), are based on predetermined profiling of cultural features (in this case accent, use of slang) and established locations—neighborhoods with high concentrations of immigrant populations. The informant, a young, white, and employed male, through his multiple interactions with the police over the years, has learned how to detect and avoid places and circumstances in which contact with law enforcement officers is likely. During the interview he compared his experiences with law enforcement officers in France and Spain. He spent his youth in the suburban area of Paris during the years of the conservative policies implemented by Sarkozy as interior minister. He described the practices employed by the French police as "fearsome" (*temible*). Even after been stopped several times in Spain, he believes he is better off in Spain than in France.

The second informant is John (a pseudonym to guarantee anonymity), an international student from Colombia. Before his arrival in Spain, John taught at the college level in Colombia. To advance further in his academic career, John decided to pursue a doctoral degree at a well-known Spanish university. On his way home to visit his family back in Colombia during the holiday season, he stopped in a large Spanish city to visit friends and stayed at a youth hostel. While at the youth hostel he was mistakenly accused of sexual harassment by a couple of young males. The hostel manager called the police. Without being further questioned John was taken to a police station, detained, and then transferred six times in 72 hours. The police never asked further questions of his accusers. His friends received a call from the police, but since his location changed so often it was difficult for them, his lawyer, and the consular officer providing assistance to know where he was being detained. He was released just in time to take the flight back to Colombia. Due to the experience of harassment at the hostel, mistreatment from police officers and various detainees, and the stress generated by his unjustified detention, he dropped out of the doctoral program and stayed in Colombia to avoid any chance of ever having a similar experience.

The described experiences of authorized immigrants who did not commit any civil or penal offense, but who, due to their immigrant condition, were targeted by law enforcement officers, show how the stigmatization by the police of presumably well-adapted and positively perceived immigrants, Colombians in this case, affects their livelihoods.

According to my informants and other interviews with persons in charge of programs for the integration of immigrants, there is permanent surveillance for unauthorized immigrants in places with large concentrations of immigrant communities (e.g., long-distance telephone booths or *locutorios* and mosques). For example, there are undercover police agents at bus stops and train and metro stations close to immigrant neighborhoods during the morning commuting hours. Persons passing by are asked for their identification documents, and those without documentation are taken to a police station. These permanent surveillance activities toward immigrants are not reported in newspapers or on TV news shows; however, they are well-known practices in immigrant communities. These internal "border control" areas in central regions of major urban centers are created by law enforcement agents to detect, detain, and expel unauthorized immigrants. These practices complement regulations and mechanisms designed to mark the distance between foreigners and nationals (Barbero, 2012). This permanent immigrant surveillance creates anxiety not only among unauthorized immigrants but also among their families and within the immigrant communities. The constant surveillance and resulting anxiety generated within the immigrant population is reflected in immigrants' behavior. Immigrants are forced to hide, to walk close to the walls, to not make any noise, to stay quiet, and if possible, to remain invisible (Terray, 2008).

Once a person is identified as an authorized immigrant by a law enforcement officer, he or she is taken to a police station. Since working and residing in Spain without authorization is considered a serious civil offense, a case is opened against the unauthorized immigrant. If requested by the detainee, a friend or family member must be reached and informed of the fact that the person is being detained and where. Authorities have 72 hours to search for previous detentions and criminal background, and based on this information and the particular circumstances of the unauthorized immigrant, the police then decide whether the detainee will be released or sent to a CIE. There are nine CIEs in Spain. These are centers designed to hold only unauthorized immigrants. The maximum number of days that a person can be held at a detention center in Spain is 60 days. If a judge has not issued a deportation order within 60 days, the immigrant is released.

I gathered information about the conditions of immigrants at CIEs located in the Iberian Peninsula or at temporary stay centers for immigrants (Centro de Estancia Temporal de Inmigrantes, or CETI) located in Ceuta and Melilla. These two types of centers are designed to enforce immigration law at different stages of the migration process. Immigrants generally avoid the CIEs, but once in Ceuta and Melilla, they usually visit the CETIs, because following due process they will have an opportunity to be transported to the Iberian Peninsula and either be released upon arrival or placed at a CIE.

According to Ley Orgánica 4/2000 (Art. 62 bis), CIEs are nonpenitentiary public establishments where detained unauthorized foreigners wait for deportation. Deprivation of freedom of an authorized immigrant must be proposed by the police and adopted by a judge. According to the law, deprivation of freedom must be the last recourse in carrying out the expulsion of an unauthorized immigrant. It is enforced once all other measures for voluntary return have been exhausted or when the person is considered a risk to the public or national security. In 2009 there were 16,590 unauthorized immigrants detained at CIEs, of whom 8,935 were deported; and in 2012 there were 11,325 unauthorized immigrants, of whom 5,924 were deported (Defensoria del Pueblo, 2014). However, the detention of immigrants in CIEs as a cautionary measure is overused (Servicio Jesuita a Migrantes España, 2014). Of the 300 immigrants interviewed in the CIEs, 221 had a previous order of expulsion due to their unauthorized status, another 54 were recent arrivals, and only 14 had a penal conviction. In addition, the difference in the number of detainees who were released from CIEs due to the impossibility of their expulsion (3,217) and the number of deported immigrants (5,924) (Fiscalía General del Estado, 2013) indicates there are a number of cases in which internment is unnecessary given the impossibility of effectively deporting the irregular immigrant from Spanish territory.

Police strategies to detect and detain irregular immigrants are reflected in the statistics on immigrant detention: out of 300 respondents, 109 were asked for documentation in the street; 12 in the metro, bus, or train; 6 in a raid; 24 were denounced by others; 7 were identified as unauthorized during their detention in prison; and, 25 were detained as unauthorized immigrants at the exit of the jail after completing a prison sentence (Servicio Jesuita a Migrantes España, 2014). Unfortunately these tactics inevitably result in the criminalization of immigrants.

There are no public statistics of the populations at CIEs. However, the report of the Jesuit Service for Migrants based its findings on a large sample of 300 immigrants they visited at CIEs in Spain. According to the results, about 38% were originally from sub-Saharan Africa, 36% from Latin America, 12% from the Maghreb (primarily from Morocco), and the remaining 14% from Eastern Europe and Asia. The majority of detainees (78%) were males. The length of time in Spain varied, with 25% of detained immigrants having lived more than 10 years in Spain, 39% between 4 and 9 years, 13% between 1 and 3 years, and 23% less than 1 year. For many immigrants, and particularly for African immigrants, Spain is the gateway into Europe. Many immigrants are on their way to other countries where their families and friends are established.

The human cost of the abusive use of CIEs to detain unauthorized immigrants is high. There is a strong and negative psychological and economic impact on immigrants and their families. The vulnerability of immigrant children is heightened due to the absence of one of the household heads who most likely was the primary earner in the household.

According to the information provided by a social worker in charge of the provision of humanitarian assistance to immigrants, unauthorized immigrants who are released from CIEs face difficult challenges. Many of them, due to their low level of education, do not understand the long-term consequences of having an order of expulsion. Those who have orders of expulsion and do not appeal are no longer subject to a regularization process. Therefore, their chances of becoming permanent residents are minimal. For an unauthorized immigrant, the prospect of finding a stable job in a weak labor market is limited, and his or her chances to overcome social and economic vulnerability are therefore bleak. In the words of my informant: "What are a group of 30 recent and unauthorized immigrants from Africa supposed to do when they are released from the CIEs in the streets of Barcelona without any guidance or support? It is a shocking experience for them, but also for the Barcelona residents. They think they are free, but in reality they are trapped."

The criminalization of immigrants is not only connected to their immigration status or their presumed culpability for a civil or penal offense; it is related to their stigmatization and the practices employed by law enforcement agents. In the following paragraphs, I will explore the cases of three immigrants who were criminalized and subject to discriminatory treatment. In all three of these cases, the Spanish judicial system proved inadequate and nonsensical on issues of racial profiling and discriminatory treatment toward foreign-born persons regardless of their citizenship or immigration status.

The first case is of Rosalind Williams, an African American woman originally from the United States who acquired Spanish nationality in 1969 (European Network of Legal Experts in the Non-discrimination Field, 2014). On December 6, 1992, at the Valladolid railway station, a police officer asked her for her identity card. Rosalind asked the officer about the reasons for the identity check. The office replied that he was obliged to check the identity of people "like her," since many of them were illegal immigrants. She filed a complaint with the Ministry of the Interior for racial discrimination and then appealed to all competent Spanish courts. She lost all appeals. In January 2001 the Spanish Constitutional Court justified the police action, because the action was an application of the racial criterion as an indicator of greater likelihood that the person concerned was not Spanish. In 2006, with the support of Open Society Justice Initiative, Women's Link Worldwide, and SOS Racismo-Madrid, Rosalind filed a complaint to the Human Rights Committee. In 2009 the UN Human Rights Committee considered that there had been a violation of the International Covenant on Civil and Political Rights by Spain.

The second case is of Beauty Solomon, a woman of Nigerian origin who had resided in Spain since 2003. In July 2005 she was arrested three times by police officers while working as a sex-worker in Palma de Mallorca (European Network of Legal Experts in the Non-discrimination Field, 2014). While purporting to carry out an identity check, the officers struck her with a stick and shouted derogatory racial insults. Beauty denounced the police brutality and alleged racial discriminatory treatment to all competent Spanish courts, including the Constitutional Court. She lost all appeals, and the Constitutional Court did not admit her claims. With the help of Women's Link Worldwide, Beauty brought the case to the European Court of Human Rights. This court concluded that Spain violated the prohibition of discrimination and of inhuman and degrading treatment by its lack of an effective investigation of the offense committed against Beauty.

The last case took place in Barcelona on April 19, 2010. Two police officers falsely accused a Romanian Roma woman who was begging on the street of physically punishing her baby daughter in public (Fundacion Secretariado Gitano, 2014). The women was sent to prison and banned from approaching her daughter. The baby was placed under state custody and remained separated from her parents for 8 months. The Romanian woman and her husband challenged the placement of her child in state custody and denounced the police officers for document forgery and false accusations. The police officers acknowledged the truth and were sentenced to 2 years in prison and ordered to pay €12,000 to the Roma family for the moral damage caused.

These events show how disruptive immigrant criminalization is in the lives of immigrants and foreign-born citizens, and how difficult, but not impossible, it is for vulnerable and stigmatized social subjects to claim fair treatment in Spain despite the spirit of Spanish legislation and European directives regarding discrimination based on racial or ethnic origin, religion, gender, age, sexual orientation, and disability.

### CONCLUSION

In Europe, despite several examples of xenophobia with respect to immigrants (Cachón, 2011), integration and immigration directives led by the European Commission have aimed at integrating *legal* migrants and EU citizens. However, the most recent strategies do not clearly set specific provisions for unauthorized immigrants, other than the emphasis on "security" of European space. The efforts to detect, detain, and expel unauthorized immigrants (e.g., see Directive 2008/115/CE, also ironically called "Return Directive," which set guidelines for the expulsion of unauthorized immigrants) have increasingly reinforced the conditions for the criminalization of immigrants in Spain regardless of the provisions considered in the law for the regularization of immigrants and the respect of their rights.

Immigrant criminalization in Spain cannot be explained by the application of a repressive and impractical legal framework, by negative and generalized opinions toward immigrants, or even by the negative effects of a long and deep economic recession on resource availability. Currently, the criminalization of immigrants in Spain can be explained by the articulation of the government's agenda through the implementation of policing practices on immigrants; the lack of understanding of the judicial system regarding racial profiling and discriminatory practices toward immigrants; and the scarcity of resources, including jobs, available for immigrants. As in the rest of the EU, the principle of individual security (for those living inside the fortress) trumps principles of human safety.

### REFERENCES

Barbero, I. (2012). *Globalizacion, estado y ciudadania. Un análisis socio-jurídico del movimiento sinpapeles.* Valencia, Spain: Tirant lo Blanch.

———. (2002). La formación de la "España inmigrante": Mercado y ciudadanía. *Revista Española de Investigaciones Sociológicas,* (97), 95–126.

———. (2009). *La España inmigrante: Marco discriminatorio, mercado de trabajo y políticas de integración.* Barcelona: Anthropos.

———. (2011). Inmigracion y conflictos en Europa. Aprender para una Mejor Convivencia. Barcelona: Hacer.

Cea D'Ancona, M. Á., & Valles Martínez, M. S. (2008). *Evolución del racismo y la xenofobia en España.* Madrid: OBERAXE, Ministerio de Trabajo e Inmigración.

———. (2013). *Evolución del racismo y la xenofobia en España.* Madrid: OBERAXE, Ministerio de Empleo y Seguridad Social.

———. (2014). *Evolución del racismo y la xenofobia en España.* Madrid: OBERAXE, Ministerio de Empleo y Seguridad Social.

Coibion, O., Gorodnichenko, Y., & Koustas, D. (2013). *Amerisclerosis? The puzzle of rising U.S. unemployment persistence* (NBER Working Paper 19600). Cambridge, MA: National Bureau of Economic Research.

Defensoria del Pueblo. (2013). *Memoria anual.* Madrid: Author.

Escamilla, M., Tomas, M., Tomas, S., Bernabé, J.M., Bernabé, S., Ripollés, J.L.D., & Menendez, I.V. (2014). "Expulsiones en Caliente": Cuando el Estado Actua al Margen de la Ley (Informe Jurídico). Madrid: Universidad Complutense de Madrid. Retrieved on June 23, 2014, from http://eprints.ucm.es.

European Network of Legal Experts in the Non-discrimination Field. (2014). *Spain 2013: Country report.* Utrecht, The Netherlands: Human European Consultancy. Retrieved on May 30, 2014, from www.humanconsultancy.com.

Eurostat. (2007). *Europe in figures: Eurostat yearbook 2006–07.* Luxemburg: Author.

Fiscalía General del Estado. (2013). *Memoria anual.* Madrid: Fiscalia General del Estado.

Fundacion Secretariado Gitano. (2014). Sentencia No. 1135. Retrieved on June 29, 2014, from www.gitanos.org/upload/37/69/Sentencia_ok.pdf.

Gobierno de España. (2007). Plan estrategico de ciudadania e integracion 2007–2010. Madrid: Secretaría de Estado de Inmigración y Emigración. Retrieved on June 3, 2014, from www.cruzrojamadrid.org/contenidos/img/File/Inmigrantes /Plan%20Estrategico%20de%20Ciudadania%20e%20Integracion%202007 –2010.pdf.

Ilustre Colegio de Abogados de Madrid. (2014). Estancia irregular: Multa o expulsion? Retrieved on June 29, 2014, from www.pueblosunidos.org.

Instituto Nacional de Estadistica. (2014). Estadisticas de variaciones residenciales. Retrieved on June 14, 2014, from www.ine.es.

Joppke, C. (2007). Beyond national models: Civic integration policies for immigrants in western Europe. *West European Politics, 30*(1), 1–22.

Malgesini, G., & Candalija, J. (2014). Dossier Pobreza de EAPN España. Retrieved on June 14, 2014, from http://www.eapn.es/ARCHIVO/documentos/dossier _pobreza.pdf.

Martin, P. (2009). Recession and migration: A new era for labor migration? *International Migration Review, 43*(3), 671–691.

Massey, D. S., & Sanchez-R, M. (2010). *Brokered boundaries: Creating immigrant identity in anti-immigrant times.* New York: Russell Sage.

Ministry of Labor and Social Security. (2013). Observatorio permanente de la inmigración. Concesiones de nacionalidad española por residencia. Retrieved on June 14, 2014, from http://extranjeros.empleo.gob.es.

Organization for Economic Co-operation and Development [OECD]. (2010). *Employment outlook 2010: Moving beyond the jobs crisis.* Paris: Author.

——. (2013). *International migration outlook.* Paris: Author.

Portes, A., & Rumbaut, R. G. (2006). *Immigrant America.* Los Angeles: University of California Press.

Servicio Jesuita a Migrantes España. (2014). CIE informe 2013: Criminalizados, internados, expulsados. Retrieved on June 14, 2014, from www.pueblosunidos.org.

Terray, E. (2008). Inmigración en la UE. La política que se proclama no coincide en absoluto con la política que se aplica. La política aplicada no pretende expulsar a la gente, sino aterrorizarla. *Viento Sur,* (98), 100–108.

Transatlantic Trends. (2014). *Transatlantic Trends Key Findings: 2013.* Washington, DC: German Marshall Fund of the United States. Retrieved on June 9, 2014, from http://trends.gmfus.org/files/2013/09/TTrends-2013-Key-Findings-Report .pdf.

# 16

# Creating Criminals

## AUSTRALIA'S RESPONSE TO ASYLUM SEEKERS AND REFUGEES

▸ *LINDA BRISKMAN AND LUCY FISKE*

Let me be clear. I'm trying to stop people illegally entering Australia by boat. That's our objective.

(Scott Morrison, Australian immigration minister, *Australian Business Review*, 2013)

### INTRODUCTION

AS IN EUROPE AND THE United States, politicians from the two major political parties in Australia have steadily and successfully sought to present asylum seeking as illegal, a phenomenon Welch (2012) refers to as "crimmigration." The "illegality" of people represents a discursive turn in contemporary migration rhetoric (Dauvergne, 2008). Although seeking asylum in Australia (including when arriving without documentation or prior authorization) does not break any law, the use of language of "illegality" by politicians and the media creates perceptions of criminal activity. This in turn underpins the dominant view of asylum seekers not as refugees in search of safety and protection but as criminal (possibly terrorist) threats (Aas, 2007). The criminalization of asylum seekers has proven to be an effective political strategy to enable national governments to show sovereign strength in a globalized world where actions of transnational corporations have greater impact than government policies on citizens' daily economic realities (McNevin, 2007). It also opens a largely unfettered space in which governments can enact punitive policies and cause serious harm and human rights violations to refugees and asylum seekers. Immigration detention is a key space in which such harm is enacted. Globally, detention of unauthorized foreigners in prison-like facilities has grown enormously in both scope and scale in the last 30 years, particularly in developed countries (Wilsher, 2012).

Criminalization of asylum seekers is also achieved in other ways, including, as the quote above demonstrates, by constructing the mode of arrival as illegal. Furthermore, the discourse of the criminal, terrorist Muslim with desires to overthrow Australian values and the Australian way of life is pervasive (Briskman, 2013), as is presenting asylum seekers as being in partnership with organized criminal networks engaged in people smuggling (Pickering, 2005). These rhetorical devices have successfully duped the Australian community into reactions of fear. Law and order politics create fertile soil for treating asylum seekers as dangerous others (McCulloch, 2008).

Crucial in the criminalization of asylum seekers in popular discourse is Australia's use of mandatory indefinite detention. Once refugees have been "caught" at the border, the Australian government detains them until their claims for recognition of refugee status are processed. Australian immigration detention centers look very much like maximum-security prisons, which is supported by the "illegal" narrative surrounding refugees and tautologically serves to reaffirm their criminality: the refugee is criminal and so is imprisoned; the refugee is imprisoned and so must be a criminal (Story, 2005, pp. 20–21). As Michael Grewcock effectively demonstrates, once asylum seekers and refugees have been rhetorically criminalized, the government is largely free to do whatever it likes to them, including enacting policies and practices of "systemic violence and abuse" (Grewcock, 2009, pp. 9–10). As Wazana (2004) posits, "In the face of international condemnation by human rights groups, the creation of such categories as the 'illegal' and the 'legal' becomes a way of 'justifying' state practices" (p. 89).

Australian asylum seeker policies and politics are encapsulated in the conservative federal government's successful electoral slogan Stop the Boats and use two linked strategies to achieve this aim: punishment and deterrence. Policies of punishment center on the use of detention within and outside Australian territorial boundaries. Deterrence policies also draw on detention and offshore processing as a threat to those who may make boat journeys, but also include interception of boats at sea, turning boats back to Indonesia, funding of immigration detention in Indonesia, funding of border patrol boats in Sri Lanka, and most recently, endeavors to hand asylum seekers directly to another sovereign power in international waters.

The Australian government goes to great lengths to ensure that the stories of actual people who are directly affected by these policies remain hidden from view and that asylum seekers are never humanized and do not get to speak for themselves.

As a contribution to countering the purposeful silencing of asylum seeker and refugee voices, this chapter draws on our many years of research and advocacy with asylum seekers and refugees in Australia and on more recent work with refugees in Indonesia. It primarily focuses on lived experiences of criminalization of asylum seeking in Australia. It draws on asylum seeker and refugee narratives from the People's Inquiry into Detention (Briskman, Latham, & Goddard, 2008), research into refugee resistance and protest (Fiske, 2012), and unpublished research by the two authors that recounts stories of hardship of asylum seekers and refugees in Indonesia who are now fearful to come to Australia by boat. Incarcerating people for the purposes of deterring others has been condemned by legal academics, as it involves treating human beings as a means to an end (Taylor, 2006), and it is improper to use the pain and discomfort of some asylum seekers to deter others (Crock, Saul, & Dastyari, 2006). All three projects privilege asylum seeker and refugee voices narrating lived realities that contrast with dominant narratives.

## PUNISHMENT

Australia maintains an extensive network of immigration detention centers on Australian territory and in Nauru (a small Pacific nation) and Manus Island, Papua New Guinea (PNG). Under the current policy framework, the vast majority of asylum seekers are detained in Nauru and Manus Island and on the small Australian territory of Christmas Island, located 2,660 kilometers from the nearest Australian mainland city of Perth. The main detention center on Christmas Island is purpose-built, based on U.S. super-max prison design, with closed-circuit television cameras monitoring every part of the center, electrified fences, and a laser-protected no-man's-land separating the internal and external perimeter fences. Rooms are cells, with steel doors, and the interior of the detention center is divided into isolatable compounds. The detention centers on Manus and Nauru are hastily erected rudimentary camps that make extensive use of transportable buildings, shipping containers, and tents. Regardless of the physical infrastructure, all detention centers are sites of imprisonment and follow carceral regimes, including multiple daily head counts, use of "management units" (separate compounds, rooms, or cells in which people can be held in group or solitary confinement) to control behavior, limitations on movement within the facilities, restrictions on communication with the world beyond detention, and at times excessive and arbitrary use of force by guards who seemingly act with impunity.

Australian law permits the use of immigration detention for "administrative purposes" rather than punishment, which would require the sanction and oversight of a court. This fine distinction, however, is lost on most detainees, who experience immigration detention as prison and as punishment for seeking asylum in Australia. "Imran" told Mark Isaacs, a welfare support worker in detention on Nauru, that he had come to the realization that seeking asylum is a crime. When Isaacs assured him it is not, Imran replied, "Well, look at us. Is this not a prison? Are we not prisoners? So therefore we must have committed a crime" (Isaacs 2014, p. 216). Unlike prisons, in which sentences are time delimited, indefinite detention provides relentless uncertainty. Furthermore, as clinical psychologist Jeanette Gibson proclaims, modern correctional facilities have far better conditions than immigration detention environments (Skelton, 2010). Immigration detainees, in contrast to citizen prisoners, are outcasts from Australian society. They are isolated by the fact of detention, the geographical location of most detention centers, their status as "noncitizens," language barriers, lack of knowledge, obfuscatory practices by officials, and by their effective criminalization in the minds of a majority of "ordinary" Australians. This isolation enables a range of harmful practices and makes it difficult for refugees and asylum seekers to get their stories of life inside detention out into the public sphere.

Upon arrival in detention all people are allocated a number, usually consisting of three letters and two to four digits (e.g., ANR-402). It has been standard practice in detention for guards and some other officials to call people only by their numbers, not their names. Osman recounted how he had asked a guard to call him by his name, the guard refused, saying it was a regulation that staff must call all detainees by number. Osman responded, "Oh God. I've got a name. Your donkey . . . your dog and your cat has got name. I'm a human like you, don't call me by number" (Fiske, 2012, p. 58).

A former detainee told the People's Inquiry into Immigration Detention that being allocated a number was particularly demeaning:

> The first day we were given a number and I was told that from now on that's how I will be known. You will be ABC123. That was one of the most difficult things for us because having your normal freedom taken away from you and at the same time you lost your name.
>
> (Briskman et al., 2008, pp. 132–133)

Another penal regime of detention that refugees have found particularly disturbing is multiple daily head counts. Such musters, often known as the "midnight census," are carried out at least once at night, disturbing sleep, as well as several times during the day. A former detainee said:

> One of the most difficult things for me too was that there were three different head counts. There was one at six in the morning, one at midnight and another at two in the morning. No matter who you are, even a baby, they will have to wake you up; you show your card or shout your number loudly.
>
> (Briskman et al., 2008, pp. 132–133)

Some 6 years after his release from detention, Mohammed remained offended by the intrusion,

> Very, very simple point I'm telling, very, very, and at night time when you're asleep they wake you up, put the torch in your eyes "Where is your ID card?" Now fuck man ...
>
> (Fiske, 2012, p. 220)

Most detainees follow Australian politics throughout their time in detention and pay close attention to refugee and asylum seeker news stories in particular. Refugees speak of their shock, frustration, and anger at being portrayed as criminals, terrorists, and threats to society. Emad spoke of his frustration at the popular portrayal of asylum seekers:

> It was very hard for us to change the image that the government gave about us to the external world. Just psychologically you get really frustrated

when you think that "oh the people that I will meet outside think that I'm a different person, you know I'm a primitive . . . I'm criminal," you know. It's very, very sad actually. But if you're inside the detention centre and let's say you have no access to legal system, you have no access to the media, you cannot talk to the management there, you cannot talk to the immigration department there, you don't have the ability to explain yourself.

(Fiske, 2012, p. 110)

Baha'adin said that he felt "more angry and upset" when he "was watching the news on there" and I heard that Phil Ruddock was saying "these people are very dangerous people and they are terrorists . . . " He used us as a bit of propaganda like "they are dangerous people, they are terrorists" or "they are criminals" and things like that."

(Fiske, 2012, p. 128)

Ibrahim believed that detention was "a plan to punish these people to be honest. This plan has been well managed by someone with high authority in the hierarchy to punish these people and to make them a good example for others . . . people are gonna think twice before they come here." Osman reached a similar conclusion, saying, "John Howard and other ministers mention many time that they keep us to send a message to the smuggler, to other people, don't come to Australia."

(Fiske, 2012, p. 130)

Mehdi explained,

We were the victim of Australian policy to just stop people coming illegally or something. We were the victim and they wanted to show people that we keep them . . . It's not a matter of "what's your story or what . . .?" it's just "keep that person." That's it. They needed to keep some people . . . for a long time to say that "We are strong against these people."

(Fiske, 2012, p. 130)

The criminalization of asylum seeking and the construction of refugees arriving by boat as a serious threat to Australia's national security supports a strong penal response from the government. This means detention in harsh conditions and it means detention that extends far beyond what might reasonably be justified as necessary to enable identification and processing of people's claims. The impact on asylum seekers is dire, particularly on Christmas Island and offshore detention sites.

Under recent government policies, asylum seekers now detained on Christmas Island, Manus, and Nauru have been there for more than a year and very little claims processing has taken place. Refugees are facing years of incarceration in inhumane conditions with no certainty of when or where they might be resettled if they are found to be refugees. Tensions have increased in all detention centers. At the time of this writing, 13 mothers detained on Christmas Island are on suicide watch and acts of self-harm have increased (Australian Human Rights Commission, 2014).

> "Voices" emanating from these actions has been discredited with accusations by Prime Minister Tony Abbott of "moral blackmail," a cynical view that denies the nature of mental illness and that overlooks the possibility that the conditions of detention may result in people reaching breaking point.
>
> ("The cruel and degrading policy of detention," 2014)

> On Nauru despair resulted in a July 2013 riot which caused extensive damage, including the burning of accommodation facilities. Those involved entered the formal justice system in Nauru, charged with offences including affray, riot and larceny.
>
> ("125 asylum seekers charged," 2013)

By far the most notorious events occurred in February 2014, when detainees on Manus Island staged a series of protests, including marching around the compound while chanting slogans. While the full circumstances of events remain unclear 6 months later, some detention staff and members of the PNG mobile squad entered the detention center and began attacking detainees, using machetes, rocks, and guns. One man was killed and 70 others injured, several of them seriously. Despite several asylum seekers witnessing the fatal attack on Reza Berati, a 23-year-old Iranian, and being able to identify his attackers by name, no charges have yet been laid. Nor have charges been laid against anyone for the multiple nonfatal assaults on asylum seekers. Criminal acts inflicted on the criminalized have to date gone unpunished, compared with Nauru, where charges were quickly laid against asylum seekers accused of causing damage to the detention facility.

Some asylum seekers attempted to contact outside agencies during the 2 days of attacks on Manus. The messages conveyed terror and fear. One Lebanese man wrote on social media, "Tonight, polices and g4s attack us again. Many peoples in the yard. Injure please we need one to help us. May be till morning they will kill us. We are human or animals." Another left a phone message on the answering machine of a nongovernmental organization (NGO) saying:

> They are injuring us . . . please, if you are the office for asylum seekers, please contact someone, or the media or anyone . . . We are not here by choice. The government brought us here by force. We are not even fighting them, we are running away from them.
>
> (Whyte, 2014)

Scott Morrison, Australia's immigration minister, when asked by a journalist about the second night of attacks, denied reports as "completely untrue" and advised that journalists should be "more skeptical of stories coming from activists" (Whyte, 2014). When it became clear that the reports of ongoing violence were in fact true, the minister changed his approach and instead laid the blame squarely at the feet of asylum seekers, accusing them of being the instigators of the violence; of breaking out from the detention center; and of provoking detention center staff, police, and local community members (Davidson, 2014).

The events on Manus Island were extraordinary, even in the Australian context, which has seen many mass hunger strikes; lip sewing; mass breakouts; riots; and the use of tear gas, water cannons, and rubber bullets to put down protests. Such events and the lack of negative political consequences for the government in Australia have been made possible by almost two decades of criminalizing and dehumanizing asylum seekers.

Arguably, protest and riot, which exacerbate both the criminalization discourse and punishment, result from governmental policies that trigger such sequences of events. Policies of criminalization create such "criminal" responses, and the criminalization discourse becomes even stronger.

## DETERRENCE

Policies of punishment are underpinned by an ideology of deterrence. By signaling to would-be asylum seekers the fate that awaits them, the clear intent is to prevent asylum seeker arrivals, and from this position the policies have been a "success." Deterrence measures not only arise from the punishment regime within immigration detention but through other extraordinary measures, such as a policy called Operation Sovereign Borders, which pushes boats at sea back to Indonesia. The criminalization discourse here is further exaggerated as an incursion on Australia's sovereign borders. It is in Indonesia that a dual deterrence narrative converges, one that criminalizes both human smugglers and asylum seekers. This occurs at sea and on land, where interdiction and interception undermine state obligations under international law (Babacan & Briskman, 2008).

Australia's blockade, an extraordinary commitment to detention and refusal of protection to asylum seekers arriving by boat, is having an impact in Indonesia, the most common departure point for asylum boats. Indonesia is not a signatory to the 1951 Refugee Convention and does not offer any pathways for refugees to attain permanent residency there. It hosts approximately 10,000 to 15,000 refugees and usually has a policy of tolerance—refugees are permitted to reside in the community while they wait for a United Nations High Commissioner for Refugees (UNHCR) resettlement to a third country or come up with their own solution, such as continuing their journey to a Refugee Convention signatory country. Refugees in Indonesia are not entitled to social security, nor can they work or start their own businesses. Indonesia is a rapidly developing country, with half the population living in poverty using the global US$2 per day measure (Handayani, 2012). The government prioritizes its citizens' opportunities to develop and maintain their livelihoods—any engagement by refugees in income-generating pursuits is seen as competing with the host community and is forbidden. The effect is that refugees in Indonesia must find ways to sustain themselves.

Prior to Australia's policy of turning boats back to Indonesia, refugees may have spent as little as a week or 10 days and up to several months in Indonesia. Refugees are now facing wait times of several years and must sustain themselves for the duration. All the refugees we met in December 2013, men and women from Pakistan, Afghanistan, Iran, and Sri Lanka, were struggling to meet their basic needs for survival.

We met with an Afghan family of three generations. They had been waiting for 6 months. Their 3-year-old daughter had been unwell when they arrived and needed surgery for respiratory problems. The cost of the surgery was prohibitive, and Samira and Yaqub were extremely worried. They had managed to get enough money together to get all surviving family members out of Afghanistan, but this left them little to survive on, much less to pay for surgery. A Pakistani family we met with an 18-month-old daughter who was also unwell relied on their friend, Jawad, a fellow refugee, to search the Internet for symptoms and remedies. Jawad explained that he "used to learn a little bit about medical." When asked about his experience he replied, "I worked in a hospital in Pakistan for seven years. I had experience as receptionist and representer of hospital in Pakistan." This is a service he also provides to other members of the Pakistani refugee community. A man we met who is perpetually struggling with skin irritations and allergies explained that the medicine Jawad recommends "sometime it work, sometimes it's not."

Many refugees facing a long wait in Indonesia rely on remittances from friends and family in Afghanistan, Pakistan, and Australia. Yaqub's friend in Afghanistan sends him money whenever he has some. His brother has a friend in Australia who has sent the family money. This story was repeated by many refugees we met, with several expressing shame and guilt—they had hoped to be in a situation in which they could work, support themselves, and send money back to help those left behind. Raya, a young Pakistani Hazara woman traveling with her younger brother, had recently sold the little jewelry she had and was worried about what would happen when those funds ran out. She estimated she could pay rent and food for another month but could not see beyond that.

The families of the Sri Lankan Tamils we met were either still in Sri Lanka or in refugee camps in India and were unable to offer any support. The group we met consisted of two families with children, one single woman, and five adult men. They were all sharing a house to keep costs down, and most received monthly financial assistance from an NGO. They all received a free meal once each day from a nearby Hindu temple, and if they pooled their resources, they could manage an evening meal each day.

They told us they had been intending to reach Australia. One family had paid cash to a smuggler, but no boat was arranged. The adult men had attempted to take a boat to Australia, but it had sunk off the Indonesian coast, killing almost 200 people. They were among a small number of survivors. The Australian government is not offering resettlement to Sri Lankans, and this group had been advised by the UNHCR to expect a 6-year wait for possible resettlement to New Zealand. The two families with children were particularly concerned about the disruption to their children's education and the long-term impact this would have on their lives.

The financial difficulties created by Australia's criminalization of asylum seeking, however, do not fully capture the emotional impact of the years spent waiting in limbo. Yaqub explained that:

> this is not the solution of our problems because we cannot do anything here. Indonesia do not have any solution for refugees and personally I think . . . it temporarily provides us safe haven. We feel much more secure than in our country. But we are very vulnerable. We can be arrested by police and they can take bribe and release us. We can be looted. We can be treated like animals, just like we are treated in our countries.

He told the story of his friend who was robbed at knifepoint one night and injured in the attack. His friend did not report the matter to police, Yaqub says,

> Because we think that if we report to police, police will prefer the statement of the local people rather than refugees. And then, just like the time . . . motorbike hit one refugee and they say you have to pay compensation for damaging my motorbike.

Indonesia does not deport refugees who have UNHCR status or who are awaiting the outcome of their case with UNHCR, but beyond this security of being permitted to remain, life is precarious. Refugees of all backgrounds that we met said that the vast majority of Indonesian people are accepting and tolerant of them. Pejman was particularly grateful for the safety he had found, saying that when he goes to the market in Indonesia he feels safe: "I don't think this person kill me? This one kill me? This one kill me? Na. In Quetta . . . in Jakarta I have not this problem. That's why I improve my mind. Here is another problem. Because of money, basically money." His neighbor, Moussa, expressed similar sentiments, saying that "in Pakistan there is a . . . genocide against Hazara people. Then we come to here for my safety, protection. I feel better here. There is miracle. The people in this neighborhood are good, not disturbing." He added, however, that he is aware of his precarious status and that because of not having formal legal status he is careful to "stay quiet" and does not go out at night.

Maimunah and Aida, a young Afghan woman and a young Iranian woman sharing a one-room apartment, had moved in just 1 week earlier, after a Molotov cocktail was thrown through the window of their previous accommodation, setting the rug ablaze. They were terrified but had not reported the matter to police for fear of their unclear legal status in the country. Nor had they told their families, as they did not want to worry them.

Pejman and Sazan, a Pakistani Hazara couple in their mid-twenties, waiting with their 18-month old daughter, said they have a good relationship with their Indonesian neighbors. Sazan had befriended her neighbor, and their daughters played together regularly, but language set limits to the possible closeness and depth of their friendship. The family also have Pakistani neighbors, but they are all men, and Sazan feels isolated and lonely. Pejman has been working full-time since he was 12 years old. He has many skills in welding, carpentry, mechanics, and tailoring. He proudly showed us his wife's clothes, explaining that he had made them all. The enforced passivity of waiting for a solution from the UNHCR is very difficult for this young man, who has been enterprising and independent for so much of his life.

> In here, because I work from class eight and now I am 26. I am jobless, so I can't sit one place. I become depress, depress. Just wait and wait. We are waiting, waiting for UNHCR. Now I have this mobile phone (only) for UNHCR. I sleep. Every day I wake and look that the battery is full, signal is coming.
>
> (Pejman)

Sazan agrees and says having Pejman at home all the time, worrying and feeling frustrated, adds to her stress. Pejman was at the site of a bomb explosion in Quetta. He was injured in the blast and has recurrent headaches and pain. His childhood friend was killed in the blast, and he saw dozens of people die around him. With little to do each day he is haunted by his memories of the explosion and its aftermath. He hopes that once he has had his UNHCR interview his "tension will be little bit decreased."

## CRIMINALIZATION, PUNISHMENT, AND DETERRENCE: WE SHALL OVERCOME

Australia's criminalization of asylum seeking has almost closed the door for desperate people in search of safe haven. This means that asylum seekers and refugees have had to find their own solutions rather than waiting for the slow heaving of multicountry bureaucracies. For asylum seekers in detention centers, political agency is apparent in the few means available to protest their plight, which compounds the criminalization discourse of border invasion through punishment for "bad" behavior within detention. Those who experience criminalization at the deterrence stage must live hand to mouth, try to keep control of their bad memories, swallow their pride, and accept a period of dependency on friends and families in parts of the world where earning a living is extremely difficult.

Parallel narratives of those on the receiving end of the politics of punishment and deterrence illustrate how criminalization of irregular migration creates suffering. The stories from inside detention illustrate the methods used for punishment purposes. Those from people waiting in limbo reveal the "successful" impact of punishment of one group to deter others and the half lives that result from this. Governments privilege national security and crime discourses in formulating responses, focusing on boats and borders. Voices of asylum seekers and refugees are discredited, and the human costs of "crimmigration" are hidden from view. Those asylum seekers and refugees who have spoken out do so in the hope that they will be heard and received with compassion. We share their aspirations.

### REFERENCES

125 asylum seekers charged over Nauru riot which caused $60m worth of damage. (2013, July 22). *ABC News*. Retrieved on May 22, 2014, from www.abc.net .au/news/2013-07-22/125-asylum-seekers-charged-over-violent-nauru -riots/4834098.

Aas, K. F. (2007). Analyzing a world in motion. Global flows meet criminology of the other. *Theoretical Criminology, 11*(2), 283–303.

Australian Human Rights Commission. (2014, July 24). New mothers on suicide watch at Christmas Island. Retrieved on July 24, 2014, from www.humanrights .gov.au/news/stories/new-mothers-suicide-watch-christmas-island.

Babacan, A., & Briskman, L. (2008). The future for asylum seekers in a changing world. In A. Babacan & L. Briskman (Eds.), *Asylum seekers: International perspectives on interdiction and deterrence* (pp. 158–165). Newcastle, UK: Cambridge Scholars.

Briskman, L. (2013). Courageous ethnographers or agents of the state: Challenges for social work. *Critical and Radical Social Work, 1*(1), 51–66.

Briskman, L., Latham, S., & Goddard, C. (2008). *Human rights overboard: Seeking asylum in Australia.* Melbourne: Scribe.

Crock, M., Saul, B., & Dastyari, A. (2006). *Future seekers ii: Refugees and irregular migration in Australia.* Sydney: Federation Press.

The cruel and degrading policy of detention [Editorial]. (2014, July 25). *The Age,* p. 16.

Dauvergne, C. (2008). *Making people illegal: What globalization means for migration and law.* New York: Cambridge University Press.

Davidson, H. (2014, February 19). Manus Island violence: Australia and PNG launch investigations. *The Guardian.* Retrieved on July 24, 2014, from www.theguardian .com/world/2014/feb/19/manus-island-violence-australia-png-investigations.

Fiske, L. (2012). *Insider resistance: Understanding refugee protest against immigration detention in Australia 1999–2005* (Unpublished doctoral dissertation). Perth: Curtin University. Retrieved on July 24, 2014, from http://espace.library.curtin .edu.au/R?func=dbin-jump-full&local_base=gen01-era02&object_id=186695.

Grewcock, M. (2009). *Border crimes: Australia's war on illicit migrants.* Sydney: Institute of Criminology Press.

Handayani, I. P. (2012, February 13). Beyond statistics of poverty. *Jakarta Post.* Retrieved on May 24, 2014, from www.thejakartapost.com/news/2012/02/13 /beyond-statistics-poverty.html.

Isaacs, M. (2014). *The undesirables.* Richmond, Australia: Hardie Grant.

McCulloch, J. (2008). Enemies everywhere: (In)security politics, asylum seekers and other enemies within. In A. Babacan & L. Briskman (Eds.), *Asylum seekers: International perspectives on interdiction and deterrence* (pp. 112–127). Newcastle, UK: Cambridge Scholars.

McNevin, A. (2007). The liberal paradox and the politics of asylum in Australia. *Australian Journal of Political Science, 42*(4), 611–630.

Packham, B. (2013, October 25). No illegal arrivals on ABC despite minister's line. *The Australian Business Review.* Retrieved from http://www.theaustralian .com.au/business/media/no-illegal-arrivals-on-abc-despite-ministers-line /story-fnao45gd-1226746316263.

Pickering, S. (2005). *Refugees and state crime.* Annandale, Australia: Federation Press.

Skelton, R. (2010, September 22). Jail better than detention centers. *The Age.* Retrieved on July 21, 2014, from http://www.smh.com.au/national/jail-better -than-detention-centres-20100921-15lei.html.

Story, B. (2005). *Politics as usual: The criminalization of asylum seekers in the United States* (Working Paper Series 26(38)). Oxford, UK: Refugee Studies Centre, University of Oxford.

Taylor, S. (2006). Immigration detention reforms: A small gain in human rights. *Agenda, 13*(1), 49–62.

Wazana, R. (2004). Fear and loathing down under: Australian refugee policy and the national imagination. *Refuge, 22*(1), 83–95.

Welch, M. (2012). The sonics of crimmigration in Australia: Wall of noise and quiet maneuvering. *British Journal of Criminology, 52*(2), 324–344.

Whyte, S. (2014, February 19). Desperate call for help as Manus rioters go on rampage with bedposts. *Sydney Morning Herald.* Retrieved on February 19, 2014, from www.smh.com.au/federal-politics/political-news/desperate-call-for-help-as -manus-rioters-go-on-rampage-with-bedposts-20140218-32yl7.html.

Wilsher, D. (2012). *Immigration detention: Law, history, politics,* Cambridge: Cambridge University Press.

# 17

# Longing to Belong

UNDOCUMENTED YOUTH, INSTITUTIONAL INVISIBILITY,
AND AMBIVALENT BELONGING IN CANADA

▸ FRANCESCA MELONI

WHEN I ASKED THE PASTOR of a church if he knew of any undocumented children who faced difficulties accessing education, his voice suddenly lowered, becoming a whisper. It was late in the evening, and there was nobody, except for the two of us, sitting in the corner of a little church in the suburbs of Montreal. The church activities had ended in the afternoon, and the rooms were dark and empty. The pastor's voice suddenly became a whisper in the shadows—a whisper that was even more of a whisper because we were alone in the room and nobody could possibly have heard us. The pastor looked at me for a moment and then said, bringing his face close to mine: "Yes, I see what you are saying. We know these situations."

I later realized that the whispering of the pastor, this intimate way of speaking and not speaking in the shadows of the church, was not merely a way of protecting the families he befriended. It was also the counterpart to the invisibility—ways of being and not being—of the everyday lives of many undocumented youth that I encountered in my ethnographic fieldwork in Montreal. As described by Coutin in her research with Salvadoran undocumented immigrants, people without legal status can be physically present but legally absent, existing in a contradictory space of nonexistence—outside national borders, hidden within certain spaces of social reality (Coutin, 2003). The fragile, yet powerful relationships that young people "living underground" establish with social institutions and people who have legal status entail a sense of extreme uncertainty. First, these relationships could be revoked at any moment, when undocumented families are deported or when they feel they are in danger of being deported; and second, youth do not usually tell people about their lack of status.

In this chapter, I would like to explore these uncertain ways of being and not being as they are experienced by the many undocumented youth I have met. In particular, I am interested in the tension that exists between the ways in which the restrictions of immigration policies frame the every-day worlds of youth and how these subjects respond to these constraints by forming different forms of social belonging. How do youth endure the uncertainty of their legal status? How do they establish their sense of belonging, when being "here" may be revoked at any moment?

In order to address these questions, I will draw on ethnographic field-work conducted with undocumented youth from Latin American and Caribbean countries in Montreal over a 3-year period. I began conducting this fieldwork in June 2010 in a multicultural neighborhood in Montreal where many undocumented families live. This exploration has been part of a wider mixed-methods research project that aims to document the health status of precarious-status pregnant women and children as well as part of a community-university partnership for access to education (Meloni, Van-thuyne, & Rousseau, forthcoming). In the next section, before exploring undocumented youth's social belonging in more depth, I will provide some context by briefly describing immigration policies in Canada and Québec.

### POLICIES OF EXCLUSION AND INVISIBILITY IN CANADA

In recent decades, Canadian policies have institutionalized—at the social, administrative, legal, and political levels—immigration precariousness, making immigrants illegal in multiple ways (Goldring, Berinstein, & Bernhard, 2009). These policies have made it more difficult to enter Canada as a permanent resident, while other temporary resident categories explic-itly do not lead to pathways to permanent residence or citizenship (Arbel & Brenner, 2013). To give an example of such restrictions, the number of people accepted for refugee claims and family reunification status has been severely restrained, compromising the right to the more inclusive political and social rights that are associated with family reunification and asylum (Ruiz-Casares, Rousseau, Derluyn, Watters, & Crépeau, 2010).

However, with regard to undocumented children, policies are much more ambivalent due to the double status of undocumented children as both *illegal* immigrants to reject and dependent *minors* in need of protection (Meloni, Rousseau, Montgomery, & Measham, 2014). Access to education is an example of this ambivalence. Even if access to public education for *all* children and youth under 18 years old in Québec is both a right and a requirement under provincial law, *free* education is provided only to legal residents of Québec. Many youth I met were often accepted into a school but were considered nonresidents—their families were therefore asked to pay high tuition fees. Moreover, they were not officially recognized as students, since they did not hold valid registration codes issued by the Ministry of Education.

Undocumented children and youth were thus situated in an ambivalent space of nonexistence. While policies failed to recognize them, youth were often unofficially accepted into schools, and they were able to establish affective relationships in this context. Their lives were shaped by "institutional invisibility" (Puggioni, 2005). Juridical norms excluded them as outsiders to the community of citizens and, in turn, limited their access to services. These exclusionary practices, on the one hand, reinforced fear among undocumented children of exposing their status and, on the other hand, created the impression among many teachers and school administrators that undocumented children did not exist at all in their school—indeed, making it seem as though they were invisible.

### FRAMING INVISIBILITY AND BELONGING

The condition of illegality, as shaped by the previously described policies, is not only a juridical status. Rather, it also permeates "migrants' everyday embodied experiences of being-in-the-world" (Willen, 2007, p. 10). It defines profoundly or in more subtle ways a particular subjective understanding of everyday life. With respect to undocumented children and youth, scholars have highlighted how a lack of legal status destabilizes their identity as "betwixt and between," in that they no longer belong to the group they are leaving and yet do not fully belong to the host society (Abrego, 2011; Gonzales, Suárez-Orozco, & Dedios-Sanguineti, 2013). According to this perspective, their ambiguous belonging and liminality act to "thwart individual autonomy and agency" (Suárez-Orozco, Yoshikawa, Teranishi, & Suárez-Orozco, 2011, p. 450).

However, in depicting undocumented youth as subjects who simply have nowhere to fully belong, we fail to consider the complex and contradictory processes in which subjects "are caught within wanting to belong, wanting to become, a process that is fuelled by yearning rather than positing of identity as a stable state" (Probyn, 1996, p. 17). I refer here to an understanding of belonging as dialectically determined by both the state and the subjects. That is, not as a homogeneous and ontologically solid state of being or a rigid exclusion between political membership and affective belonging (Yuval-Davis 2006), but rather as foreground in a principle of noncoherence, an ambivalent and contradictory construction of being and becoming, belonging and longing to belong (Gibson-Graham, 2011; Lobo & Ghosh, 2013).

In what follows, I will unpack this complex process by showing the ways in which youth understand their everyday experiences and the world in multiple and contradictory forms that lie at the same time both *within* and *beyond* four different social and symbolic spaces: (1) the everyday habits they establish "here"; (2) the transnational ties to their home country, over "there"; (3) a sense of larger self, an "us," composed of the family relationships and the network of peers met at school and in other social spaces, with whom they establish affective relationships; and (4) a "living future," a virtual potentiality of the present that already shapes their lives and their ways of being.

### BEING "HERE"

Alicia, a young undocumented girl I met in Montreal, is 15 years old. She arrived in Canada from Jamaica in 2008 with her younger sister and her mother. At the time of this writing, she has been deported to her home country, along with her family. As soon as she knew of her family's deportation order, she started to avoid her peers at school. She told me that she was not even able to tell her boyfriend that she had to leave. She could not look him in the eye. She was so angry, she told me, because she and her brother did not want to leave Canada. "Why would you like to stay here?" I asked her. Alicia replied:

> Everything, you know. Here you have more things, you can take a metro or a bus and you can go everywhere. And I am used to here. I have my boyfriend. I have my very good friend, she is from Spain. I don't get along with Canadians, they are too cold. But I call my friend and I say: What are you up

to? And we plan things together. In Jamaica I don't have a friend like that, someone I can call when I have things to tell.

"I am used to here." Alicia's words echo the words of many youth I met. These words do not express a clear statement of belonging—a firm sense of possession. Rather, they entail a sense of acceptance and adaptation to a particular physical and emotional space—"here." Alicia got used to living here, although it had been her mother's choice to migrate to Canada. She had to align herself with an array of new habits that were completely foreign to her. Interestingly, Alicia got used to "here" by establishing a network of everyday affective and social relationships. As she put it, "I am used to here. I have my boyfriend. I have my very good friend." In this sense, her everyday habits cannot be separated from the affective relationships to which they are attached.

Yet Alicia already foresaw the loss she will suffer. Immigration authorities will separate her from her boyfriend and from her very good friend. For a moment, her eyes were wet: "My friend says she will miss me. And I will miss her, too. It will be hard without her." How do youth cope with loss and absence—a loss that is always present, if not in reality, at least in its potentiality? How can they endure when their being here—their "everything," as Alicia put it—is undermined by their "deportability" (De Genova, 2002), the possibility of being deported?

In order to answer, or partially answer, these questions, we first have to understand youth's lives as containing a manifold and complex dimension that goes beyond merely the habits of daily life and beyond a stable sense of attachment. Youth learn to live and to grow with the potential disruption of their everyday worlds. For instance, many youth told me they were constantly afraid of telling anyone about their status because they were afraid others would not understand their situations or because they feared exposing their status to immigration authorities. They knew that in order to preserve their everyday worlds, they had to hide a part of who they were. Yet even if their peers did not know their "entire story," they often knew, or perhaps imagined, "something." An undocumented girl explained to me: "I've never told my entire story, yet my friends know something. Even my closest friends, they just know that I cannot travel abroad with them. They know that I have to pay higher tuition fees than them. They know I cannot enter a bar with them. But they don't know more than that."

### BEING "THERE"

A youth's sense of his or her own story cannot thus escape from a transnational dimension, that is to say, from the transnational ties and memories to which he or she is attached and from the possibility of being deported. However, youth who left their home countries at a young age, went to school, and established affective relationships in the countries of arrival often felt a sense of estrangement from their own cultural communities (Castro-Salazar & Bagley, 2010). For instance, Roberto, a young undocumented boy from Mexico, explained to me that he did not have any Mexican friends:

> At first, when I arrived here, I spent a lot of time with Mexicans. But then I said to myself: Why should I have Mexican friends since I am here in Canada? I would like to meet people from other countries and to learn French. Then I decided to try a little bit, and now I don't have any Mexican friends anymore. I speak only with Québécois and people from other countries. And all Mexicans are gone anyways and I am alone now. They went back to their country.

Roberto was caught between a "double absence" (Sayad, 2004), a double estrangement that was also a double, always incomplete, form of belonging. On the one hand, he partially belonged to his Mexican peers and to the church where his family and many Mexican immigrants would go. This world is a world of departure and uncertainty, constantly shaped by loss. Roberto, referring to the many Mexican friends of his family who have been deported, told me, "All the Mexicans are gone anyways and I am alone now."

On the other hand, he developed relationships with others who were not part of his cultural community. He started to play volleyball three times per week; he started to go out with a Québecoise girl. His social networks were primarily established in his neighborhood: he went to a park to play with his friends, and his girlfriend lived only 10 minutes' walking distance from his apartment. And yet the social ties he established in Montreal were always undermined by the presence of a "there" he partially belonged to—the community of Mexicans who are gone now.

The ambivalence between being here and there, however, does not necessarily put youth in an empty space of despair. Youth also resignify their lived reality and constraints by evoking new ways of symbolically, if not physically, being "there." For instance, Carlos, a young, undocumented boy who worked 15 hours per day to earn his living, told me that when he had some free time, he used to take pictures for himself and for his friends. He proudly showed me his new professional camera and explained:

> My lawyer says he cannot do anything about my situation. The law has changed. It is too hard and I am afraid to go back to my country. That is why I like to do photography and take pictures, because I just want to get away from this, because I am always thinking about this and it is on my mind. I started to take pictures when I came to Canada. It helps me think of something else.

Thus, for many youth, being "here" always extends to the perceived reality of "there" through a physical or an imagined space. But it also extends beyond a defined boundary of themselves. Indeed, their being is also entangled with the affective relationships they establish with their peers and their family. It evokes the presence of an "other," someone for whom they can exist without the need to narrate their entire story. It evokes the presence of an "us" in which their sense of self is rooted.

### BEING "US"

Elizabeth crossed many countries as an unaccompanied minor and has lived illegally in the United States and Canada. She was imprisoned twice: once at the U.S. border and another time in Canada. Yet despite the trauma, she found her own way to survive. "You don't forget. But you have to live with it, you have to survive," she told me. As she explains, a number of different people helped her survive:

> What kept me alive was my family, my brothers, my sisters, my aunts; but also, I chose life. I saw myself in different people. When I saw people on the street or people with no rights, people living illegally, I saw myself in those people. So I got the strength, I got the inspiration to live, to be a good person, but to also find ways to help people like that. I grew up a community in so many ways. And I built a community, by engaging myself in an organization that helps people and cases like mine, so that they can have some justice.

This ability to survive her past traumatic experiences and to "keep herself alive," as she put it, was made possible by the support of her family, with whom she kept in contact through "the community" she established during all those years, and by her "seeing herself in different people in need." The experience of "growing up" a community and the different activities and social justice engagements that she took part in were a source of strength for Elizabeth, her inspiration and motivation to live on despite adversity. A way to become new kinds of "we," new kinds of "I," in relation to and in spite of the pain she suffered.

Moreover, this community made her alive politically and socially. It was an essential way of making herself socially and politically recognized as an entitled member of the polis. Interestingly, when her refugee claim was refused in Canada and she was arrested, her friends and her "community" of peers organized a series of public demonstrations, asking the government if she could be granted refugee status on humanitarian and compassionate grounds. Following 3 months of detention and several public demonstrations, Elizabeth finally received refugee status in Canada.

### BEING "IN FUTURE"

As youth imagine and form themselves in new forms of pluralities, they also imagine themselves as "living futures." A living future is more than a hope, it is more than simple will, more than a not-yet (Anderson, 2006). It shapes youth's ways of being in the present. Roberto's life, for instance, was profoundly shaped by a clear desire. He was firmly determined to come back to Canada, even if his family decided to leave following a deportation order: "I really would like to come back. I will try hard to come back here, after. I would like to have a family and to have children. I would like to come here to work, or to study. And to have a better future."

Yet it is quite unlikely that Roberto will succeed in coming to Canada with legal status. In recent years, multiple policies have closed the door to Mexican immigrants, who now face the impossibility of obtaining a permanent migratory status (Canadian Council for Refugees/Conseil Canadien pour les Réfugiés, 2010). Perhaps Roberto's hope emerged from the very impossibility of entering Canada with a permanent migratory status. As Anderson (2006) points out, hope has a contradictory place in relation to everyday life. There is some despair folded into becoming hopeful: hope always emerges in relation to specific diminishments or disillusionments or in relation to "bad encounters" that affect us with sadness. The present is haunted by the fact that "the conditions that make it possible to hope are strictly the same as those that make it possible to despair" (Marcel, 1967, p. 101).

Yet this hopefulness, which begins from a discontinuity and a disillusionment, "paradoxically enables the enactment of good tendencies and latencies which fold into those relations that diminish" (Anderson, 2006, p. 744). And, sometimes stubbornly, youth insist on carrying on their dreams. Michael, a young boy, drew the picture of a smiling doctor and recounted his greatest dream:

> My biggest dream is to become, one day, a doctor, and to help people. We left our life in our country because my family was a victim of violence. We had to leave our country because of our fear. Now that we live underground without legal status, I am sad to see that same fear in the eyes of my parents. Even if we have to hide, my dream will never change. And it will never change. Even if some people try to stop me from succeeding, I will fight to carry on my dream.

Youth's ways of being are thus also ways of being in the future. Their representations of their future, by virtue of their call, can come to affect their present. These representations may be a thought, a dream, or a totally imaginary entity, they may be revocable or transitory, and they do not have to be accomplished or to even exist: their being in future, as an unmanifested goal, "will suffice" (Pierce, 1933, p. 292). A youth's being is, in essence, a being in future, which he or she can actively carve and shape.

## CONCLUSION

This is, after all, a meditation on frail forms of agency, dreams, hopes, and not-yets that are already, in some way, niches of reality. Perhaps, as I have suggested, at the core of the strength of many of the youth I met and of their capacity to survive uncertainty lies the possibility or hope of creating new opportunities in life through affect and belonging. Gilles Deleuze holds that affects are based on a representation, "There is the idea of the loved thing, to be sure, there is an idea of something hoped for" (Deleuze, 1978, p. 16). However, to express this desire and this hope, it is "necessary to have an idea, however confused or indeterminate it may be, of what is willed" (Deleuze, 1978, p. 17). It is thus essential to have a desire—something, even if unclear, to long for and to exist for. As Povinelli points out, an affect is not nothing. But it is also not something definite, meaning that it is not a realized thing or the accomplishment of something. It is rather a force of existing, "a space of potentiality where new forms of life can emerge" (Povinelli, 2011, p. 9). In this sense, this affect or the establishment of a desire for social (and political) existence is a way to express agency—both the nothing and the something. It is both the illusion and the potentiality of agency or, to be more precise, the possibility of opening new spaces for something that could be or could simply not be.

The youth I encountered in my fieldwork often had different, complex, and sometimes paradoxical ways of establishing their belonging, through affect and hope, within intricate and shifting webs of interdependence made up of family, peers, and transnational ties. Most of the time, these youth were situated in a double ambivalence, since they vacillated between the possibility and desire to belong and the impossibility of fully belonging—they are and they are not "here" (Abu El-Haj, 2007). I hold that two reasons may explain the ambivalence of youth's belonging. First, youth cannot fully belong, because others (immigration authorities, teachers, school administration, peers) fail to recognize them (Butler, 1997). But second, their ambivalence protects them from being wounded by the constant possibility of deportation and with it, the possibility of being removed from the social world they have built in Canada and being separated from the persons for whom they care. Youth distance themselves, to some extent, from the ways others define them as excluded or partially excluded from the social and political community. They are unsure whether the new forms of life they hope for (i.e., the possibility of being recognized as entitled members of a community) will ever be realized or perhaps will just come to nothing.

It is crucial to ask ourselves questions about these new possibilities of life for which youth hope. How will we listen to them? How will we recognize them? Will they become something? Will they remain anything? To be sure, these are not only abstract questions. The needs of youth and their families are urgent and pressing. Their ways of establishing affective relationships and their longing to belong are entangled with their everyday lives and interactions with different social spheres (primarily their families, schools, peers, and neighborhoods), which sometimes may over-lap with ours. Questions of access to health care or school are becoming increasingly relevant at the public and political levels, since these individuals, who are mostly invisible and whose existence we often forget, now come to disturb us. They ask for citizenship, they demand access to services and education. But they also say that, whether we want it or not, they already exist in some forgotten spaces within our societies, the in-between spaces.

As such, youth's ways of understanding their place already defy the boundaries of national membership, even if we do not recognize them. These boundaries oppose jus soli, according to which every child born in a national territory is a citizen, and jus sanguinis, according to which a child is entitled to citizenship not by place of birth but by having a parent who is citizen. In contrast, youth's stories seem to tell us that in order to be an entitled member of a community, it does not matter where you are born or who your parents are. Instead, what matters deeply is how you establish your affective ties and how you decide to belong, partially belong, or con-tradictorily belong, somewhere and to someone.

## REFERENCES

Abrego, L. J. (2011). Legal consciousness of undocumented Latinos: Fear and stigma as barriers to claims-making for first and 1.5 generation immigrants. *Law & Society Review, 45*(2), 337–370.

Abu El-Haj, T. (2007). "I was born here, but my home, it's not here": Educating for democratic citizenship in an era of transnational migration and global conflict. *Harvard Educational Review, 77*(3), 285–316.

Anderson, B. (2006). Becoming and being hopeful: Towards a theory of affect. *Environment and Planning D, 24*(5), 733–752.

Arbel, E., & Brenner, A. (2013). Bordering on failure: Canada-U.S. border policy and the politics of refugee exclusion. Cambridge: Harvard Immigration and Refugee Law Clinic Program.

Butler, J. (1997). *The psychic life of power: Theories in subjection.* Stanford, CA: Stanford University Press.

Canadian Council for Refugees/Conseil Canadien pour les Réfugiés. (2010). Protecting rights in a fair and efficient refugee determination system: Submission to Parliament on Bill C-11, 5 May, 2010. Montréal, QC, Canada: Author.

Castro-Salazar, R., & Bagley, C. (2010). "Ni de aquí ni from there." Navigating between contexts: Counter-narratives of undocumented Mexican students in the United States. *Race Ethnicity and Education, 13*(1), 23–40.

Coutin, S. B. (2003). *Legalizing moves: Salvadoran immigrants' struggle for US residency*. Ann Arbor: University of Michigan Press

De Genova, N. (2002). Migrant "illegality" and deportability in everyday life. *Annual Review of Anthropology, 31*(1), 419–447.

Deleuze, G. (1978). Transcripts on Spinoza's concept of affect (pp. 1–28). Retreived from http://www.gold.ac.uk/media/deleuze_spinoza_affect.pdf.

Gibson-Graham, J. (2011). A feminist project of belonging for the Anthropocene. *Gender, Place and Culture, 18*(1), 1–21.

Goldring, L., Berinstein, C., & Bernhard, J. K. (2009). Institutionalizing precarious migratory status in Canada. *Citizenship Studies, 13*(3), 239–265.

Gonzales, R., Suárez-Orozco, C., & Dedios-Sanguineti, M. C. (2013). No place to belong: Contextualizing concepts of mental health among undocumented immigrant youth in the United States. *American Behavioral Scientist, 57*(8), 1174–1199. doi: 10.1177/0002764213487349

Lobo, M., & Ghosh, S. (2013). Conversations on belonging: Women of Indian heritage speak. *Journal of Intercultural Studies, 34*(4), 410–417. doi: 10.1080/07256868.2013.821218

Marcel, G. (1967). Desire and hope. In N. Lawrence & M. O'Connor (Eds.), *Readings in existential phenomenology* (pp. 312–331). Englewood Cliffs, NJ: Prentice-Hall.

Meloni, F., Rousseau, C., Montgomery, C., & Measham, T. (2014). Children of exception: Redefining categories of illegality and citizenship in Canada. *Children & Society, 28*(4), 305–315. doi:10.1111/chso.12006

Meloni, F., Vanthuyne, K., & Rousseau, C. (forthcoming). Ethics, interdependence and agency: Rethinking ethical issues in anthropological research with children and youth. *Anthropological Theory*.

Pierce, C. S. (1933). *Collected papers of Charles Sanders Pierce*. Cambridge: Harvard University Press.

Povinelli, E. (2011). *Economies of abandonment: Social belonging and endurance in late liberalism*. Durham, NC: Duke University Press.

Probyn, E. (1996). *Outside belongings*. New York: Routledge.

Puggioni, R. (2005). Refugees, institutional invisibility, and self-help strategies: Evaluating Kurdish experience in Rome. *Journal of Refugee Studies, 18*(3), 319–339.

Ruiz-Casares, M., Rousseau, C., Derluyn, I., Watters, C., & Crépeau, F. (2010). Right and access to healthcare for undocumented children: Addressing the gap between international conventions and disparate implementations in North America and Europe. *Social Science & Medicine, 70*(2), 329–336.

Sayad, A. (2004). *The suffering of the immigrant.* Malden, MA: Polity.

Suárez-Orozco, C., Yoshikawa, H., Teranishi, R. T., & Suárez-Orozco, M. M. (2011). Growing up in the shadows: The developmental implications of unauthorized status. *Harvard Educational Review, 81*(3), 438–473.

Willen, S. (2007). Toward a critical phenomenology of illegality: State power, criminalization, and abjectivity among undocumented migrant workers in Tel Aviv, Israel. *International Migration, 45*(3), 8–38.

Yuval-Davis, N. (2006). Belonging and the politics of belonging. *Patterns of Prejudice. 40*(3), 197–214.

# 18

# Migrants and Justice in Qatar

*TIME, MOBILITY, LANGUAGE, AND ETHNOGRAPHY*

▸ ANDREW GARDNER, SILVIA PESSOA,
AND LAURA HARKNESS

## JUSTICE, GULF MIGRATION, AND THE LIVED EXPERIENCE

THE LIVES AND EXPERIENCES EXPLORED in this chapter are the subject of a large, multifaceted, ethnographic research project conducted between 2010 and 2013 in Qatar. One component of that multifaceted ethnographic project (a component supported by a grant from the Open Society Foundation) sought to use ethnographic methods to assess the experiences of transnational labor migrants and their access to justice.[1] Forty-nine individuals—or "subjects"—were interviewed as part of this component of the project, and a longer, detailed report encapsulates their experiences and the project's findings (Gardner, Pessoa, & Harkness, 2014). The report concluded with a set of policy recommendations intended to incrementally improve the efficiency of the existing pathways to justice open to labor migrants in Qatar. This chapter focuses less intently on those policy recommendations and instead considers several of the recurring threads woven through many of the migrant narratives our research team gathered in the field. These threads describe some of the forces that confound migrants' pursuit of justice in Qatar.

Notably, this paper is not as directly about "illegal" migrants. The migrants interviewed for this project were in the midst of the challenging task of navigating the threshold between legality and illegality and were doing so in a complicated foreign environment. More directly, the chapter explores the governance of foreign migrants and the criminalization of the portions of migrant agency that conflict with the interests of the state, with those of corporations and migrants' employers, and with some of the citizens and foreigners who profit from these migrants' labor. This *migration system*, in place not only in Qatar but also in the neighboring Gulf States, now comprises the third-largest transnational migration flow in the contemporary world (after North America and Europe). In that sense, this chapter also helps shift our attention to other migrations and other experiences in our contemporary world. In this case, millions of migrants from around the Indian Ocean world encounter this migration system at a destination also in the global South.

Migration to the hydrocarbon-rich Gulf States of the Arabian Peninsula, once an odd and understudied footnote in the contemporary era of global mobility, has more recently emerged as a lightning rod of global attention.[2] Qatar and the neighboring Gulf States (Kuwait, Saudi Arabia, Bahrain, United Arab Emirates, and Oman) all rely heavily on foreign labor forces. In most of these states, this foreign workforce represents a majority of the total workforce, and in several of these states foreign populations are an absolute majority of the total population. Qatar is a particularly extreme example of these demographics: on the Qatari peninsula today, citizens are outnumbered more than nine to one by foreign workers. The men and, less frequently, women who make up this foreign workforce come from a variety of different places. Most come from South Asia—places like India, Bangladesh, Nepal, Pakistan, and Sri Lanka—but substantial portions of the migrant population come from elsewhere, including Africa, Southeast Asia, and other parts of the Middle East.

Migrants to the region are governed by the *kafala*, or sponsorship system. This system, in place for decades and with roots that stretch back much further, ties individual migrants to a particular job and a particular employer. Both scholars and advocates (and those of us who believe we straddle that threshold) have long contended that this system structures problematic relations for migrants (Eelens, Schampers, & Speckmann, 1992; Gardner, 2005, 2010a, 2010b; Longva, 1997, 1999). Sponsors who often profit from both those who immigrate and work are unequally empowered, so a migrant's fate depends almost entirely on the character of his or her sponsor. And beyond that sponsor's character, that fate depends on the sponsor's concern, oversight, and organizational skill. Many migrants have never met their sponsors but instead deal with the other end of a hierarchy that begins with the migrant's supervisor, that supervisor's manager, perhaps one or two higher positions, and a foreign owner in business with a citizen-sponsor. Indeed, low-skilled labor migrants are at the bottom end of complex hierarchies of institutions, structures, and contracts that typify labor relations in a busy, global, and cosmopolitan hub.

When relations with their employers go awry, some migrants seek justice. Most commonly, in the justice system they seek the salaries they believe are owed to them, although they occasionally enter the justice system to pursue other issues. Most of the cases we came to learn about involved $1,000 or $2,000, and occasionally a bit more. The Qatari state provides migrants with two avenues to justice. First, there is arbitration at the Department of Labor Relations. This typically involves explaining problems, phone calls to the employer, and occasionally a meeting. Intransigent or absent employers are beyond the department's reach. Second, there is Labor Court. This court hears cases, and it is notable that many migrants whose cases are heard there eventually achieve their goals. We found migrant encounters with Labor Court to be much less common than those with the Department of Labor Relations, however.

We also concluded that the state-provided avenues to justice were the centerpiece of a more complex array of institutions and junctions that recurred in migrants' pathways toward justice. Migrants' respective embassies, diasporic community leaders, other institutions, and an assortment of acquaintances often facilitated their pursuit of justice. Roommates and friends loaned these migrants money or gave them food to help them endure periods with no income. Some migrants sought an "illegal" job, defined in Qatar as any work for anyone other than the sponsors/employers who brought them to the peninsula. This is known as "absconding" in the Gulf States and is criminalized under the *kafala*. The Ministry of the Interior was also involved in migrants' journeys toward justice. The ministry might imprison and/or deport them. In other circumstances, it might release them from their sponsors, thereby freeing them to work elsewhere.

In summary, the *kafala* is the key characteristic of this migration system, and it shapes many of the circumstances that result in migrants seeking justice. Notably, the *kafala* criminalizes the free movement of labor and empowers individual sponsors/employers. The justice system in Qatar, as detailed here in both institutional form and through the lived experiences of labor migrants, essentially functions to manage frictions internal to this migration system and the labor relations it arranges. Despite the clarity of this theorized functionality of this justice system, it is a complex, byzantine, and foreign amalgamation of laws, institutions, and norms. Navigating the complexities of this foreign justice system posed a significant challenge to all the migrants we interviewed. After collating these migrants' narratives of their time in the justice system, we identified three threads woven through those experiences: time, space, and language. Each is described here.

### TIME AND THE CHRONOLOGY OF JUSTICE IN QATAR

One of the recurring themes in the experiences of the migrants interviewed for this project concerned the long delays that were part and parcel of the adjudication process. The timelines of justice in Qatar are an issue that is noteworthy on its own, but when comprehended against the backdrop of the *kafala* and the transnational migration industry that has evolved around it, the long timelines of migrant justice in Qatar can be envisioned as a serious, chronic hindrance to the administration of justice. Consider Rajendra's[3] experience.

In June of 2010, Rajendra arrived in Qatar to work as a driver for a construction company. He was told his salary would be QR 1,500 (US$412) per month. After 16 months of work, he and his fellow workers, Filipinos, Sri Lankans, Indians, and Nepalese, had only been paid for a few months of work. The employees decided to stop working until the matter was resolved. They went to the Department of Labor Relations in the Industrial Area, which Rajendra, like many other foreign migrants, referred to as the "Labor Court." They went to this office three times, but their employer's representatives failed to attend any of these appointments. The case was then referred to another branch of the Department of Labor Relations. After three additional meetings at this other branch, the company's owner finally appeared. He agreed to provide the workers plane tickets to return home and to pay them 25% of their pending salary. The workers agreed to this arrangement, but the owner failed to return to the office. Instead, he came to their labor camp, where he offered to pay for their plane tickets home and provide them 1 month's salary, nothing more. The workers rejected this proposal. After they returned to the Department of Labor Relations, their case was referred to the Labor Court, which Rajendra, like most migrants, called "high court." Rajendra and the other workers went to Labor Court and were given a date to return in 2 months. When they returned 2 months later, they were told to return again in 10 days. The pattern of being told to return 10 days later continued a few more times, because the owner of the company failed to appear for any of these hearings.

While the case was in "high court," Rajendra and the other workers went to the Human Rights Department of the Ministry of Interior. There they were advised to continue with the court case for the next three or four months until it was concluded. They were told that upon the case's conclusion they would receive a release (or No Objection Certificate) legally permitting them to change sponsors and therefore employment. However, it was difficult for them to survive while waiting for the outcome of the court case. They borrowed money from friends for food, and the company owner told them they must leave the company-provided labor camp. The owner finally came to the Human Rights Department and agreed to give them a release if they withdrew their case. Rajendra and the majority of the other workers acquiesced, withdrew their case, and received the release from their sponsor.

With the release, Rajendra was able to obtain a job with a different company where his friend worked. The conditions at the new company seemed relatively good, although he would have preferred to have received the salary owed to him and to have simply returned to Nepal. This, however, did not seem possible—the case had been dropped, but he felt powerless in the justice system. As he summarized,

> I have gained some knowledge from this process that our category of people cannot fight with the Labor Court in Qatar, because we could not win the case. I just felt that. So it would be better if we did not think of going to court. I have met some friends here that are still fighting with the court. Some are still fighting after two years ... So I realized that we could not win our case against the owner by the court here in Qatar.

Many different issues coalesce in these stories and those other migrants we interviewed that describe migrants' experiences with the justice system. But like many of those other stories, Rajendra's experience reveals how time and the chronology of justice are significant aspects of his experience and his decisions. Like most migrants, Rajendra waited for the company to address his issue for many months. When he finally embarked on his journey through the justice system, he faced a complex, bureaucratic, and multifaceted system that was difficult to navigate. Consecutive meetings at one juncture of this justice system were followed by months of waiting for follow-up appointments. Indeed, these elongated timelines to justice were typical of all the migrants we interviewed for this project. Rajendra's willingness to accept the owner's proposal to withdraw the court case, and the widespread desire by many migrants to simply return home no matter how much money they are owed, results from these long timelines to justice.

Notably, many migrants would willingly pursue their cases if they could continue working and continue earning a salary while doing so. But during those many months of process and indecision, migrants often have no income at all, for they are typically refusing to work (or disallowed from working) for the sponsors/employers against whom they have filed a case. Those sponsors/employers have often failed to pay them their promised salaries, and under the strictures of the *kafala*, are simultaneously the only people who can legally employ them. By criminalizing migrants' mobility in the labor market, the *kafala* locks migrants in place. Moreover, many migrants reported that their employers, who were typically defendants in their legal cases, frequently made their situation even more difficult by turning off the electricity (and therefore air conditioning) at their labor camps and sometimes forcing them to depart their only accommodation. In summary, as Rajendra's narrative reveals, the long timelines to justice in the Qatari justice system are a practical and everyday impediment to the administration of justice and oftentimes compel foreign migrants to abandon the pathways to justice provided to them by the state.

### MOBILITY, URBAN SPACE, AND JUSTICE IN QATAR

Mobility provides another conceptual thread that connects migrants' experiences and challenges in Qatar's justice system. In general, migrants in contemporary Qatar and throughout the Gulf live an enclaved, marginalized existence in spatially segregated portions of the cities and their peripheries. In Qatar, many foreign migrants live in the Industrial Area, at the outskirts of Doha, or in Al Khor, north of the city. They are bussed to their worksites and then back to their camps. Labor camps and other assigned migrant dwellings are typically located some distance from the city center, and recent zoning policies in Doha have sought to extend and formalize this segregation. This impulse to segregate the foreign workforce is, indeed, a region-wide phenomenon, for Qatar's plans clearly echo the plans in other Gulf States to build "bachelor cities" and other offstage spaces to accommodate the foreign workforce.

While this spatial segregation and the enclaving of the foreign population is often morally challenged by scholars ensconced in Western norms and ideas, it poses a significant *practical* challenge to migrants seeking to address issues in Qatar's justice system. Public transportation services to many of the enclaves and segregated spaces that accommodate the foreign workforce are partial at best, and the costs of this transportation put it out of reach of most transnational migrant workers. While many migrants wish to access and utilize Qatar's complex justice system, they often simply cannot get to the places they are required to be, and when they do so, it is only with great difficulty and expense.

Shanti's migration experience is illustrative of this reality. Shanti was 18 years old when we interviewed him, and he came as part of a group of men from his village in Nepal to work as a general laborer. When they arrived at their labor camp for the first time, there was no space for them: there were already 14 workers packed in the single small room leased by the company, so the new arrivals from Nepal slept in the open air on the roof. All of the men had paid QR 3,500 (US$961) for their work visas in Nepal, and although they had been promised a salary of QR 1,000 (US$275) by their labor broker in Nepal, after 4 months in Qatar they had yet to see any of their salary. Shortly thereafter, their employer told them there was no more work for them. They took their issue to the Nepali embassy. Officials at the embassy called the company's manager, a Pakistani immigrant himself, but nothing was resolved. Returning to the embassy, the men were told to take their case to court. Recalling this juncture in his experience, Shanti noted, "They gave us a paper to take to the labor court. But we don't have any money to go there! How can we go?"

Although Shanti's comments pertain to a single juncture of his interaction with the justice system, they portray how mobility in contemporary Doha is a formidable challenge for many migrants, particularly for those who are simply not being paid. The issue is compounded by the fact that many laborers only have access to company-provided transportation—another "benefit" that is often rescinded when laborers pursue claims against employers in the ministries or courts. These challenges are redoubled by the bureaucratic nature of the Qatari justice system: migrants are often advised by their embassies to bring their case to the Department of Labor Relations, which then may transfer their case to other branches of the department that in turn may forward their cases to the court system. The geographical distribution of these institutions in the city, combined with the repeated visits that are often necessary, put foreign workers with little or no mobility at a significant disadvantage and stymie their pursuit of justice.

All of this suggests that mobility can be conceptualized as a significant impediment to the carriage of justice in Qatar. The Qatari justice system requires migrants' repeated presence, often at different locations. Their lack of mobility in the city impedes their attempts to seek justice. For transnational workers with little or no income, the costs of attending these appointments are substantial, and these costs function as a systemic disruption to the state's intent of providing migrants with a clear and achievable avenue to justice. In discerning the role that immobility plays in the carriage of justice in Qatar, we can also envision how the criminalization of migrant agency rests atop a foundation of factors and circumstances beyond those codified in law. In this case, labor relations and the arrangement of labor in the built space of the city comprises a set of recurring challenges undergirding their position in law.

## LANGUAGE AND JUSTICE IN QATAR

As previously noted, the population of foreign workers in Qatar and throughout the Gulf comes from a wide and diverse variety of sending states. The majority come from a handful of South Asian states, and while some arrive with a functional understanding of English and/or Hindi, few are fluent in Arabic. Arabic remains the official language of the state and the various institutions in Qatar's complex justice system. This project's wide-ranging interviews with both migrants and experts suggested that language itself comprises a major impediment to the administration of justice for the foreign population. Migrants almost uniformly lack an understanding of how this system works and what decisions are being made about their case. In the most basic terms, this is visible in the recurring confusion about the courts and ministry but is also woven into their experiences in the courtroom. For many migrants, the most acute and noticeable junction where this issue confronts them is in their appearances at the Labor Court or at the Department of Labor Relations.

Udit's experience in the justice system is illustrative. A Nepalese labor migrant, Udit had been promised a salary of QR 800 (US$220) by a labor broker in Nepal. When he arrived in Qatar, however, he was informed that he could either accept QR 500 (US$137) per month or he could go back to Nepal. He accepted this salary as his fate. His job as a "helper" in a crew of workers meant that some days he helped a plumber, other days he worked as an electrician's assistant. Although the recurring nonpayment of his promised salary was an ongoing problem, Udit and other workers entered the justice system because, after many months, the company employing them had failed to provide them with proper identification—and, more specifically, with their residency permits. Without that residency permit, he and the other workers feared being caught by the police and deported.[4] The risks to his and his family's financial survival in Nepal were overwhelming: "We would lose all our belongings, the cash owed to us by the company, everything. That is why we went to the labor court." His experience in the court, though, was not promising. "They talked a bit to the people who could speak a little Arabic and that is all," he recalled.

Rajendra, whose experience was previously described, faced chronic nonpayment of the salary promised by his employer. After 16 months in Qatar, he had been paid only sporadically: he estimated he had been paid for only a few months of work. Then his employer told him there was no more work. When he brought his case to court, he noted that he depended on "some friends who could speak a little Arabic and English, too. [In court] there was one person sitting near the Qatari who spoke Hindi words, so it was easy to translate for us. That guy was from Pakistan." Like Rajendra, Rakesh had pursued the nonpayment of his salary in the justice system. In his description of his experience in the Qatari justice system, he noted that the tea boy, a male office servant, actually did much of the translation during his appearance at the Department of Labor Relations. Rakesh noted to us that he had no idea if the tea boy did a good job with the translation, as Rakesh obviously could not understand the Arabic portion of the translation.

The preparation of documentation and forms necessary for migrants to deliver to the Labor Court or the Department of Labor Relations is also affected by linguistic issues. Those documents must be prepared in Arabic, and entrepreneurial typists are a common fixture at many of the ministries in contemporary Qatar. Rakesh noted that he paid one of these typists QR 10 (US$2.75) for preparing a necessary document. While seemingly minimal, these costs are formidable in the lives of these migrants, particularly in those situations in which migrants have no income.

Finally, without a doubt these same linguistic issues and the segregation of the foreign population also percolate into the widespread misunderstandings about this complex and multifaceted justice system. As periodically noted throughout this chapter, one of the largest struggles for our research team was identifying which institutions in the Qatari justice system the project's participants were referring to in our interviews. Almost ubiquitously, foreign migrants referred to the Department of Labor Relations as "court," and to the Labor Court itself as "high court."

In a recent presentation at the University of Puget Sound in Tacoma, Washington, Jorge Barón, the executive director of the Northwest Immigrant Rights Project, noted that American migration and detention laws are like a foreign language and that part of his project's outreach mission was simply translating law and process into a framework comprehensible to detainees. Similarly, in Qatar, the law and procedures related to migration and the institutional framework are a byzantine, complex system, even for natives. This puts most labor migrants in a double bind: law, metaphorically understood as a "foreign language," is also written, codified, and adjudicated in a language literally foreign to almost all labor migrants in Qatar. The result, readily observed in the interviews conducted for this project, is a vast and significant lack of comprehension of the Qatari justice system. Most labor migrants do not know what institutional component of the justice system they are interacting with, and they have little idea about what that institutional component is empowered to adjudicate. They do not understand the proceedings during their time in these institutions; they struggle to comprehend how to navigate the justice system; and their stories and experiences are also poorly understood by judges and other officials. In this particularly cosmopolitan and heterogeneous context, language is clearly another impediment to the administration and adjudication of justice.

Again, this thread connecting many migrants' experiences in the justice system points to a field of issues beyond criminalization in law. Their struggle to navigate the thresholds of that criminalization is fettered not only by their immobility, as discussed in the previous section, but also by language they encounter in the justice system. In Qatar and elsewhere in the contemporary world, this is a result of the increasing diversity of transnational migrant demography.

## CONCLUDING THOUGHTS

This chapter, and the project it describes, was centrally grounded in the lived experiences of migrants in the Qatari justice system. Notably, these experiences were not anecdotal flourishes intended to illustrate or highlight conclusions derived from an analysis of the taxonomy of the legal system. Instead, in the ethnographic tradition, these migrants' experiences were the foundation of data from which this legal system was mapped and from which our conclusions were drawn. Among other notable qualities, this analytic method ensures that those conclusions and the policy recommendations that emerged from them are deduced not from the legal system as it is envisioned or imagined to work but rather from the legal system as it is encountered and experienced by migrants who are struggling to utilize it.

Additionally, the breadth of the ethnographic scope of inquiry often yields other (and perhaps unforeseen) analytic vista points. Because the interviews and experiences surveyed here explored issues beyond the ambit of the legal system itself—such as the migrants' households in the sending states, their experiences in the migration system that brought them to the Arabian Peninsula, and their experiences in the city itself—one can see the forces at work in their decisions to continue in the justice system or abandon their pursuits, or one can better contextualize their frequently reported challenges of making scheduled appointments in the Qatari justice system. From another angle, the holistic nature of ethnographic inquiry frames Qatar's justice system as another juncture in a complex, transnational migration system. A deep and sustained engagement with migrants' experiences and migrant voices are an essential component of this holism.

The combination of the criminalization of the migrant "other" and the pervasive role of illegality in these migrants' experiences is a more complicated topic here. Foremost, any analysis of the migration system that brings transnational labor migrants to the Arabian Gulf States immediately calls into question the European and American tether of our understanding of migration as a whole, the assimilative and democratic norms that underpin that understanding, the parity of these migrants' experiences with the often-disenfranchised minorities in the democratic West, and the racial politics that shape both the migrant experience and our scholarly understanding of that experience. Amid those tectonic differences between the predominant Arabian migration system and the Euro-American one upon which most of our understandings are constructed, however, criminalization and illegality remain potent ingredients of both systems and certainly shape these migrants' decisions and everyday experiences. In the Qatari migration system, criminalization and illegality harness and bind migrants to unequal relations with their employers and sponsors. They are the means by which migrants are governed and through which the structural violence endemic to this migration system is enabled, orchestrated, and deployed.

### REFERENCES

Amnesty International. (2013). Qatar: The dark side of migration: Spotlight on Qatar's construction sector ahead of the World Cup. Retrieved on June 21, 2014, from www.amnesty.org/en/library/info/MDE22/010/2013/en.

Eelens, F., Schampers, T., & Speckmann, J. D. (1992). *Labour migration to the Middle East: From Sri Lanka to the Gulf.* London: Kegan Paul International.

Gardner, A. (2005). *City of strangers: The Transnational Indian community in Manama, Bahrain* (Doctoral dissertation, Department of Anthropology, University of Arizona). Available from Ann Arbor, MI (UMI No. 3182610).

——. (2010a). *City of strangers: Gulf migration and the Indian community in Bahrain.* Ithaca, NY: Cornell University Press.

——. (2010b). Engulfed: Indian guest workers, Bahrain citizens and the structural violence of the kafala system. In Nicholas De Genova & Nathalie Peutz (Eds.), *The deportation regime: Sovereignty, space and freedom of movement* (pp. 305–349). Durham, NC: Duke University Press.

Gardner, A., Pessoa, S., & Harkness, L. (2014). *Labour migrants and access to justice in contemporary Qatar.* London: London School of Economics.

Human Rights Watch. (2003). *Dubai: Migrant workers at risk.* New York City: Author.

——. (2006). *Building towers, cheating workers: Exploitation of migrant construction workers in the United Arab Emirates 8.18.* New York: Author.

——. (2009). *"The island of happiness": Exploitation of migrant workers on Saadiyat Island, Abu Dhabi.* New York: Author.

——. (2010). Rights on the line: Human rights work on abuses against migrants in 2010. Retrieved on August 2, 2014, from www.hrw.org/reports/2010/12/12/rights-line-0.

——. (2012a). *Building a better World Cup: Protecting migrant workers in Qatar ahead of FIFA 2022.* New York: Author.

———. (2012b). *For a better life: Migrant worker abuse in Bahrain and the government reform agenda*. New York: Author.

International Trade Union Confederation. (2011). Hidden faces of the Gulf miracle. *Union View, 21*(May), 1–24.

Longva, A. (1997). *Walls built on sand: Migration, exclusion and society in Kuwait*. Boulder, CO: Westview.

———. (1999). "Keeping migrant workers in check: The *kafala* system in the Gulf." *Middle East Report, 211*(Summer), 20–22.

Pessoa, S., Harkness, L., & Gardner, A. (2014). Ethiopian labor migrants and the "free visa" system in Qatar. *Human Organization, 73*(3), 205–213.

**NOTES**

1. The project findings described here resulted from a project funded by the Open Society Foundation's International Migration Initiative in 2012. This project was constructed on the base of a large, multiyear project entitled Foreign Labor in Qatar: An Empirical Sociological Analysis, made possible by a grant from the Qatar National Research Fund under its National Priorities Research Program (award 09-857-5-123). This chapter's contents are solely the responsibility of the authors and do not necessarily represent the official views of the Qatar National Research Fund.

2. See, e.g., Amnesty International, 2013; Human Rights Watch, 2003, 2006, 2009, 2010, 2012a, 2012b; International Trade Union Confederation, 2011; and the substantial quantity of journalism that followed these reports.

3. Rajendra, like all the names that appear in this chapter, is a pseudonym.

4. See Pessoa, Harkness, & Gardner (2014) for details on the lived experience of undocumented migrants in Qatar.

# 19

# Resistance to the Criminalization of Migration

*MIGRANT PROTEST IN GREECE*

▸ *GEORGIOS KARYOTIS AND DIMITRIS SKLEPARIS*

### INTRODUCTION

IT HAS BECOME COMMONPLACE TO argue that questions about migration provoke almost inherently and typically exaggerated anxieties about its impact on host societies. The trend is for citizens in the Western world to perceive migrants predominantly as a threat to the economy, to a particular way of life, and not least, to public order. Receiving states, on their part, have adopted immigration laws and policies that are designed to restrict flows of, primarily but not exclusively, irregular migrants. These include measures to reinforce borders, to expand criminal sanctions for migration offenses, to facilitate detention and deportation processes, and to tighten conditions of entry and stay (Parkin, 2013). This phenomenon of conflating migration, crime, and security, observed in both public attitudinal surveys and state policies, is at the heart of the so-called criminalization of migration.

A plethora of studies in the literature seek to analyze the discursive process through which the migrant-criminal thesis is constructed. Among others, they identify political and media discourses (Buonfino, 2004), security practices (Basaran, 2008), institutional configurations (Karyotis, 2007) and forms of governmentality (Bigo, 2002) as crucial in the top-down framing of migration as a menace. What these emphatically highlight is that criminalization occurs as a result of a process wherein elites and publics, in a given context and within specific structures, reach a shared understanding that migrants are inferior and/or threatening, which is irrespective of any "objective measurements of how dangerous they really are" (Waever, 1996).

In fact, criminalization is not only found to be counterproductive to migration management and detrimental to migrant human rights (Guild, 2010) but is also, counterintuitively, unrelated to increases in either crime rates or immigration flows (Palidda, 2011). Instead, periods of sociopolitical instability and economic downturn produce the greatest supply (in the form of hostile elite discourses) and demand (in the form of rising public threat perceptions) for intensified criminal-migrant frames (Melossi, 2003).

While both the process and implications of criminalization continue to inspire heated academic debates that cross disciplinary and theoretical divides, how migrants themselves experience and react to criminalization remains poorly understood. The scarcity of empirical data such as surveys that would shed light on the migrant experience and attitudes is partly to blame for this relative imbalance in the literature, which this collective volume seeks to address. A stronger underlying reason, arguably, derives from the way criminalization itself is conceived. The emphasis tends to be on the interplay between three types of actors: securitizing actors, commonly political and security elites who portray migration as a threat; facilitating actors, such as the media, who popularize the threat image by reproducing the official discourse; and an empowering audience, such as the citizens within a state, who evaluate these cues against competing representations, and, accordingly, develop positive or negative attitudes toward migration (Buzan, Waever, & de Wilde, 1997). Migrants themselves, on the other hand, are often ignored, because they are seen as the passive protagonists and subjects of criminalization and lack agency and a voice to impact upon how migration is framed and managed.

Greece offers an ideal setting for exploring overlooked dynamics relevant to the criminalization of migration. It is a country with persistently high anti-immigration attitudes since the unexpected inflow of migrants in the early 1990s and has been undergoing a severe economic crisis since 2010 and has been forced to rely on external rescue packages to prevent involuntary default on its debt. Drawing on discourse analysis and a set of face-to-face interviews with migrants who staged a 44-day hunger strike in January 2011, the aim of this chapter is twofold: first, to analyze the impact of criminalization and of the economic downturn on the migrant experience; and second, to explore the migrants' attempt to resist and react to their criminalization through organized protest action. The first section sets the stage for the analysis by looking at the national context and migration patterns.

The second section discusses the migrants' own evaluations of their lived experiences and mobilization. The third section then reflects on the discursive strategies that migrant protesters themselves employed to influence migration discourse and policy.

## THE CRIMINALIZATION OF MIGRATION IN GREECE

The tectonic geopolitical shifts resulting from the end of the Cold War transformed Greece from an emigration country into a de facto immigration country. An estimated 1 million irregular migrants, mainly from Albania (about 65%), the Balkans, and Eastern Europe, arrived in the 1990s to a country with a population of about 11 million citizens (Karyotis, 2012). While Greece was the final destination for those migrants, a second wave, with different characteristics, followed with the turn of the millennium. Migrants originating mainly from Asia and Africa arrived irregularly, seeking to use Greece as a transit destination to other western European countries. However, due to the Dublin II regulation and the intensification of internal European Union (EU) border controls (e.g., FRONTEX), they became trapped in Greece.

This sudden influx activated a defense mechanism on the part of the state, with political elites, security professionals, and the mass media all contributing to the discursive criminalization of migration (Karyotis, 2012; Karyotis & Skleparis, 2013; Swarts & Karakatsanis, 2012). The discourse of political elites in particular emphasized the need to fortify the borders, protect national identity, and curtail the development of socio-economic threats that migrants were deemed responsible for, such as an alleged increase in crime rates, although there was little objective evidence in support of these claims (Antonopoulos, 2005; Antonopoulos, Tierney, & Webster, 2008; Karydis, 1998).

Law and migration policy equally projected the message that migration is a threat that has to be curtailed. The country's first immigration law, introduced in 1991, and subsequent amendments to its legal framework were driven entirely by security considerations and were designed to prevent the entry and stay of migrants. For instance, Law 1975/1991 adopted very narrow definitions of asylum and family reunification; excluded irregular migrants from welfare services, including health care (except in emergency cases) and education; and criminalized any form of solidarity from the private sector, such as access to housing, public transport, and employment (Karyotis, 2012). In the absence of any provisions for integration and with all routes to regular immigration effectively sealed off, the emphasis of the authorities was on hardening and militarizing the external border through, for example, the establishment of new border guard forces in 1998 and, later, the construction of a 10.5-kilometer fence across its northern border with Turkey in 2012 (Karyotis & Skleparis, 2013).

With limited opposition to the dominant criminalization frame on migration, it is not surprising that a ubiquitous moral panic ensued (Antonopoulos, 2005). One of the most persistent causes of public insecurity was the perception that migration is linked to criminality. For instance, 84% of Greek citizens in 1993 felt that migrants pose a public order threat (Kiprianos, Balias, & Passas, 2003), a view shared with an overwhelming 92% of police officers, who in a 2006 survey thought migrants were partly or exclusively responsible for the perceived increase in criminality (Antonopoulos et al., 2008). What is perhaps paradoxical is that despite these collective public anxieties toward migrants, most Greeks reported that they had not been personally affected by their presence and had often developed friendship ties with them (Kasimis, Papadopoulos, & Zacopoulou, 2003). Accelerated economic growth and recognition that the overall economic impact of migrants, including irregular ones, was positive, facilitated some tentative moves toward liberalizing policy on the eve of the new millennium. Even so, the adoption of a series of one-off regularization programs (in 1998, 2001, 2005, and 2007), which granted amnesty to categories of settled migrants, lacked a long-term perspective, while the 2005 action plan for the social integration of immigrants (Law 3386/2005) was not implemented in practice (Triandafyllidou et al., 2013). The onset of the Great Recession in December 2007 and the subsequent severe Greek debt crisis of 2010 put an abrupt end to any hesitant moves toward liberalization. The state, at both discursive and policy levels, retreated to a harder stance on immigration, while public anti-immigration attitudes and support for far-right parties reached new heights (Karyotis & Skleparis, 2013).

Immigration emerged as one of the most salient issues, alongside the austerity debate, in the run-up to and aftermath of the 2012 parliamentary elections. Surveys of Greek members of the Parliament and their voters revealed that all parties, with the exception of the radical left SYRIZA, exhibited varying degrees of anti-immigration bias (Karyotis, Rudig, & Judge, 2014).

More tellingly, even SYRIZA voters did not connect with their party on this issue and instead perceived migration as a threat. What this might point toward is that economic crises compress the space for political alternatives and provide fertile ground for intolerance. Tensions between migrants and citizens in Greece did indeed intensify, resulting in social segregation, vigilantism against migrants, and racial violence. For instance, the Network for the Recording of Incidents of Racist Violence identified a 20% increase in incidents of racist violence in 2012 over 2011 (Karyotis & Skleparis, 2013).

The picture that emerges is that Greek migration management is characterized by short-termism, knee-jerk reactions, and incoherent policies, indicative of its inability to shake off the established frame that, fundamentally, migration remains "an unwanted burden for the country" (Triandafyllidou, 2009, p. 174). The criminalization of migration also has an unquestionably detrimental impact on the human rights of migrants, with arbitrary discrimination based on ethnic and racial characteristics, inhumane conditions in detention centers, and even threats of physical violence described by nongovernmental organizations (NGOs) as routine (Human Rights Watch, 2013).

Against this backdrop, some 300 immigrants residing irregularly in Crete traveled to Athens and Thessaloniki in January 2011 and commenced a hunger strike that lasted for 44 days. Supported by solidarity groups and NGOs, the hunger strikers put their lives at risk but achieved some concessions from the state with regard to their legal status. Their number, 300, is reminiscent of a heroic episode in ancient Greek history, when Leonidas and the Spartans willingly stood to their inevitable death against the massive Persian army in pursuit of higher objectives (Walsh & Tsilimpounidi, 2012). The difference, however, is that while the Spartans' sacrifice is glorified and celebrated, the migrants' battle soon faded into obscurity, after a short period of visibility. Drawing on a set of face-to-face interviews with these migrant protesters, the next section discusses their profiles and motivations and assesses their own evaluations of their protest action and of the impact of criminalization on their lives.

## PROFILES AND LIVED EXPERIENCES OF THE HUNGER STRIKERS

The previous section contextualized the two-decade-long process of criminalization of migration in Greece. The analysis indicates that this was driven by elite discourse and state policies and negotiated with citizens, who experienced a heightened sense of anxiety toward the "other." The main opposition to this has come from NGOs such as the Human Rights Watch and intergovernmental organizations such as the United Nations High Commissioner for Refugees (UNHCR), with some moderate successes, including the clearance of antipersonnel mines Greece maintained across its northern border until 2009 (Karyotis & Skleparis, 2013). Migrants themselves had scarce, if any, opportunities to make any impact on immigration discourse or policy.

This changed somewhat with the debt crisis that exploded in Greece in 2010. Not only did it have a tremendously negative effect on economic conditions, but it also provoked unprecedented levels of anti-austerity protest (Rudig & Karyotis, 2014). In such a climate of intense general mobilization and rising economic deprivation, migrant activists found fertile ground to attempt to make their own grievances heard. Drawing on the experience of previous sporadic and fragmented migrant marches and motivated by the worsening socioeconomic conditions, a migrant movement with a more coherent basis started to emerge.

Instrumental to this was the support from social networks and NGOs. Members of the Migrants Forum in Crete, a local NGO, proposed a hunger strike, originally penciled in for November 2010, when a new restrictive immigration law was being pushed through Parliament. Participants residing in Crete irregularly were recruited by volunteers on a door-to-door basis, and a decision was reached to host the hunger strike simultaneously in two major cities, Athens and Thessaloniki. With support from other local sympathizers, the protesters traveled by boat and occupied symbolic public spaces, commencing the strike on January 25, 2011. In total, 287 people took part, following a few last-minute withdrawals, with 237 protesters in an unused building of the Athens Law School and a further 50 in the Labor Center in Thessaloniki.

The hunger strike, a form of activism that in Greece and Europe falls outside the normal "protest repertoires" (Tilly, 1995, p. 26), captured media and public attention and provoked passionate reactions of sympathy and condemnation. Support came from migrant groups and networks, NGOs, antiracist and university student bodies, labor associations, neighborhood initiatives, anarchist collectives, and left-wing political parties. Some of these joined forces to create the Initiative for Solidarity, which, among other actions, organized demonstrations in support of the hunger strikers. The protesters themselves formed their own collective body, the Assembly of Migrant Hunger Strikers (AMHS).

Our face-to-face interviews, held in Crete in July 2012, allowed us to take a closer look at the profiles and attitudes of the hunger strikers. By the time of the survey, 100–120 of the 287 participants had permanently left Greece and a further 40–50 were on holiday. About 20 individuals refused the invitation to participate. In total, 52 interviews, each lasting approximately 30 minutes, were conducted using an original structured questionnaire that included both open- and closed-ended questions. The research was funded by the Carnegie Trust, whose support is gratefully acknowledged, and was carried out in accordance with the standard code of practice for research including human beings; no individuals can be identified from the data collected.

All of our respondents were nationals of Maghreb countries: 48 from Morocco, two from Algeria, and two from Tunisia. Most were in their mid-to-late twenties and single (92%). In terms of their employment status, 40% were working full-time, 37% part-time, and 19% were unemployed. Nationwide unemployment in Greece at the time of the survey was about 25%. The majority of migrants found employment opportunities in the construction sector and in the tourist industry and agriculture. As was also the case with citizens, the impact of the economic downturn had been uniformly detrimental to their living conditions, with 90% noting that their lives were worse (62% much worse) compared with the time before the crisis. The reduction of employment opportunities was cited as the main problem by almost all respondents, closely followed by the increase of racism and the prevalence of anti-immigration discourses.

Criminalization of migration, inevitably, increases migrant insecurity. Almost one out of every two (46%) of our respondents reported that they had been a victim of some form of abuse, either verbal (21%), physical (15%), or both (10%). The frequency of abuse varied. For some migrants it occurred once (10%), for others two to five times (25%), with 11% reporting they had been abused more than five times. When asked to describe in an open-ended question who abused them, the most common answers by far were "the police" and "fascists," the latter presumably a reference to supporters of the extreme-right Golden Dawn party, who have been linked to persecution of migrants. Only a small minority referred to Greeks in general as the culprits of racist attacks, although some did note that they had expected people to be kinder.

We asked participants to express their level of satisfaction with various aspects of their lives that might have been affected by the criminalization of migration (Figure 19.1). An overwhelming majority (90%) were, unsurprisingly, dissatisfied with the state's illiberal immigration policy (81% very dissatisfied). Similarly, 89% of respondents were unhappy with their access to the labor market (77% very dissatisfied), an indication of both the impact of the economic crisis and of criminalization, considering the legal provisions of heavy penalties for employers who hire undocumented migrants.

Nevertheless, in other areas, the restrictive laws did not seem to be enforced, and formal exclusion did not affect the migrants' daily lives. For instance, respondents were satisfied with their access to the housing market (80%), public transportation (77%), and health care (50%), despite the threat of penalties to citizens who provided these services to irregular migrants. Furthermore, a minority (38%) expressed dissatisfaction with how they were treated by citizens in general, which is perhaps lower than we might have expected, given the aforementioned high abuse rates and the increased public exposure that activism entails. When these are read in conjunction with other studies that find that citizens often develop friendship

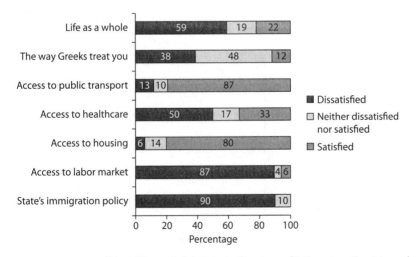

FIGURE 19.1. **Possible Effects of the Criminalization of Migration.** Participants' levels of satisfaction with various aspects of their lives.

ties with migrants (Kasimis et al., 2003), it suggests that criminalization does not result in a total exclusion from access to certain rights and services, as "non-status migrants experience different degrees and forms of exclusion in their daily lives" (Monforte & Dufour, 2011, p. 203).

When asked to evaluate their involvement with a range of actors, specifically with regard to their hunger strike, our interviewees were very positive about the solidarity groups, strike organizers, and immigrant associations but were very critical of the way the government and the police managed the issue (results plotted in Figure 19.2). With the government refusing to negotiate until the health of many of the strikers reached critical levels, a deal was finally brokered on March 9, 2011, to end the protest, as its escalation was damaging the government's reputation and legitimacy (Dingley & Mollica, 2007). The migrants' demand for full regularization was rejected, but some moderate ad hoc concessions were made, including being granted a biannually renewable status of "indefinite tolerance" and special permission to visit their home countries. For most these were not enough. On a scale of 0 to 10, where 0 means "not at all," and 10 means "absolutely," the mean average for respondents' who retrospectively believed that the goals of the hunger strike were achieved was just 3.1, although on a personal level they felt that participation helped them grow as individuals and was something to be proud of.

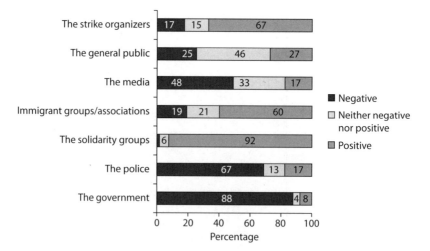

FIGURE 19.2. **Opinions on Actions Toward the Hunger Strike.** Participants' evaluations of the involvement of a range of actors in regard to their hunger strike.

Our data also allow us to see a snapshot of migration pathways and evaluate the participants' overall migrant experience in Greece. The majority of respondents, 73%, had been residing in Greece for more than 5 years. Only a small percentage, 9%, came to Greece regularly on a student or tourist visa. The remaining 91% entered the country irregularly via Turkey, through Samos (33%), Patmos (20%), other islands (18%), or the borders in northern Greece (21%). Figure 19.3 plots responses about the drivers of their decisions to emigrate. The most important motivation was to use Greece as a transit destination to another EU state (69%). Pursuit of better living conditions (64%) and employment (62%) were also important drivers, but fear of persecution in their home countries was not (8%). Findings also debunk some of the myths about other pull factors, such as presumed knowledge of welfare provisions and presence of existing migrant communities, which do not apply in the cases of those we interviewed. Overall, 40% expressed a desire to settle permanently in Greece, despite criminalization, with the rest seeking to move elsewhere in the EU or return to their home countries.

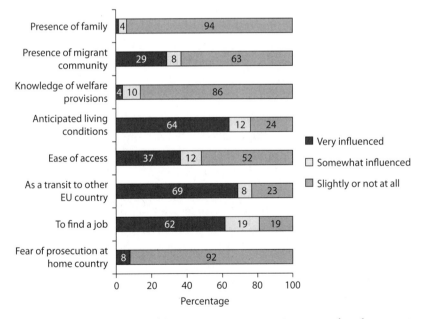

FIGURE 19.3.  **A Snapshot of the Migrant Experience**. Participant data showing migration pathways and evaluating the participants' overall migrant experience in Greece.

## FRAMING THE PROTEST MOVEMENT

In addition to the performative act of the hunger strike, the migrant protesters sought to make an impact on debates relevant to the criminalization of migration through 15 press statements. Discourse analysis is employed in this section to explore their collective framing of the protest action. The assembly's first public statement on January 23, 2011, introduced the protesters to the public as "migrant men and women, refugees from all over Greece . . . [who] came here to escape poverty, unemployment, wars and dictatorships" (AMHS, 2011a). Our individual-level survey data challenge the accuracy of this statement. All protesters were in fact male, residing in Crete, exclusively from Maghreb countries, while very few had been persecuted in their home countries. However, the all-encompassing and open identity adopted here was designed to maximize its potential to mobilize support from the more than 1 million migrants across Greece, in whose name the hunger strike was conducted (Jasper, 2004).

Accordingly, the protesters underlined that the main aim of their collective action, as framed, was the regularization of all undocumented migrants in Greece (AMHS, 2011a), to dispel any suggestion that they were driven by either individualistic motives or any underlying psychological conditions (McGregor, 2011; Silove, Steel, & Waters, 2000). In this respect, they specifically emphasized: "[W]e are not mentally disordered. We started a fight through our own conscious processes. Our morale is very high and we don't need any kind of psychological support" (AMHS, 2011b).

The protesters repeatedly and emphatically stated that they were fully conscious of the risks they were taking: "We risk our lives because, either way, there is no dignity in our living conditions," and "We would rather die here than allow our children to suffer what we have been through" (AMHS, 2011a). They expressed certainty that their struggle was a just one and a source of commitment, self-legitimacy, and pride: "We will exit this building either as winners or dead" (Dama, 2011). Thus, they portrayed their hunger strike as their last resort to pressure the government to address their grievances deriving from the criminalization of migration: "We do not have any other way to make our voices heard, to raise awareness of our rights" (AMHS, 2011a).

The protesters also strategically framed their collective identity as being first and foremost workers, irrespective of their ethnicity or legal status, by underlining that their struggle seeks to "send a message to every Greek and foreign worker to rise up. . . . This strike belongs to all of us" (AMHS, 2011c). Their irregular status was not hidden but attention was shifted away from it: "Whether by regular or irregular entry, we came to Greece and are working to support ourselves and our families. We live without dignity, in the dark shadow of illegality" (AMHS, 2011a). By constructing an image of themselves as suffering workers, who did their best to provide for their families, they tried to humanize their struggle and generate empathy among Greek citizens, who were experiencing relatable economic hardship at the time. After all, key to criminalization is the construction of adversarial identities ("us" versus "them"), which the protesters sought to reimagine as not being based on ethnic/citizenship grounds but on economic/class ones.

Related to this, both the hunger strike as a form of protest (Simeant, 1998) and its framing as a labor movement were designed to appeal to left-wing audiences in particular. The protesters pointed a finger at "the West," the "multinational companies and their political servants," for the economic crisis, echoing the discourse of left-wing parties (AMHS, 2011a). They rejected the scapegoating of migrants, emphasizing instead that their vulnerable position as irregular migrants enables employers and state agencies to benefit from the "harsh exploitation" of their labor. However, they highlighted the fact that this applies to migrants and citizens alike and thus made a plea to "our Greek fellow workers, everyone suffering exploitation, to stand with us" (AMHS, 2011a).

Despite the role of various social networks in the organization of the protest, the hunger strikers defended the independence of their actions, rejecting allegations that they were pawns in a bigger political game: "We take our decisions by ourselves during the assemblies we hold, and we do not get influenced by external factors" (AMHS, 2011d). Reiterating this point, they insisted: "We, 300, took the initiative for that kind of struggle, without the intervention of political parties, organizations and individuals" (AMHS, 2011e). Finally, they underlined that they were not victims and they should not be portrayed as such: "We are not those piteous, destitute migrants, deprived of housing, work and clothes that the media are describing." Instead, they portrayed themselves as active political agents who "came to fight, for as long as our bodies will allow us, for our rights and for a life with dignity" (AMHS, 2011d).

### CONCLUSION

This chapter analyzed both the top-down process and the impact of criminalization on migrants' lives. It demonstrates that the prevalence of restrictive frames and policies in Greece to manage migration is very detrimental for its subjects, the migrants themselves, who experience increased levels of insecurity, abuse, and deprivation. While an accurate assessment of this would require the comparison of our findings with a sample of the migrant population who did not participate in protest action, our data give a good indication of how migrants experience criminalization. What is somewhat comforting is that even in such hostile conditions, there appears to be a degree of solidarity that exists within society. As our analysis demonstrates, migrants experience different degrees and forms of exclusion that are lower than the legal framework prescribes in relation to certain rights and services, such as housing and health care.

The other key point to take away from the Greek case is the demonstrable desire and ability of irregular migrants to escape invisibility, even temporarily, and popularize their grievances. What is important in this area is that the discourses of the protesters did not only result from the daily experiences of the actors within mobilizations, as Della Porta and Piazza (2008) claim. Instead, the framing of the hunger strike by the protesters was markedly strategic, seeking to make links with potential allies among both migrants and citizens to maximize the impact of their message. Admittedly, the protesters achieved less than they desired from the hunger strike. However, the alliances built, the socialization experience gained, and the visibility they received has planted a seed for a challenge to criminalization that is likely to find fertile ground once the economic conditions, mainly, and the political environment improve.

It is worth concluding by reminding ourselves that criminalization of the "other" is not a new phenomenon in human history, and it both can and should be resisted. The 1847 Annual Report of the American Institute (1848) of the City of New York eloquently captures this sentiment:

> The tide of emigration which now sets so strongly toward our shores, cannot be turned back. We must receive the poor, the ignorant, and the oppressed from other lands, and it would be better to consider them as coming filled with the energy of hope for happier days, and more useful labors, than they

found at home. No one, I presume, seriously believes they come with bad intentions, and then whose fault is it that they live here in cellars more filthy than the cabins of whose wretchedness we hear so much, and for whose existence, half the blame is thrown upon the government they have left. Let us first cast the beam from our own eye. We are parties to their degradation, inasmuch as we permit the habitation of places, from which it is not possible improvement in condition or habits can come. We suffer the sub-landlord to stow them, like cattle, in pens, and to compel them to swallow poison with every breath. They are allowed, may it not be said required, to live in dirt, when the reverse, rather, should be enforced.

(American Institute, 1848)

## REFERENCES

American Institute. (1848). Sixth Annual Report of the American Institute of the City of New York: Made to the Legislature, March 25, 1848. Albany. Retrieved on June 11, 2014, from http://archive.org/stream/annualreportofam61847amer /annual reportofam61847amer_djvu.txt.

Assembly of Migrant Hunger Strikers (AMHS). (2011a, January 23). Statement of the Assembly of Migrant Hunger Strikers [in Greek]. Retrieved on June 15, 2014, from http://hungerstrike300.espivblogs.net/2011/01/23/statement-of-theassembly -of-migrant-hunger-strikers.

——. (January 23 in 2011b). Announcement to society [in Greek]. Retrieved on June 14, 2014, from https://allilmap.wordpress.com.

——. (January 25 in 2011c). Press release decision of the Assembly of Migrants on hunger strike [in Greek]. Retrieved on June 14, 2014, from https://allilmap .wordpress.com.

——. (January 23 in 2011d). Decision of the Assembly of Migrant Hunger Strikers [in Greek]. Retrieved from http://blog.occupiedlondon.org/2011/01/27/483 -decision-by-the-assembly-of-the-300-hunger-strikers-of-the-law-school/.

——. (April 8 in 2011e). Announcement of the hunger strikers [in Greek]. Retrieved on June 14, 2014, from https://allilmap.wordpress.com.

Antonopoulos, G. A. (2005). The limitations of official statistics in relation to the criminality of migrants in Greece. *Police Practice and Research, 6*(3), 251–260.

Antonopoulos, G. A., Tierney, J., & Webster, C. (2008). Police perception of migration and migrants in Greece. *European Journal of Crime Criminal Law and Criminal Justice, 16*(4), 353–378.

Basaran, T. (2008). Security, law, borders: Spaces of exclusion. *International Political Sociology, 2*(4), 339–354.

Bigo, D. (2002). Security and immigration: Toward a critique of the governmentality of unease. *Alternatives: Global, Local, Political, 27*(1), 63–92.

Buonfino, A. (2004). Between unity and plurality: The politicization and securitization of the discourse of immigration in Europe. *New Political Science, 26*(1), 23–49.

Buzan, B., Waever, O., & de Wilde, J. (1997). *Security: A new framework for analysis.* Boulder, CO: Lynne Rienner.

Dama, G. (2011). Lives below zero [in Greek]. *Enet English.* Retrieved on May 29, 2014, from www.enet.gr/?i=news.el.article&id=257380.

Della Porta, D., & Piazza, G. (2008). *Voices of the valley, voices of the straits: How protest creates communities.* New York: Berghahn Books.

Dingley, J. C., & Mollica, M. (2007). The human body as a terrorist weapon: Hunger strikes and suicide bombers. *Studies in Conflict and Terrorism, 30*(6), 459–492.

Guild, E. (2010). *Criminalisation of migration in Europe: Human rights implications* (Issue Paper). Strasbourg, Germany: Council of Europe Commissioner for Human Rights.

Human Rights Watch. (2013). Unwelcome guests: Greek police abuses of migrants in Athens. Retrieved on May 29, 2014, from www.refworld.org/docid/51bae3274.html.

Jasper, J. M. (2004). A strategic approach to collective action: Looking for agency in social- movement choices. *Mobilization, 9*(1), 1–16.

Karydis, V. (1998). Criminality or criminalization of migrants in Greece? An attempt at synthesis. In V. Ruggiero, N. South, & I. R. Taylor (Eds.), *The new European criminology: Crime and social order in Europe* (pp. 350–367). Oxon, UK: Routledge.

Karyotis, G. (2007). European migration policy in the aftermath of September 11: The security-migration nexus. *Innovation: The European Journal of Social Science Research, 20*(1), 1–17.

——. (2012). Securitization of migration in Greece: Process, motives and implications. *International Political Sociology, 6*(4), 390–408.

Karyotis, G., & Skleparis, D. (2013). Qui bono? The winners and losers of securitising migration. *Griffith Law Review, 22*(3), 683–706.

Karyotis, G., Rudig, W., & Judge, D. (2014). Representation and austerity politics: Attitudes of Greek voters and elites compared. *South European Society and Politics, 19*(4), 435–456. DOI:10.1080/13608746.2014.977478

Kasimis, C., Papadopoulos, A., & Zacopoulou, E. (2003). Migrants in rural Greece. *Sociologia Ruralis, 43*(2), 167–184.

Kiprianos, P., Balias, S., & Passas, V. (2003). Greek policy towards immigration and immigrants. *Social Policy & Administration, 37*(2), 148–164.

McGregor, J. (2011). Contestations and consequences of deportability: Hunger strikes and the political agency of non-citizens. *Citizenship Studies, 15*(5), 597–611.

Melossi, D. (2003). In a peaceful life: Migration and the crime of modernity in Europe/Italy. *Punishment & Society, 5*(4), 371–397.

Monforte, P., & Dufour, P. (2011). Mobilizing in borderline citizenship regime: A comparative analysis of undocumented migrants' collective actions. *Politics & Society, 39*(2), 203–232.

Palidda, S. (2011). A review of the principal European countries. In S. Palidda (Ed.), *Racial Criminalization of Migrants in the 21st Century* (pp. 23–30). Farnham, UK: Ashgate.

Parkin, J. (2013). *The criminalisation of migration in Europe: A state-of-the-art of the academic literature and research* (Working Paper No. 61, Liberty and Security in Europe Papers). Brussels: Centre for European Policy Studies.

Rudig, W., & Karyotis, G. (2014). Who protests in Greece? Mass opposition to austerity. *British Journal of Political Science, 44*(3), 487–513.

Silove, D., Steel, Z., & Waters, C. (2000). Policies of deterrence and the mental health of asylum seekers. *Journal of the American Medical Association, 284*(5), 604–611.

Swarts, J., & Karakatsanis, N. M. (2012). The securitization of migration: Greece in the 1990s. *Journal of Balkan and Near Eastern Studies, 14*(1), 33–51.

Tilly, C. (1995). *Popular contention in Great Britain, 1758–1834*. Cambridge: Harvard University Press.

Triandafyllidou, A. (2009). Greek immigration policy at the turn of the 21st century: Lack of political will or purposeful mismanagement? *European Journal of Migration and Law, 11*(2), 159–178.

Triandafyllidou, A., Dimitriadi, A., Maroufof, M., Hatziprokopiou, P., Gemi, E., Nikolova, M., & Yousef, K. (2013). *Migration in Greece: People, policies and practices* (Working Paper). Athens: ELIAMEP/EUI.

Waever, O. (1996). European security identities. *Journal of Common Market Studies, 34*(1), 103–132.

Walsh, A., & Tsilimpounidi, M. (2012). The disappearing immigrants: Hunger strike as invisible struggle. *Theory in Action, 5*(2), 82–103.